An historical and chronological treatise of the anointing and coronation of the Kings and queens of France, from Clovis I. to the present King ; and of all the sovereign princes of Europe. ... Faithfully done from the original French.

Nicolas Menin

ECCO
PRINT EDITIONS

An historical and chronological treatise of the anointing and coronation of the Kings and queens of France, from Clovis I. to the present King ; and of all the sovereign princes of Europe. ... Faithfully done from the original French.
Menin, Nicolas
ESTCID: T123498
Reproduction from British Library
Titlepage in red and black. The ornaments are those used by Henry Woodfall. With three final advertisement pages.
London : printed for W. Mears ; S. Chapman ; and J. Woodman, 1723.
xvi,333,[3]p.,plate ; 8°

ECCO

Eighteenth Century
Collections Online
Print Editions

Gale ECCO Print Editions

Relive history with *Eighteenth Century Collections Online*, now available in print for the independent historian and collector. This series includes the most significant English-language and foreign-language works printed in Great Britain during the eighteenth century, and is organized in seven different subject areas including literature and language; medicine, science, and technology; and religion and philosophy. The collection also includes thousands of important works from the Americas.

The eighteenth century has been called "The Age of Enlightenment." It was a period of rapid advance in print culture and publishing, in world exploration, and in the rapid growth of science and technology – all of which had a profound impact on the political and cultural landscape. At the end of the century the American Revolution, French Revolution and Industrial Revolution, perhaps three of the most significant events in modern history, set in motion developments that eventually dominated world political, economic, and social life.

In a groundbreaking effort, Gale initiated a revolution of its own: digitization of epic proportions to preserve these invaluable works in the largest online archive of its kind. Contributions from major world libraries constitute over 175,000 original printed works. Scanned images of the actual pages, rather than transcriptions, recreate the works ***as they first appeared.***

Now for the first time, these high-quality digital scans of original works are available via print-on-demand, making them readily accessible to libraries, students, independent scholars, and readers of all ages.

For our initial release we have created seven robust collections to form one the world's most comprehensive catalogs of 18th century works.

Initial Gale ECCO Print Editions collections include:

History and Geography
Rich in titles on English life and social history, this collection spans the world as it was known to eighteenth-century historians and explorers. Titles include a wealth of travel accounts and diaries, histories of nations from throughout the world, and maps and charts of a world that was still being discovered. Students of the War of American Independence will find fascinating accounts from the British side of conflict.

Social Science

Delve into what it was like to live during the eighteenth century by reading the first-hand accounts of everyday people, including city dwellers and farmers, businessmen and bankers, artisans and merchants, artists and their patrons, politicians and their constituents. Original texts make the American, French, and Industrial revolutions vividly contemporary.

Medicine, Science and Technology

Medical theory and practice of the 1700s developed rapidly, as is evidenced by the extensive collection, which includes descriptions of diseases, their conditions, and treatments. Books on science and technology, agriculture, military technology, natural philosophy, even cookbooks, are all contained here.

Literature and Language

Western literary study flows out of eighteenth-century works by Alexander Pope, Daniel Defoe, Henry Fielding, Frances Burney, Denis Diderot, Johann Gottfried Herder, Johann Wolfgang von Goethe, and others. Experience the birth of the modern novel, or compare the development of language using dictionaries and grammar discourses.

Religion and Philosophy

The Age of Enlightenment profoundly enriched religious and philosophical understanding and continues to influence present-day thinking. Works collected here include masterpieces by David Hume, Immanuel Kant, and Jean-Jacques Rousseau, as well as religious sermons and moral debates on the issues of the day, such as the slave trade. The Age of Reason saw conflict between Protestantism and Catholicism transformed into one between faith and logic -- a debate that continues in the twenty-first century.

Law and Reference

This collection reveals the history of English common law and Empire law in a vastly changing world of British expansion. Dominating the legal field is the *Commentaries of the Law of England* by Sir William Blackstone, which first appeared in 1765. Reference works such as almanacs and catalogues continue to educate us by revealing the day-to-day workings of society.

Fine Arts

The eighteenth-century fascination with Greek and Roman antiquity followed the systematic excavation of the ruins at Pompeii and Herculaneum in southern Italy; and after 1750 a neoclassical style dominated all artistic fields. The titles here trace developments in mostly English-language works on painting, sculpture, architecture, music, theater, and other disciplines. Instructional works on musical instruments, catalogs of art objects, comic operas, and more are also included.

J Clark sculp. 1723

AN
Hiſtorical and Chronological
TREATISE
OF THE
ANOINTING
AND
CORONATION
OF THE
Kings and Queens of FRANCE,

From *CLOVIS* I. to the Preſent King;

And of all the Sovereign PRINCES of *Europe*.

To which is Added,

An Exact Relation of the CEREMONY of the CORONATION of *LOUIS* XV.

By M. *MENIN*,

Counſellor to the Parliament of *Metz*.

Faithfully done from the Original French.

LONDON;

Printed for W. MEARS, at the *Lamb* without *Temple-Bar*; S CHAPMAN, at the *Angel* in *Pallmall*; and J. WOODMAN, at *Cambden's-Head* in *Bow-ſtreet*, *Covent-Garden*. M.DCC.XXIII.

TO THE

KING.

SIR,

THE *Historical Treatise of the Anointing and Coronation of the Kings of* France, *and the other Christian Princes of* Europe, *which I have the Honour to present to*

YOUR MAJESTY, *ought not to appear but under the Auspices of Your August Name; for it gives an Account of the Anointing and Coronation of all the Kings of this Great Monarchy, which is only a Preparation for your own. All your People, and the whole* European *World expect the Day of that Pomp with Impatience.*

May you, SIR, *in receiving the Sacred Unction, receive likewise the Fulness of those Graces it confers: May you have the Piety of* ST. LOUIS, *the Wisdom of* CHARLES *V. the Goodness and Affection for your People which shone in* LOUIS *XII. the Valour, Courage, and Firmness of* HENRY *IV. the Justice of* LOUIS *the XIIIth, the Grandeur and Magnanimity of* LOUIS *XIV. May you,* SIR, *in one word, unite in your self alone all the Glorious Perfections which those Great Kings, of*

whom

whom you descend, have only divided: But your August Person is already adorn'd with all these Virtues.

The happy Inclinations which Heaven has given to YOUR MAJESTY, *and have appeared from your Infancy, cultivated by the Care of those Illustrious Hands, that form your Royal Education, display themselves, and improve daily. We discover in you all that can make a Prince accomplished, all bespeaks a Reign glorious and fortunate; the first Times are happy Presages of it, and the Regency of a Prince, whose sublime Spirit, attended with all Great Qualities, has carried its Views to the Glory of* YOUR MAJESTY, *and the Good of the Nation, still the more confirms our Hope and Assurance.*

We have nothing more remaining, SIR, *but to continue our Prayers for the Length of a Reign, which ought not to have any Bounds at all set to it.*

These are, SIR, *the Vows of Subjects, of all Ranks, in your Kingdom, and particularly of him who is, with a most profound Respect,*

SIR,

YOUR MAJESTY'S

Most Humble, Obedient,

and Faithful Servant,

and Subject,

MENIN,

Counsellor to the Parliament of Metz.

THE

PREFACE:

OR,

Advertisement to the Reader.

SO many Books have been publish'd, on the Anointing and Coronation of our Kings, that we should have been silent upon that Topick, had not several Persons, equally distinguish'd by their Learning and Rank, persuaded us, that our

Collections upon the Facts and Circumstances, relating to the Anointing and Coronation of the Kings of *France*, and the other Sovereign Princes of *Europe*, which are not sufficiently treated of, or even mention'd, in the General Histories, nor in the Great Ceremonial of *France*, would be the more favourably receiv'd, as we have reduced them to the most narrow Limits, tho they might afford Materials for several Volumes.

In our Abridgment, we have taken proper Care to omit nothing that is essential, and to answer sufficiently the Titles of our Chapters, to give a just Idea of our Subject, and a Solution of what we proposed that is certain and well authoriz'd. In our Chronology, we have follow'd the most exact Authors, and in doubtful Points the most common Opinion.

The Reader may possibly be surprized, that we have not formed particular Chapters on the Miracle of the Holy Vial, the Oriflame, and each of the Royal Habits and Ornaments. But as to the first Article, we imagined it would be a Disparagement to the Truth of it, to speak more than we have written about it, on the Baptism and Anointing of *Clovis*; and all the Dissertations we can make upon it, are short of the

the Teſtimonies of St. *Remy*, and the Authors we have quoted.

As to the Oriflame, and the Royal Habits and Ornaments, we have ſpoken enough of them in the Text and Notes, in ſuch Places where it has been proper to do it. We have taken the ſame Courſe with reſpect to the Lords, whoſe Buſineſs it was to attend the Holy Vial, and thoſe who were to ſupport the Canopy, under which that precious Treaſure was convey'd from the Church of St. *Remy*, to the Cathedral of *Rheims*, on the Day of the Coronation.

As to what remains, we give an expreſs Precaution, that none either ought, or can draw any Advantage or Conſequence from the Ranks, or Order of Sitting; nor from the Diſpoſition of the Places, Theatres, Steps, and Scaffolds, which we have mention'd in this Work; not only, becauſe they have vary'd, almoſt at all Coronations, for particular Reaſons, of which the Hiſtorians have not informed us; but further, becauſe only Meſſieurs the Grand-Maſter, and Maſter of the Ceremonies, have it in their power to adjuſt them: ſince it is only in their Regiſters that we can find all the Lights that are proper to clear that Subject.

It

It is on this account, that we have forborn to name the Peers, Great Officers, and Lords, who *ought* to represent, and to assist at the Coronation, however they are at present pointed out; in hopes that the Grand Master, and Master of the Ceremonies, will some time be pleased to give such Reports of those Affairs to the Publick, as are equally profitable and curious.

TABLE OF THE CHAPTERS.

Sect.

THE

THE

APPROBATION

Of M. the Abbot RICHARD, *Dean of the Canons of the Royal and Collegiate Church of* St. Opportune *at* Paris, *Prior, Lord of* Regny, *and* l'Hôpital, *Under* Rochfort, *Censor Royal.*

I HAVE read by the Order of Monseigneur the Keeper of the Seals, a Manuscript, entitled, *An Historical and Chronological Treatise of the Anointing and Coronation of the Kings and Queens of* France, *from* Clovis *to the present King, and of the other Sovereign Princes of* Europe; *by M* MENIN, *Counsellor of the King in his Court of Parliament at* Metz.

M. *Menin* has perfectly answer'd the Idea given by his Title: The whole Work is distributed in great Order, what is the more

more laudable in him, is, that he has advanced nothing, which he has not proved by the Authority of the best Authors, which he quotes. It is not a bare Description of the Ceremonies of a Coronation, but a curious Account of their Rise and Progress. His Enquiries are full of profound Learning, we view in them the Date and Settlement of Christianity in each of the Kingdoms of *Europe*; and though the Matter of every Chapter might have furnished an entire Volume, he has contracted it to a small Compass, without leaving out any thing of Importance. So far, that I can assure my Lord, the Keeper of the Seals, that this Work will be very useful and agreeable to Posterity. In making it publick by the Impression of it, a great Satisfaction will arise to the *French* Nation, and to all the Kingdoms of *Europe*. This Magistrate promises likewise an exact Relation of all that shall pass in the Ceremony of the Coronation of *Louis* XV. That will be printed at the End of this Treatise, after I have read and sign'd it.

At Paris, *this 4th of* September, 1722.

The ABBOT RICHARD,

Censor Royal.

A N

A N

Hiſtorical and Chronological

TREATISE

OF THE

Anointing and Coronation of the Kings and Queens of *France*.

CHAP. I.

The Original of the Conſecration and Anointing of Kings, as well before as ſince Chriſtianity.

THE Conſecration of Kings by Anointing, is not meerly a Ceremony of Cuſtom or Uſage, introduced by Men, but it is an Act more ſacred and myſterious, as it is of Divine Command and Inſtitution, and imprints a Character like that of the Holy Sacraments. The Unction of Kings, says a (*a*) Father of the Church, commenc'd upon *Saul*: it was continued in *David*, and *Solomon*; and all the Kings of *Judah*, and *Israel*, were anointed after their Example.

Indeed, we are appriz'd from the Scripture, that the *Hebrews*, who experienc'd the Favours of Heaven more than any other Nation, as they were guided by the Spirit of God himself, in the management of their State, growing weary of their Judges, demanded the Government of a King: That the Prophet *Samuel* oppos'd their Design, till God commanded him to anoint *Saul*, the Son of *Kish*, to be the Sovereign (*b*) of his People. That *Samuel* obey'd, and taking *Saul* apart, he pour'd a small Vial of Oil upon his Head, to anoint him King, and (*c*) embrac'd him, as a Salute to his new Dignity, with these Words: (*d*) *Behold the Lord hath anointed thee to be Captain over his Inheritance*, [*and thou shalt deliver his People out of the Hands of their Enemies.*]

(*a*) St. *August.* in Psalm 104 and 144

(*b*) Thou shalt anoint him to be Captain over my People *Israel*, that he may save my People out of the hand of the *Philistines*. 1 *Sam* 4.

(*c*) Kiss'd him *Eng. Vers*

(*d*) Then *Samuel* took a Vial of Oil and pour'd it upon his Head, and said, Is it not because the Lord hath anointed thee to be Captain over his Inheritance?

This

This Unction was repeated in *Gilgal* (*e*) where *Saul* was recogniz'd, and confirm'd King before all the People. And immediately after his anointing, they offer'd to (*f*) God Sacrifices, and Peace-Offerings, to give thanks to the Lord for his Favours, and obtain a peaceable Reign, and Succour against his Enemies.

Thus *Saul* is the first anointed King, but his Reign was not long, he was (*g*) rejected by God for his Disobedience: *David*, who was full of Goodness and Wisdom, was chosen in the place of him, and God again directed *Samuel* to anoint him (*h*).

The Scripture adds (and we are therefore oblig'd to mention it, in proof, that the anointing of Kings confers upon them at the same time, a variety of heavenly Gifts and Graces unknown to other Men) that from the Instant of this mysterious Oil's be-

(*e*) All the People went to *Gilgal*, and there they made *Saul* King before the Lord in *Gilgal*, and there they sacrificed Sacrifices of Peace-Offerings. 1 *Sam.* 11.

(*f*) Who had already chosen him King in a solemn Assembly of all the Tribes of the *Jews*, or the People of *Israel*, gather'd together at *Mispah*, by a secret Order of Providence. 1 *Sam* 8.

(*g*) It repented the Lord, that he had made *Saul* King over *Israel*. 1 Sam. 15

(*h*) The Lord said unto *Samuel*, fill thy Horn with Oil, and go, I will send thee to *Jesse*.— And the Lord said, Arise, anoint him, for this is he. Then *Samuel* took the Horn of Oil, and anointed him (*David*) in the midst of his Brethren. 1 *Sam.* 16.

ing pour'd upon the new King, the Spirit of God fill'd *David*, and quitted *Saul* (*i*).

Saul and *David* were not the only Kings of *Iſrael* that received this Unction; *David*, when far advanc'd in Age, and foreſeeing the Diviſions that would ariſe after his deceaſe among his Children, by the deſire they all had to be Maſters of the Kingdom, himſelf nam'd his Son *Solomon* for his Succeſſor: He made him ſit upon his Throne during his Life, and cauſing him to ride upon a Mule adorn'd with a rich Equipage, he order'd him to be conducted in Triumph to the Town of *Gibon*, to be anointed King of *Iſrael* by *Zadok* the High Prieſt (*k*), which was done with great Magnificence, with the Sound of Trumpets, and joyful Acclamations of the People, who ſaid with a loud Voice, *Let the King live for ever*. Eng. Ver. *God ſave the King*.

The ſame Scripture tells us, that the Oil uſed in conſecrating the Kings of *Iſrael* was ſo ſacred, that they preſerv'd it carefully in (*l*) the Tabernacle. And *Tertullian* aſſures

(*i*) And the Spirit of the Lord came upon *David* from that Day forward— But the Spirit of the Lord departed from *Saul* 1 *Kings* 16

(*k*) Cauſe *Solomon* my Son to ride upon mine own Mule, and bring him down to *Gibon*, and let *Zadok* the Prieſt anoint him there, that he may come and ſit upon my Throne for he ſhall be King in my ſtead, and I have appointed him to be Ruler over *Iſrael*, and over *Judah*. 1 *Kings* 1

(*l*) So *Zadok* the Prieſt took an Horn of Oil out of the Tabernacle, and anointed *Solomon*, and they blew the Trumpet, and all the People ſaid, *God ſave King* Solomon.

ſures (*m*) us, That after the Kingdom was confirmed in the Houſe of *David*, they ever uſed the ſame Unction that was perform'd and inſtituted by *Samuel*, which they affirm to have laſted near the ſpace of 900 Years; that is to ſay, till the Deſtruction of *Solomon*'s Temple, where it was preſerv'd.

The Kings of *Syria* likewiſe receiv'd an Unction; and the Prophet *Elijah* was expreſly order'd by God to anoint *Hazael* (*n*): And ſince the King was bound to be a Guardian of the Laws, and eſpecially of the Laws of God, he receiv'd, for that purpoſe, the Tables of the Law from the Hands of the *Levites*, with a Promiſe to maintain and keep them. Thus it was, that the High-Prieſt *Jehoiada*, having ſet things in order for the anointing of *Jehoaſh*, Son of *Ahazia*, firſt put the Crown upon his Head, and gave him the Book of the Law, then anointed him, all the People crying aloud, *Let the King live* (*o*).

This Anointing, and theſe Ceremonies, have ſo near a Reſemblance with the Inauguration of our Kings, that they ſeem to have been tranſmitted down to us, notwithſtanding the prodigious Interval of Ages

(*m*) B. 1 of his Hiſtory

(*n*) And the Lord ſaid unto him (*Elijah*) anoint *Hazael* to be King of *Syria*. 1 Kings 14. 15

(*o*) 2 *Chron*. 23 11. Then they brought out the King's Son, and put upon him the Crown, and gave him the Teſtimony

past since the Destruction of the Kingdom of *Israel* (*f*) and *Juda* (*g*), till the Conversion of *Clovis*, the first Christian King of this Monarchy (*h*), for it is certain, as the Fathers of the Church have remark'd, that before (*i*) Christianity there was no Anointing but with the *Jewish* People, among whom the Anointed of the Lord, the King of Kings, was prophesy'd and expected. and since it is as certain, that after the Faith of Christ was publish'd in the World, the first Christian Kings that were anointed were the Kings of *France*; it is evident, that our Monarchs hold the same in the new Law from God himself, as the *Hebrews* receiv'd it in the antient, and that it was not introduc'd among our Princes by any other Example.

(*f*) *Hosbea*, the last King of *Israel*, was subdu'd by *Shalmanezar*, and his Kingdom was overthrown, *Anno Mundi* 3283, 721 Years before Christ, and 250 after it was separated from that of *Juda*. Jos. Antiq. Jud. 2 Kings 18. 9.

(*g*) *Zedekiah*, and his Kingdom of *Jerusalem*, were conquer'd by *Nebuchadnezzar*, *Anno Mundi* 3416, 588 Years before Christ, and 387 after it was divided from that of *Israel*. 2 Kings 25. Joseph.

(*h*) *Ann.* 496, *Clovis* was converted to Christianity, was baptiz'd, and receiv'd the Holy Unction, miraculously sent from Heaven, for his Inauguration, in the Church of St. *Remy at Rheims.*

(*i*) *Non alibi ungebantur*, &c. Priests and Kings were no where anointed but in that Kingdom where Christ was prophesy'd, and whence he was to come. *S. Aug. in Psal.* 64. *Tertull. l.* 13

In

In short, tho' *Constantine* the Great, and *Theodosius* (*) the Younger, were the first Sovereign Princes who submitted to the Gospel; tho' *Constantine* was baptiz'd, confirm'd, and receiv'd the Eucharist a few Days before his Death, about the Year 337, tho' after him *Theodosius* the Younger, and many of his Successors, receiv'd the Benediction, the Sword, and Crown of the Empire from the Hands of the Patriarch of *Constantinople* (*k*), yet we do not find that any of them were anointed, as Kings or Emperors, till the Reign of *Andronicus* junior, who was not elected till the Year 1327 (*l*), many Ages after *Clovis*, in whom this Unction was renew'd, about the Year 496, by the visible Order of God (*m*) himself, either because the first Emperors, after *Constantine*, had fill'd the Church with Schisms and Heresies, and so render'd themselves unworthy of this Anointing, by the Inconstancy of their Faith, or because the

(*) Emperors of *Constantinople*. *See* Zonaras, Eutropius, Baronius, P. Alexander de Concordia Sacerdotii & Imperii.

(*k*) *See* Socrat. Hist. lib. 7. Theodoret Hist lib. 5. c. 35.

(*l*) Joan Cantacuzen in Andron. juniorem.

(*m*) And after the Baptism of *Clovis*, while St. *Remy*, Archbishop of *Rheims*, waited for the Holy Oil to inaugurate the King, a Pillar brought him from Heaven the Holy Vial to the Altar, containing the precious Balm with which our Kings, since *Clovis*, have ever been anointed. This Miracle happen'd in the Church of St. *Remy*, at *Rheims*, on *Christmas* Night, *Anno* 496. *See* Greg de Tours, l. 2. Aimoin. l. 1. Hincmar & Mezeray Hist.

Eternal Wiſdom was pleas'd to reſerve this Prerogative for ſuch Princes, as were to be the true Protectors of the Law of Grace, and the eldeſt Sons of the Goſpel.

CHAP. II.

What kind of Ceremonies was ſubſtituted in the place of Anointing, after the Deſtruction of the Jews, *till the Eſtabliſhment of Religion, and the Revival of Anointing in Chriſtian Kingdoms.*

THO' the Anointing of Kings was only practis'd among the *Hebrews*, and not introduc'd into any other Kingdoms before Chriſtianity; yet God, who has a particular Care of Monarchs, whom he makes the Delegates of his Supreme Authority here below, has always inſpir'd even the moſt barbarous People, plung'd in the Darkneſs of Paganiſm and Idolatry, with Sentiments of Love, and Veneration for their Kings: ſo that all Nations of the World, from their firſt Original, have obſerv'd, and ſtill

ſtill keep up ſome Ceremonies of Show and Splendor in the Election and Coronation of their Kings or Governours, which tho' they differ according to the Manners, Laws, and Cuſtoms of each People in particular, yet all tend to the ſame purpoſe, which is to ſtamp a ſingular Character upon the Prince, that points out his Greatneſs, and the Authority he has over his People; and creates a due Fear and Reſpect to his Government.

Thus the *Aſſyrians*, the *Chaldeans*, the *Medes*, or *Perſians*, whoſe Empire was extinguiſh'd by that of the *Greeks*, the Emperors of *Conſtantinople*, whoſe Place is now fill'd by the *Ottoman* Princes, the Kings and Emperors of *Rome*, as well before as after the Conſuls, the *Egyptians*, from their *Pharaohs* to the Invaſion of the *Perſians*, and from the Conqueſt of *Alexander* the Great to Queen *Cleopatra* II. the *Chineſe*, whoſe Empire was ſettled above 2960 Years before Chriſt, and ſubſiſts to this Day; the *Tartars*, the *Japoneſe*, the *Aſiatic* and *European Turks*, and all Nations of the World, from the earlieſt Date of their Monarchy, bound themſelves, in a voluntary manner, to certain Ceremonies, for the Election and Coronation of their Kings: and notwithſtanding the Clouds of Idolatry, that cover'd the true Light from them, yet they called upon Heaven, after their manner (if we may have the freedom to uſe that Phraſe of their ſuperſtitious Worſhip) to obtain that Strength, Courage, and Conduct for their new King, as was requiſite for a proper Government of their People.

Thus it was, for Inſtance, that the *Perſians* brought the new Succeſſor to the Throne to *Perſepolis* (after the Death of their Emperor) into the Temple of *Pallas* (*n*) accompany'd with the Princes, the Great Officers, the Prieſts and People, to receive there the Diadem from the Hands of their Pontiff, or Chief Prieſt.

There, after the Sacrifices, the new King, cloth'd with Royal Habits and Ornaments, was conducted, in pompous Apparel, to the Chair of *Cyrus*, on a Throne of (*o*) unrivall'd Magnificence; where, being ſeated, he receiv'd the Homage of his People: The Chief Prieſt himſelf and the Princes fell in Proſtration upon the Ground before him,

(*n*) *Cyrus*, who is look'd upon as the firſt King of the *Perſian* Empire, was Son of *Cambyſes* and *Mandane*, Daughter of *Aſtyages*, King of the *Medes*. This *Cyrus* united the *Perſian* Empire with that of the *Medes*, and, by his Conqueſts, was Sovereign of the *Eaſt*, *Anno Mundi* 3468, and 536 Years before Chriſt. He dy'd in the Year 3475, 529 Years before Chriſt, and 7 Years after the Reduction of all the *Eaſt* to his Empire. *Joſeph. Ant. l.* 11. *Euſ. Chron. l.* 60. *Petav. l* 10. He magnificently built this Temple of *Pallas*, to proclaim and crown there the Kings of the *Perſians*. Xenophon in Cyropædia

(*o*) *Peliſtratus* tells us, that the Throne of the Kings of *Perſia* was under an Arch of Sapphire, repreſenting the Heavens, and the Stars, and ſupported by Golden Columns, enrich'd with precious Stones. *See* Quint. Curt. l. 4.

and

and paid him a profound Adoration, as if his Coronation plac'd him in the Rank of the Gods.

But not to deviate too far from our Subject, or to enlarge upon any (as we propos'd) but Christian Kings and Emperors, and particularly the Kings of *France*, we will pass to what concerns them, without staying longer on the Antient or Modern Practice of Infidels, in regard to the Inauguration and Crowning of their Kings.

CHAP. III.

What Ceremonies were used in France, *for the Coronation of our Kings, before that of Anointing; and whether it be true, that the Kingdom of* France *was Elective, and not Hereditary, till the Second Race of our Kings.*

THE two Nations of the *French* and *Gauls* were so blended together, in the Constitution of the Kingdom, that they made only one People, and imparted their Ceremonies and Customs reciprocally to one another.

another. But thoſe of the Antient *Gauls* prevail'd in the Inauguration of our Firſt Kings; ſo that, when the *Gauls* pitch'd upon the moſt Noble among the *Druids* (who bore the Character and Reſemblance of our Princes at preſent) for their Chief or General, and came to his Election, the Principal Men of the State rais'd him aloft upon a large Shield, and bearing him upon their ſhoulders, to ſhew him to the People, they carry'd him, array'd in Royal Robes, about the Aſſembly, (which was held in a crowded Plain) and often about the whole Army; with the Sceptre, and Hand of Juſtice, before him, with the Sound of Muſical Inſtruments, and the Acclamations of the People. Thus *Pharamond*, the firſt King of this Monarchy, was elevated and crown'd, with the Conſent of his Father *Marcomirus*, General of the *French* Army, in the Year 420, from the Birth of Chriſt. This was all the Ceremony, that was obſerv'd in the (*p*) Inauguration of his Son *Clodion*, and his Succeſſors, as far as the Anointing and Coronation of *Clovis*: I ſay, his Son *Clodion*, and his Succeſſors; for it is an Error to think, as (*q*) ſome Hiſtorians pretend, that

(*p*) *Pharamond* founded his Kingdom on the Ruins of the *Roman* Empire, then poſſeſs'd by *Honorius*, and *Arcadius*, Sons of *Theodoſius* the Great: in the Year of our Lord 420. *See* Favin Tacit. Hiſt. l. 4. Greg. de Tours. Aimoin.

(*q*) Father *Daniel* and others.

the

the Kingdom of *France* was Elective, till the second Race of our Kings; for before *Pharamond*, the Founder of this Monarchy, Male Issue was call'd to the Succession of the Government, when they were capable of it, and Females were excluded from it by the Salic Law, which was in use before, and confirm'd by *Pharamond*, when that Prince came to establish himself among the *Gauls* (*r*).

The most certain Proof we can give of the Observation of this Law, is the Genealogical Series of all our Kings, by which, beginning at *Pharamond*, we see, they all ascended the Throne, from Father to Son, from Brother to Brother, or from the nearest Relation of the Royal Blood in default of Issue Male. Thus *Clodion* having succeeded *Pharamond*, his Father, in the Year 431, left *Merovæus* his Son Heir of his Crown, in the Year 451, who, ten Years after, left his Kingdom to his Son *Childeric*, Father of *Clovis* I. who, at the Age of Fifteen Years, took the Throne, in the Year 485: since which time it is easy to see, that the Crown of *France* has ever belong'd to the Nearest in Blood, without the least Mention of Election, while there were any Heirs of the Blood-Royal.

(*r*) In the Year 420, from the Birth of Christ. *See* l Orig. des Franç avant Clovis, *by* Mezeray, Recueils de Pithou, &c.

Therefore

Therefore we must not believe, that the Crown of *France* was not Hereditary, till the Emperor *Lotharius*, *Ludovicus Germanicus*, and *Carolus Calvus*, assembled at *Messen* (*s*), agreed among other things, by a solemn Treaty, that, after their Death, their Children should succeed to their Estates; since they had each the Part, that was assign'd them by their Father, and their Uncles had no share of it (*t*): because this Treaty was only a Confirmation of the Salic Law; as it is easy to apprehend by another solemn Act, made between *Louis the Stammerer* and *Louis* King of *Franconia* (*Frankenlandt*) his (*u*) Cousin; by which, they declar'd, That they held their Kingdom by a Successive Right; and that it ought by that Right of Succession to pass to Posterity. Which cannot be understood of the first Establishment of a New Right, but of the Approbation and Confirmation of one that was Antient, and in Practice before.

(*s*) Upon the River *Meuse*, near *Maestricht*.
(*t*) Annal Bertin apud Chesn tom. 3.
(*u*) Done at *Furon*, November 1. 878. *See* Aimoin. l. 5. c. 36. & Annal. Bertin. ad ann. 878.

CHAP.

CHAP. IV.

When and how Christianity and the Anointing of Kings began in France.

THE World had long been oppreſs'd with the Tyranny of the Prince of Darkneſs, when the Sun of Righteouſneſs aroſe to diſperſe it; the earlieſt Beams of his Light were extended to the *Gauls*, almoſt as ſoon as to the other Provinces of the Empire, and *France* was enlighten'd with the Goſpel by the preaching of many Apoſtles and their Diſciples, about (*w*) the Empire of *Decius*.

Several Churches were afterwards founded (*x*) by the firſt Biſhops of the *Gauls*; but when the Perſecutions of the Pagan Emperors put them in Confuſion, and *Conſtantine*, for ſome time, could hardly ſet them on a better footing; after him they

(*w*) St. *Luke*, St. *Philip*, St. *Paul*, and St *Creſcent* his Diſciple

(*x*) By *Photinus* at *Lyons*, *Creſcent* at *Vienne*, *Trophimus* at *Arles*, *Maximus* at *Aix*, *Paul* at *Narborne*, S. *Saturninus* at *Toulouſe*, S. *Gratianus* at *Tours*, S. *Denys* at *Paris*, S. *Auſtronomus* at *Clermont*, S *Martial* at *Limoges*. *See* Papyr Maſſon. Notit. Epiſc. Gall. Mezeray. Hiſt. avant Clovis.

were

were extremely disturb'd by the *Arian* Heresy, and almost entirely destroy'd by the Incursions of the Barbarians: So that there was not an Orthodox Prince in *Christendom*, till *Clovis* I. Son and Successor of *Childeric*, at the Sollicitation of the Queen *Clotilda* (*y*), his Consort, and persuaded and instructed by the Exhortations and Catechisms of St. *Remy*, Bishop of *Rheims*, and of St. *Vaast*, became himself an Apostle, and preach'd the Faith of Jesus Christ, tho' no more than a simple Catechumen: so that his Officers, Soldiers and People that heard him, were surprizingly convinc'd, as he had been, of the Truths of the Gospel, and loudly profess'd, that they would adore no other God, but him that was preach'd by St. *Remy* (*z*).

Of the Baptism, Anointing, and Coronation of Clovis I *of the Name, and the first Christian King.*

Clovis had fill'd the Throne of his Fathers about fourteen Years, having come to it by the Right of Succession, and with the Ceremonies commonly observ'd till that time, when he was converted to the Faith of Christ, was baptiz'd, anointed, and in-

(*y*) *See* Sainte-Marthe, Gall. Christ.

(*z*) Mezeray Hist de Fr. lib. 1. Sainte-Marthe. Fredegaire Hist. Epitom. ch. 23.

augurated

augurated King by the Hands of St. *Remy*, Archbishop of *Rheims*.

This great Action, the Memory of which will be immortal, was perform'd at *Rheims*, in the Church of St. *Remy*, on the Night of *Christmas-Eve*, in the Year of Christ 496. It was accompany'd with all the Pomp imaginable; the Streets of the City were cover'd with Tapestry, the Churches with white Linen, and the Baptistery, near the Gate, was magnificently adorn'd; the Air was fill'd with rich Perfumes, and the Light of Flambeaux and Tapers dispell'd the Gloom of the Night from that August Place. St. *Remy*, who led the King by the Hand to the Font. (*a*) gave him a short and pathetick Exhortation, and History has left us the Terms of it: "Humble thyself, (*b*) O *Si-*" *cambrian!* burn what thou hast wor-" shipp'd, and worship that which thou hast " burnt." After this the King profess'd his Belief in one God, and three Persons; and St. *Remy* baptiz'd him in the Name of the Father, and of the Son, and of the Holy Ghost, while the Bishops, who were present, holding him by his Arms, immerg'd

(*a*) Mezeray Hist de Clovis, l 1. Claude Fauchet, sur les Antiq. & Hist. Gaul. &c. Jean Savaron, sur la Vie de Clovis. Hincmar's Vie de St. Remy.

(*b*) From the Name of his Country, for he was originally of *Sicambria*, Mitis depone, Sycamber, adora quod incendisti, & incende quod adorasti. *S. Martl.* & *Mezeray.*

him (*c*) in the Sacred Laver, into which Three Thousand *French* deſcended after him. The King's Siſters follow'd him in the way of Salvation, and renounc'd their Idolatry (*d*).

Afterwards the King enter'd the Church, in order to his Confirmation, which was perform'd, in the firſt Times, on the Day of Baptiſm, and to be anointed and conſecrated a Chriſtian King, after the Example of the Kings of *Iſrael*, who were anointed, by the Order of God himſelf, for the Government of his People.

(*c*) For many Ages the Baptiſm of Catechumens was perform'd by immerging them thrice in the Water. The Women were rang'd on one Side, and the Men on the other, and they were all naked in the ſame Baptiſtery, having only a Veil between them, that made the Separation. They were undreſs'd by Perſons of the ſame Sex, the Men by Deacons, and the Women by Deaconeſſes, and their Reſpect for this great Myſtery took away the Shame of their Nakedneſs. But St. *Gregory the Great* hearing that the *Arians* of *Spain* us'd this Ceremony, in ſign of the three Natures they maintain'd in the three Perſons of the Godhead, ordain'd the ſingle Immerſion only. If the Catechumens did not behave themſelves well, they contented themſelves with ſprinkling them. *See* Ivo Carnot. Mezeray avant Clovis

(*d*) *Clovis* had two Siſters, *Allcofleda* and *Landechilda*: the firſt, on renouncing Idolatry, was baptiz'd, the ſecond only receiv'd the Holy Chriſm of Confirmation, for ſhe was an *Arian*, and Hereticks were not baptiz'd, ſince Baptiſm was conferr'd in the Name of the Father, the Son, and the Holy Ghoſt, and they did not believe the Conſubſtantiality of the three Perſons, but, on the contrary, would imply, by the Form, a Diverſity of Natures. *Hiſt de France de Mezeray, l 6.* S *Gregory de Tours*, in his *Chron.* collected by *Fredegarius*, chap 21.

It

It was in this moment of Grace that Heaven, in favour of the Conversion of *Clovis* and his Family, gave him visible Marks of its Protection, for him, his Successors, and the Kingdom of *France*, by the Present which it made him of the *Sainte* (*e*) *Ampoulle*, the Holy Vial (*f*), miraculously brought from Heaven by a Dove, in the sight of all the Assistants, and set upon the Altar, where St. *Remy* expected the Holy Oil, that could not soon enough be convey'd, on account of the Multitude that fill'd the Church, and by the Divine Gift of healing the King's-Evil (in touching only the Hand of the Distemper'd) which was conferr'd by God, at the same time, upon *Clovis*, and his Successors in the Kingdom.

St. *Remy*, whom Heaven distinguish'd by its Favour, confirm'd the King with the ordinary Chrism that is used in anointing of Bishops, and anointed him, as King, with the precious Liquor sent down from Hea-

(*e*) *Hincmar's* Life of St. *Remy*, *chap* 21. And behold a Dove, fairer than Snow, suddenly brought down a Vial in his Mouth, full of Holy Oil, all that were present were delighted with the Fragrancy of it, and when the Archbishop had receiv'd it, the Dove vanish'd

(*f*) *Aimoin. l.* 1. *c.* 16. *de l' Hist. de France.* For when he that bore the Chrism was absent, and kept off by the People, lo! suddenly no other, doubtless, than the Holy Spirit appear'd in the visible Form of a Dove, who, carrying the Holy Oil in his shining Bill, laid it down between the Hands of the Minister.

ven (*g*), to anoint that Prince, and his Successors to the Crown (*h*).

The first Care of *Clovis*, after his Baptism, was to re-establish the Churches and Bishopricks destroy'd by the Irruption of the *Vandals*, and by a marvellous Effect of Grace, his Conversion was so great a Turn of State to him, that the *Gauls*, who look'd upon him as an Usurper, and who were desirous of the Dominion of the *Roman* Emperors, while he was an Idolater, lov'd and esteem'd him as their Natural and Lawful Prince, since he enter'd into the Bosom of the Church, so that *Clovis* avow'd himself, and publickly own'd, that it was only from this Day he began to reign, and the *French*

(*g*) When the Holy Chrism was wanting, immediately a Snow-white Dove, descending from Heaven, brought the Vial with the Chrism, out of which the blessed Pontiff anointed the King. *St. Antonin. Som. Hist. Tit.* 11. *cap.* 2.

Charles VII in a Letter of *Garde Gardienne*, granted to the Religious of *St. Remy*, in the Year 1423, speaking of the Holy Vial, says thus "The Sacred Vial, out of which "we and our other Predecessors, Kings of the *French*, by "the Indulgence of the most High, were anointed and con-"secrated"

(*h*) Some Authors have asserted, that the Escutcheon, seeded (*or* powder'd, *we shall use either Term indifferently*) with Fower-de-Luces, and the Oriflamb, were deposited that same Night, by an Angel, in the Hands of an Hermit, in the Solitude of *Joyenval* However that be, our Kings us'd this Standard a long time, and erected it whenever they engag'd the Enemies of the Faith. The *Garde-Oriflamme*, or Post of Keeper of this Banner, was a great Office of the Crown, and it is pretended it was burnt, with the Maid of *Orleans*, by the *English*, under *Charles* VI. *See* Favin. Hist of Navarre.

Monarchy

Monarchy to be confirm'd among the *Gauls* (*t*).

CHAP. V.

Of the Lasting Prerogatives of the Kings of France, *and the Ceremony of their Anointing in general since the Conversion of* Clovis.

THE visible Protection with which Heaven has favour'd our Kings ever since the Conversion of *Clovis*, the Heavenly Unction with which they are anointed, the Purity and Constancy of their Faith, are the inexhaustible Springs of those Gifts and Privileges which raise them above the Greatest Kings of the Earth, and which have justly acquir'd them the eminent Titles of Eldest Sons of the Church, and most Christian Kings.

Indeed they were not only the first Converts to the Faith of Christ, but they have yet another Advantage, that none of them, since the Conversion of *Clovis*, has ever been charg'd with Heresy; when all the other Princes of *Europe* fell in with the Errors of

(*t*) See the Charter of the Foundation of the Abbey of *St. Remy*, reported by F. *le Cointre*.

Arius, or into other Schisms afterwards. Their Faith has never vary'd, they have always been attach'd to the Church as true Sons to their Mother, they have never separated from her; they have defended, protected, and enrich'd her with great Revenues, at the very time when she has been the most afflicted. Thus their Power has been extended, they became the first Emperors of the *West*, and foreign Nations have paid that Reverence to them, that they call them, by way of Excellence, *Kings of the Kings of the Earth* (*k*).

It is for this Reason that the Church has omitted nothing that is the most sacred, great, and respectful for the Ceremony of their Anointing; which tho' it was ever attended with a noble Preparation, yet has come to Perfection by just Degrees of Time, and is now become the most August and Solemn Ceremony in the World. I think I might define it, by saying, that *the Anointing and Coronation of the Kings of* France *is the most high and authentick Act of the Nation*; by which the Prelate, who has a Right to perform it, gives the new King, in the Church appointed for it, a Holy and Celestial Unction, and clothes him with Royal Ornaments, assisted by the Prelates,

(*k*) See the Epistle of St. *Gregory the Great* to *Childebert*, and *Matthew Paris*, the *English* Historian, *Papyre Masson*, *du Tillet*, and *Mezeray*, of the Kings of *France*.

the

the Peers, the Princes, and Nobles of the Kingdom, in the Presence of all the Powers of *Europe*, or of their Ambassadors, in the View of the most distinguish'd Subjects of all the Orders of this Monarchy, and of all the People there assembled (*).

CHAP. VI.

By what Bishop, and in what Place, the Ceremony of Anointing and Crowning the Kings of France, *is ordinarily discharged.*

THE Archbishops of *Rheims* claim the single Right and Possession of Anointing the Kings of *France*; they aver, that *St. Remy* gain'd them that Privilege; which was confirmed to them by several Popes, when they conferred upon them the Primacy of the *Gauls*, and the Title of *Legates born* of the Holy See, and that the Bulls of *Alexander* III. and *Innocent* III.

(*) The Archbishop of *Rheims* pretends to the sole Right of anointing and crowning the Kings of *France*, and that this Ceremony ought to be transacted in his Church. This is what we will examine in the following Chapters, where you will find the Reasons why I do not speak of the Archbishop, nor the Church of *Rheims*, in this Definition.

kept in the Cathedral Church, have forbidden all other Prelates, but the Archbishops of *Rheims*, to anoint the Kings of *France*, or give them the first Coronation (*l*), according to antient Usage.

Some Authors (*m*) are of the same Opinion; and they pretend, that the Vicarship of the Holy See is annexed to the Church of *Rheims*, since the Time of *St. Remy*; and that *Louis* VII. granted by a solemn Law to the same Church and its Archbishops, the exclusive Privilege of Anointing the Kings of *France* (*n*). Yet our more knowing Historians maintain the contrary; they pretend, that this *Vicariat* was only conferred on the Person of St. *Remy*; but that the Dignity by no means passed to his Successors (*o*) That as to the Right of anointing our Kings, *Hincmar*, Archbishop of *Rheims*,

(*l*) The Bulls run thus ——— We *Alexander*, Bishop, &c. do ordain, That none have Power to anoint the King of the *French*, but the Archbishop of *Rheims*, or set the first Crown upon him, as it has obtained by antient Custom.——— We *Innocent*, &c ordain, That none shall anoint or crown the King of the *French*, but the Archbishop of *Rheims*, as your Church in particular has been hitherto accustomed, even in the Vacancy of the See; which we confirm to you and your Successors by Apostolical Authority

(*m*) F *Ru ard*, Art ; of Preface to the Edition of *Greg de Tours* *Marlot* Theatr of Honour.

(*n*) *Du Tillet* says, That the Arret was given by the King himself in the Hall of the Archbishoprick of *Paris*, between the Archbishop of *Rheims*, and the Archbishop of *Sens*, in the Year 1179. *See* Favin Theat. d'Honneur.

(*o*) *See* F. le Cointre, ad ann. 535. p. 59. tit. 1.

de-

declares well, that he had not that Right, exclusive of all other Bishops; in the Discourse and the Account he gave in the Church of *Metz*, to the Bishops of the Province of *Treves*, at the time of the Coronation of *Carolus Calvus*, in the Year 869.

That 200 Years after him, *Gervase de Bellême*, Archbishop of *Rheims*, having advanced, at the Coronation of *Philip* I. in the Year 1059, that from *St. Remy*, the Archbishops of *Rheims* had a Grant from Pope *Hormisdas* of an exclusive Privilege to anoint and crown our Kings; and that *Radulphus*, Successor to the said Archbishop of *Rheims*, having, after him, maintained the same Proposition at the Coronation of *Louis* VI. called *the Fat*, performed at *Orleans*, in the Year 1108: *Ivo*, Bishop of *Chartres*, confuted their Pretension, in his Epistle, written on occasion of the Coronation of *Louis* VII.

That, in fine, it was no longer than since the Year 1179, that *Louis the younger*, having caused his Son *Augustus* to be crowned by Pope *Innocent*, obtained of him, in favour of *William*, Cardinal of *St. Sabine*, Brother of his Wife *Alice*, and Archbishop of *Rheims*, a Bull, which gave to the Archbishops and Church of *Rheims* the eminent Privilege of crowning our Kings. But that, notwithstanding this Bull, the Choice of the Church and Bishop for that

Cere-

Ceremony, always depended on the Pleaſure, Devotion, and Convenience of their Majeſties; who appointed it when, and where they pleas'd, ſometimes in one Place, and ſometimes in another, and always by that Biſhop they pitch'd upon (*p*).

So that, without entering into an Examination of the Merit of theſe different Opinions, in order to decide a Conteſt of this Importance: We will only ſay, that tho' our Kings may, abſolutely ſpeaking, ſingle out the Place where they will be crown'd, at their proper Choice, or the Biſhop that ſhall diſcharge that Function; yet we may fairly pronounce, that the Place, and the Prelate deſigned for it, are the Cathedral Church of *Rheims*, and its Archbiſhop; becauſe almoſt all our Monarchs, ſince *Clovis*, have preferred them to all others, for this great Ceremony: whether, becauſe the Miracles, ſhewn by the Interceſſion of *S. Remy*, at the Baptiſm of *Clovis*, appear to have marked the Place where his Succeſſors were to be crowned, and the Prelate who ought to have the Honour of it; or whether there is no City where it can be managed more properly, than in that where the precious Balm,

(*p*) See Letter the 70th of *Ivo*, Biſhop of *Chartres*, upon the Complaint of the Clergy of *Rheims*, on occaſion of the Crowning of *Lewis* VII. Doublet, in Hiſt. Sandyoniſ. c. 1. fol. 373. F. Sirmond, chap. Car. Cal. Mezeray Hiſt. de France, t. 2. p. 74.

ſent

sent from Heaven for this August Ceremony, was preserved for so many successive Ages, or, in short, that Custom might seem to pass into a Law.

This Determination of a fixed Place, and Bishop for it, is conformable to the Practice of the greatest Monarchies; they all have their Places assign'd, and consecrated, as we may say, by the Order of God, and the Consent of the People, for the Ceremonies of Pomp, and solemn Preparation. Thus the Temple of *Jerusalem* was built with that Magnificence, to oblige the People to resort thither, for the Worship of the true God; and there they performed their Sacrifices, by the High-Priest (*q*). The Tables of the Law were there deposited; there they crowned the Kings of *Judah*, and (*r*) the Royal Oil was preserved.

Thus likewise the *Romans* elected their Consuls in the *Campus Martius*, and after returned to the *Capitol*, to confirm that Election, in the Presence of their false Gods, and to (*s*) thank them with Sacrifices.

The Inauguration of the antient Kings of *Persia*, all Pompous as it was, was not done at *Suza*, the Capital of that Monarchy, but at some Leagues distance, in a

(*q*) See Flav. Joseph. Oper. Antiq. Jud. c. 6. & 10.
(*r*) Joseph. Hist. Jud. 1 Sam. 9. 1 Kings 1.
(*s*) Tit. Liv. c. 2. & 5.

certain

certain Borough, and by the Chief Prieſt appointed for it (*t*).

The Coronation of the Emperors of *Conſtantinople*, before the Conqueſt of it by the *Turks*, was always done in the Church of *St. Sophia*, the moſt magnificent Temple of that Time (*v*).

Amongſt us, that is, in Chriſtian Kingdoms, the Solemnity of a Coronation is rarely held in a Capital City, or in the Place of the ordinary Reſidence of a Monarch. There are other Places marked out for it.

In *Germany*, the Coronation of the Emperor was always at *Aix la Chapelle*, one of the fineſt Towns of the Empire, till the Year 1558, that *Ferdinand* and his Succeſſors were crowned, ſome at *Frankfort*, and others at *Ratisbon*, by the Archbiſhop of *Mentz*, who alone enjoys that Privilege.

In *Spain*, this Ceremony is at *Toledo*.

In *England*, at *Weſtminſter*, a City adjoining to *London*, by the Archbiſhop of *Canterbury*.

(*t*) Amm. Marcell. c. 30. tells us, it was at *Paſagardis*, and that the Chief Prieſt *Surina* performed the Ceremony.

(*v*) This noble Edifice was begun by *Juſtin*, and finiſhed by *Juſtinian*, both Emperors of the *Eaſt*, who dedicated it to the Divine Wiſdom, under the Name of *Sancta Sophia*. The *Turks* have only kept the Dome ſtanding, which was the Choir of the antient Church, which they uſe at preſent as a Moſque. *See* Grelot Voyage de Conſtantinople.

In

In *Poland*, at *Gnezna*, by the Archbishop of that Place.

In *Denmark*, at *Lunden*, a famous City of *Schonen*, separated by an Arm of the Sea from *Copenhagen*, the ordinary Residence of the *Danish* Kings.

In *Hungary*, at *Presburg*, since the taking of *Alba Regalis*, where at other times this Ceremony was performed.

In *Sweden*, at *Upsal*, seven Leagues from *Stockholm*. And thus in other Nations.

So that we may reasonably affirm, that every Kingdom has its City, Town, Place, and Prelate appointed for this purpose. We may at the same time easily prove, that this Privilege was not given at random to the Places and Prelates that enjoy it; but mostly, because they were the first Witnesses and Ministers of the Conversion and Coronation of their first Princes, that were Converts to the Faith, or on the Score of other memorable Events. Hence it is (*x*), that they are with reason jealous of so great a Pre-eminence; which gives them the Advantage of partaking in the most August Action of a Kingdom; and always use their Efforts to preserve it. But Usage and Possession are no Bar against the Will of Sovereigns, who may set them aside, and change them at their pleasure, when the Juncture or Occasion demands.

(*x*) Ivo Carnotensis. Epist. 70. Marlot. Theatr. d'Hon. cap. 1.

CHAP.

CHAP. VII.

Whether all the Kings of France *of the first Race, were anointed as Kings; whether it was always at* Rheims: *or whether this Royal Unction commenced before* Pepin, *Founder of the second Race.*

IT would be difficult to prove, that all the Succeſſors of *Clovis*, even they of the firſt Race, were anointed as Kings. Some Hiſtorians pretend, on the contrary, that he was only anointed as a Chriſtian; that the Regal Unction was not uſed in *France* before *Pepin*, Author of the ſecond Race; and that *Louis the Stammerer* was the firſt King of *France*, that was anointed as King by the Archbiſhop of *Rheims*. But if Hiſtory does not aſſure us poſitively that all our Kings from *Clovis* to *Pepin* received the ſacred Unction, as Kings, it does not permit us to doubt the uſe of it long before the Reign of *Pepin*; and that the Sons of *Clovis* were anointed, as he was before.

St.

St. Remy himſelf informs us, that *Clovis*, after his Converſion, received on the ſame day Baptiſm, Confirmation, and the Sacred Unction, to reign with more Luſtre over his People.

Hincmar, Archbiſhop of *Rheims*, who liv'd in the eighteenth Century, aſſures us of the ſame (*y*.)

And the holy Apoſtle of *France* (z) makes it evident, that he continued the Ceremony of the Anointing in the Perſons of the four Sons of *Clovis* (*a*), who divided the Kingdom after him. Therefore, after theſe authentick Proofs, and eſpecially that of the Saint, who was the Inſtrument of God in the Converſion of *Clovis*, we cannot doubt, but that Prince and his Children were anointed as Kings; and, by conſequence, the Royal Unction was in uſe a long time before the Reign of *Pepin*.

Many learned Hiſtorians and Antiquaries aſſure us, that *Childebert* I. *Cherebert* or *Aribert*, *Chilperic* I. *Dagobert* I. *Childeric* II.

(y) In the Will of *St. Remy*, in *Flodoard*, lib. 1. & 2. he ſays, *Excepto genere*, &c. *i. e.* Having received the Royal Family, (ſpeaking of that of *Clovis*) which, in honour of Holy Church, and Defence of the Poor, I and my Brethren, elected to the Royal Dignity for ever, baptiz d, took from the Holy Font, ſealed with the ſevenfold Gift of the Spirit, and ordained to the Crown by the Unction of the ſame holy Chriſm.

(z) In Capitular. Car Calvi.

(*a*) That Royal Iſſue (ſays *St. Remy* in the Place quoted) ſo often conſecrated to God by my Benediction.

Theodoric,

Theodoric or *Thierry* I. *Childebert* II. and *Dagobert* II. were all anointed (*b*).

So that all the Foundation which ſome had to affirm, this Cuſtom did not prevail in the firſt Race of our Kings, was, that ſince the firſt of our Nation, long after *Clovis*, retain'd the Practice of elevating them upon a Buckler, like the antient *Gauls*, they could not perſuade themſelves, that a Practice introduced by the Pagans was compatible with ſo holy a Ceremony, as that of anointing: but, (*c*) as all the Hiſtorians agree, that the Change of Religion under *Clovis*, made no Innovation in Cuſtoms that were indifferent to the Chriſtian Faith, and eſpecially were not ſuperſtitious; we cannot doubt, without diſcarding the more juſt Opinion, but the Ceremonies of Elevation upon the Buckler, and of Anointing, were practis'd before the Reign of *Pepin*.

(*d*) So that we may ſay with aſſurance, that as all the Kings of *Iſrael* and *Judah* were

(*b*) *Waltramne*, *Ivo* of *Chartres*, *Belleforeſt*, and *J. Chen.* in Vit. Epiſc. Remenſ. Doublet in Hiſt Sandyoniſ.

(*c*) Chron. Greg. de Tours. *Pepin* is exalted to the Kingdom by the Election of all *France* to the Throne, with the Conſecration of Biſhops, and the Homage of Princes, as the antient Order requires, with his Queen *Bertradane*. Chron. Bertin. more clearly. *Pepin* was elected King, after the manner of the *French*, and anointed by the Hand of *Boniface* the Archbiſhop, and choſen by the *French* to the Kingdom.

(*d*) The Annals of *Metz* are not leſs deciſive. He ordained the moſt pious Prince *Pepin*, to be King of *France*, with the Holy Unction, according to the manner of his Predeceſſors. *Queicet Tom.* 3.

anointed,

anointed, after the example of *Saul* and *David*, tho' the Scripture only ſpeaks of ſome that received it. Thus thoſe of *France* imitated *Clovis* and his Sons in this holy and ſalutary Rite; tho' it is not expreſsly mentioned in the greateſt Part of our Hiſtories.

All the difficulty is, where, and how the Succeſſors of *Clovis*, to the ſecond Race, were anointed.

Hiſtories and Annals are ſo obſcure upon theſe Facts, that it is almoſt impoſſible to meet with a perfect Inſtruction from them. Nevertheleſs (*e*) ſome think, that it was the Oil of the holy Vial, preſerved in the City of *Rheims*.

(*f*) Others think, that after the Death of *Clovis*, the Kingdom being divided among his four Sons, who reign'd each as a Sovereign, in the extent of his Diviſion, with the Title of King of *France*, that is; *Thierri*, King of *Metz*; *Clodomir* of *Orleans*; *Childebert* of *Paris*; and *Clotharius* of *Soiſſons*. each of them was anointed in a Church, and by a Biſhop of his Dominions. That thus the Kings of *Orleans*

(*e*) See *St. Thomas*, *Vincent* of *Beauvais*, and *St. Antonin*. *Will. Brit.* in his *Philippide*, tells us the ſame in theſe Verſes

Quo Rex ſacratus fuit, idem primus & omnes
Poſt ipſum Reges Francorum ad Sceptra vocati,
Quando coronantur, Oleo ſacrantur eodem.
From Clovis *all with Sacred Oil are crown'd.*

(*f*) Ivo Carnot. Dupleix, Hiſt. de France.

and *Paris* were anointed by the Biſhops of *Celtic Gaul*, thoſe of *Soiſſons* by a Biſhop of that City; and the Kings of *Auſtraſia*, who reſided indifferently at *Rheims*, or at *Metz*, were anointed with the Oil of the holy Vial, by the Archbiſhop of *Rheims*.

In ſhort, ſome oppoſe this Opinion, and maintain (*g*), that as the Kings of *Paris* alone bore their Arms, Sapphire three *Flower-de-Luces*, Topaz; others having them of a different Colour and Metal. ſo none but they were anointed with the holy Vial, and crowned in the City of *Rheims*; that the other Kings were crowned with the uſual Unction, and by ordinary Biſhops, in the principal Cities of their Government.

But the difficulty of conceiving, how, in the Diviſion of the Kingdom, the Kings of *Paris* could be anointed in a City that was out of their Allotment, and the Jealouſy, Diſtruſt, and Diſcord, that almoſt always prevailed among theſe Princes, give a great Prejudice to this Opinion, ſo that the preceding Notion is the more probable, and the leſs ſubject to Inconveniences.

As to what remains, in the uncertainty of the Hiſtory recited above, we cannot determine for either Party.

The greateſt Certainty we have, as to the firſt Race of our Kings, call'd the *Mero-*

(*g*) Favin. Theatr. d'Honneur, & de Chevallerie, & Du Tillet.

vingian,

vingian, which reign'd 332 Years, (consisting, in Number, of 22 Kings, reckoning only those of *Paris*; but 37, if you take in all that bore that Title, as well in *Austrasia*, where there was but one, residing at *Metz*, as in *Neustria*, where there were sometimes three, who held their Seat, some at *Orleans*, others at *Soissons*, others at *Paris*,) is, that they mostly preserved the antient Usages of the *Gauls*. Baptism, and the Anointing, did not soften their Barbarity; they were fierce and bloody; to the time of *Clotharius* II. That King, and his Successors, except *Childeric* II. shew'd themselves much more humane and religious than their Predecessors (*h*). Some are of opinion also, that the Kings of the first Race did not wear a Crown, but only a Diadem; and they remark upon their Coins now remaining, that their Foreheads are encompassed with a Wreath seeded, or studded, with Pearls (*i*).

But, since we will not advance as certain, such Facts, as are too obscure in History, about the Anointing of the Kings of the first Race, we will pass to the second; beginning with *Pepin the Short*. Since

(*h*) *See* Mezeray, Hist de France. Cl Fauchet, des Antiq & Hist. Gauloises. Gerauld de Cordemoy, Hist de France, lib. 1. & 22.

(*i*) *See* Charles Patin Introduct a l'Hist. par la connoissance des Medailles, & le Science des Medailles du Pere Joseph Jesuite. Les Antiq. de la Gaule Belg. par R. de Wassebourg.

whom, all Authors agree, not only about the Coronation of our Kings, but about the Place and Time of the Ceremony.

CHAP. VIII.

A Chronological and Historical Table of the Kings of France, *of the Second and Third Race; containing the Names of the Cities or Towns where they were anointed and crown'd; as also of the Popes, Cardinals, Archbishops, or Bishops, who perform'd the Ceremony, and the Date of their Coronation, to this Day.*

PEPIN *the Short* (k), the 22d, or, according to others, the 23d King of *France*, was anointed and crown'd, the first time, in the Cathedral Church of (l) *Soissons*,

(k) *Pepin the Short*, Son of *Charles Martel*, and *Rotrude*, was Master of the Palace, and elected King of *France* by the Advice of Pope *Zacharias*, in a Parliament assembled at *Soissons*, in the Place of *Childeric*

(l) *Childeric* was depos'd and banish'd to the Monastery of St. *Himeran* at *Ratisbonne*, where he dy'd, according to the Account of St. *Bertin*, in the second Year of the Coronation

sons, by *Boniface* Archbishop of *Mentz*, as Legate of the Holy See, and Commissarial Governour of the Church of *Rheims*, then vacant, in the Year 751. But the second time (*m*) in the Church of St. *Denys* in *France*, with his Queen *Bertha*, and his two Sons, *Charles*, afterwards call'd *The Great*, and *Carloman*, by Pope *Stephen* III. who came into *France* in *August*, in the Year 754.

CHARLEMAGNE (*n*) the 23d King of *France*, and first Emperor of the *West*, was anointed, the first time, in the

nation of King *Pepin* *Pepin* was rais'd upon a Target, according to antient Custom, plac'd upon the Royal Throne, and anointed with the blessed Oil, says *Mezeray*, that this Unction (according to the Word of God, *Touch not mine Anointed*) might serve as a Shield to his Person, and a Softening of his Authority *Hist de Pepin de Bref.*

(*m*) It is doubted by many, whether *Pepin* was twice anointed and crown'd as King of *France*. They agree only about the Coronation at St. *Denys* in 754, and deny that at *Soissons* in 751, for so, say they, there would be two Unctions in four Years, of the same King, for the same Kingdom, which is contrary to the Discipline and Usages of the Church, not allowing a Repetition of Anointing for the same purpose. But as we find a Variety of Cases where it has been repeated, we must think it was an established Custom at certain Junctures, after the Example of the Kings of *Israel* and *Judah*, who were often anointed, when Occasion or Necessity requir d

(*n*) *Pepin the Short* dying *September* 26 in 768 *Charles* and *Carloman*, his Sons, succeeded him, and, by the Consent of all the Nobles, they were recogniz'd Kings, enthron'd, and invested with the *Regalia* on the same Day, the first at *Noyon*, the second at *Soissons*, *Carolus & Carlomannus elevati sunt in Regnum, uno Die simul, Carolus in Noviomo, & Carlomanus Suessionis Civitate.* *See* the Annals of *Eginard*, and the Life of *Charlemagne*, by *le Moine*.

Church of St. *Denys* in *France*, during the Life of *Pepin* his Father; and with him, and Queen *Bertha*, his Mother, and *Carloman*, his Brother, by Pope *Stephen* III. who came into *France* in *August*, or, according to others, in *July* 754. The second time at *Noyon*, by . . . in 768, immediately after the Death of *Pepin*; the third time, as King of *Lombardy*, in the Town of *Monza*, by the Archbishop of *Milan*, in the Year 774; the fourth time at *Rome*, as Emperor of the *West*, by Pope *Leo* III. on *Christmas*-Day, in the Year 800, by the Consent of *Nicephorus*, Emperor of the *East*. *Charlemagne* had been thirty two Years King of *France*, when he ascended the Throne of the *Western* Empire.

CARLOMAN was anointed, the first time, at St. *Denys*, with *Pepin* his Father, Queen *Bertha* his Mother, and *Charlemagne* his Brother, by Pope *Stephen* III. in the Month of *July*, or *August*, 754.

The second time at *Soissons*, after the Death of his Father and Mother, on the Day, that his Brother *Charlemagne* was anointed at *Noyon*, by . . . . in the Year 768.

LOUIS I. call'd the *Debonnair*, the 24th King of *France*, and Emperor of the *West*, was anointed, the first time, at *Rome*, as King of *Aquitaine*, in the Presence of his Father *Charlemagne*, by Pope *Leo* III. in the Year 800.

The

The second time at *Rheims*, as Emperor of the *West*, with *Hermengarde* his Queen, Daughter of Count *Hildegrand*, of the House of *Saxony*; by Pope *Stephen* V. who came for that purpose from *Rome* to *France*, whither he brought two Crowns of Gold; one, set with precious Stones, for the King, the other plain for the Queen, towards the end of *July*, or the beginning of *August* in 816 (*o*).

CHARLES II. called *the Bald*, 25th King of *France*, and Emperor of the *West*, Son of *Louis* I. and his Successor, was anointed the first time at *Rome*, as King of the *Romans*, or *Lombards*, by Pope *Sergius* II. in the Year 846.

The second time at *Limoges*, as King of *Aquitaine*, by . . . . . in 854, in the Month of *October*.

The third time at *Metz*, in the Church of St. *Stephen*, as King of *Lorain*, by *Hincmar* (*p*), Archbishop of *Rheims*, *Septemb.* the 9th, in the Year 869.

(*o*) Pope *Leo* III dying, as soon as *Stephen* V was in possession of the Chair, he commanded all the *Roman* People to promise and swear an Oath of Fidelity to *Louis the Debonnair*, as their Emperor of the *West*, and having by his Legates requir'd a Permission to come to *France*, he arriv'd, by the King's Consent, at *Rheims*, two Months after his Advancement to the Holy See, and having declar'd the Subject of his Voyage to the King, he anointed and crown'd him Emperor of the *West*, &c *Mezeray Tom* 1.

(*p*) *Lotharius*, King of *Lorain*, having departed this Life in the Town of *Plaisance*, *Charles the Bald* succeeded him in the Kingdom of *Lorain*, which was a part of that of *France*.

LOUIS II. call'd *the Stammerer* (*q*), the 26th King of *France*, and Emperor of the *West*, second Son of *Charles the Bald*, and Queen *Hermentrude*, having receiv'd at *Compiegne* the Sword, Scepter, Crown, and Royal Robes, by which his Father vested him in the Kingdom, was anointed and crown'd, by Consent of all the Nobles, by *Hincmar*, Archbishop of *Rheims*, *Decemb.* 8. 877. or, according to others, 878 (*r*).

He was anointed and crown'd, as Emperor of the *West*, a second time at *Troyes*, by Pope *John* VIII. who took Refuge in *France*, to avoid the Fury of *Carloman*, eldest Son of *Louis* I. who pretended to the Empire, *Septemb.* the 7th, 879.

LOUIS III. call'd *the Lazy*, 27th King of *France*, and his Brother *Carloman*, were anointed and crown'd Kings in the Abbey of St. *Peter* of *Ferrieres* in *Gatinois*, by *Ansegise*, Archbishop of *Sens*, in 880.

(*q*) The Bishops, who assisted at this Coronation, were *Adventius* Bishop of *Metz*, *Otbo* of *Verdun*, *Arnold* of *Toul*, *Francus* of *Liege*, all in the Province of *Treves*, with those of the Province of *Rheims*, who had at their Head their Archbishop *Hincmar*. In right Order this Coronation had belong'd to the Bishop of *Metz*, because it was his Church, or to the Archbishop of *Treves*, as Metropolitan, if he had one at that time, yet the Archbishop of *Rheims* perform'd the Ceremony, after he declar'd that he did it only as the most antient consecrated Bishop, and that they of *Treves* sollicited and appointed him to it in the Absence of their Metropolitan, which proves that *Rheims* is not the only Place for it. *F. Sirm. in Car. Calv.*

(*r*) *See* le Contin. d'Aimoin l. 5. c. 36. Mezeray, Hist. de Fr. l. 10. Annal. Bertin. ad An. 878. Tom. 2.

After

After the Death of *Louis* and *Carloman*, there was an Interregnum of one Year, the Kingdom ſhould have come to *Charles the Simple*, poſthumous Brother of theſe two Princes, but ſince *Charles* was not then above five Years old, and the *Normans*, Enemies of *France*, occaſion'd great Diſturbances in the Kingdom, the Abbot *Hugo*, or *Eudo*, his Tutor, thought there was a Neceſſity for a brave and valiant Prince to repulſe them; therefore he called into *France* *Carolus Craſſus*, King of *Lombardy*, of *Germany* (*s*), and Emperor of the *Weſt*, and Couſin of *Louis* and *Carloman*.

CHARLES, call'd *the Fat*, 28th King of *France*, and Emperor of the *Weſt*, was crown'd and anointed, the firſt time, as King of *Lombardy*, at *Milan*, by the Archbiſhop of that Place, in the Year 880.

The ſecond time at *Rome*, as Emperor of the *Weſt*, by Pope *Adrian* III. in the Year 881.

We do not find that *Charles the Groſs* (*or the Fat*, *le Gras*, or *le Gros*) was anointed

(*s*) *Louis the Stammerer* being extremely ſick at *Compiegne*, ſent the Regalia to *Louis*, his eldeſt Son, and order'd the Nobles to crown him, which was punctually diſcharg'd. The two Brothers were crown'd together in their Youth. It does not appear that the Archbiſhop of *Rheims* then complain'd, that the two Kings were crown'd by another, which alſo confutes the Opinion, that the Crown was elective. Neither of them left any Poſterity, *Louis* dy'd *Auguſt* the 4th, in 882. and *Carloman*, *December* the 6th, in 884. *See* Albert. Chron. ad Ann. 884. Le Cointre. Aimoin l. 5. c. 39.

or crown'd as King of *France*, ſo that the moſt knowing Hiſtorians only look upon him as Tutor and Regent during the Minority of *Charles the Simple*, and do not comprehend him in the Number of our Kings of the Name of *Charles*. He acquitted himſelf with great Conduct and Succeſs in his Regency, but degenerated ſo much a little after, and became ſo ſpiritleſs, that his Subjects abandon'd him, and were forc'd to depoſe him, on the ſcore of his Indolence, Supineneſs, and Diſhoneſty, in the Month of *January*, in the Year 887; ſo that he dy'd in Poverty, and, according to ſome, was poiſon'd, or ſtrangled, in a Village of *Suabia*, in *January* 888. He was the laſt King of *France* who poſſeſs'd the Empire, the *Germans* having expell'd him, and choſen *Arnould* in his ſtead, the Baſtard Son of his Brother *Carloman*

And as *Charles the Simple* was not above eight Years of Age, at the time of the Retreat and Departure of *Charles the Groſs*, the Eſtates, aſſembled at *Compiegne*, deſir'd *Eudo*, Count of *Paris*, Duke of *France*, and Prince of the Blood, to take upon him the Tuition of the young Prince, and the Regency of the Kingdom, which he accepted with Regret, tho' it was an Honour due to his Birth (*t*).

(*t*) *See* Chron. Alb ad Ann 884 Chro Flo Chen. tom. 2 p 638 Mezer Hiſt de Fr l 10. Du Chene, tom. 3. p. 356. Annall Metenſ ad Ann. 887, & 888.

Eudo,

Eudo, *Eudes*, 29th King of *France*, Son of *Robert* I. call'd *the Valiant*, and *Adelaide*, Daughter of the Emperor, *Louis the Debonnair*, was elected and crown'd at *Compiegne* by *Gauthier*, or *Vautier*, Archbishop of *Sens*, in *January* 887; tho' *Compiegne* did not belong to his Metropolitan Church, but to that of *Rheims*.

We do not find that he was anointed, tho he bore the Title of King, and tho' History tells us that he was crown'd as such. But we ought not to be surpriz'd at it, because he was only crown'd for a time, that is, during (*u*) the Minority of *Charles the Simple*, and he only govern'd *France* as Tutor of that Monarch (*x*).

It was then the Custom for the Regents to take the Title of Kings in their Charters, and date them by the Years of their Reign, and for Kings themselves not to use that Style till the Day of their Coronation and Anointing, when they came to full Majority; unless the Kings, their Fathers, acting by their Sovereign Authority, occasion'd them to be crown'd, during their Life, or commanded it to be done as soon as possible when they dy'd, without waiting for their Majority: or, in short, that the Nobles of

(*u*) Chron. Marchienf. l. 2. c. 19. Annal. Metenf. Rheginald ad Ann. 888. Du Chene, tom. 3. pag. 355, &c.

(*x*) Chron. Floriac Chen. tom 2. pag. 638. *See* Baluf. Append ad Capitul. col. 1515, & 1517. Mabill. Diplom. pag. 296. Ivo Carnot. l. 4.

the

the Kingdom supply'd the Defect, by crowning the young Prince at any Age whatever. This Custom of crowning the Regent Kings continu'd till the 12th Age, according to some Authors, not only in *France*, but in the Empire of *Constantinople*, where *John* of *Brienne* was crown'd King, being Regent of the Empire, during the Minority of the Emperor *Baldwin* of *Courtenay*, in 1229, when the *French* Kings were Masters of the *Eastern* Empire (*y*).

CHARLES III. call'd *the Simple*, the 30th King of *France*, posthumous Son of King *Louis the Stammerer*, and of Queen *Adelaide*. When he came to the Age of twelve or thirteen Years, the Nobles of the Kingdom assembled, and recogniz'd his Right to the Crown, for the *French* had no other Kings but those that enjoy'd the Crown by the Right of Birth, and the Order of Succession: insomuch that they sent a Deputation to him in *England*, whither his Mother had convey'd him, and at the Prayer of his People he return'd to *France*, where he was anointed and crown'd at *Rheims*, by *Foulques*, or *Fouques*, the Archbishop, *Feb.* 27. 893 (*z*).

Eudo, two Years after, restor'd the Kingdom to *Charles the Simple*, and acknow-

(*y*) Du Cange des Emper. de Constant. p 88. & Du Bouchet. sur l'Hist. de Courtenay, p. 66.

(*z*) *See* Annal. Metens & Rhegin. ad Ann. 892. Mezer. Hist de Franc l 10 tom 1.

ledg'd

ledg'd him as fole King of *France*; and this Monarch, to repay his Services, fhar'd the Government with him, giving up to him the Provinces of the *Loire*, to hold and govern them (but under his Name) according to an Agreement made between them in the Year 894, which was the firft of the Reign of *Charles the Simple*, and the feventh of that of *Eudo*, or rather of his Regency (*a*).

After the Death of *Eudo*, which happen'd at *la Ferre* in *Picardy*, on the 3d of *January* 898, *Robert* his Brother, Count of *Paris*, and Duke of *France*, difpleas'd that *Charles the Simple* had reunited to his Domain the Part he had given to *Eudo*, rais'd a Commotion, and would divide the Kingdom with *Charles the Simple*, as his Brother *Eudo* had done; and by the Affiftance of fome Malecontents, he caus'd himfelf to be anointed at *Rheims* by *Hervé*, then Archbifhop, *June* the 20th, 922 (*b*): but *Charles* flew him with his own Hand, in a Battel near *Soiffons*, *June* 15. 923.

All Authors do not agree about thefe two laft Facts, but however that be, *Robert* cannot pafs for King; he is an Ufurper, who did not fucceed in his Enterprize.

(*a*) *See* Papyre Maffon, l. 1. *of his Annals of* France. Mezeray Chron. Rheg. ad Ann. 892. Ann. Metenf. ad Ann. 893.

(*b*) Ann. Bert. ad Ann. 898. Flodoard. Marlot. & Mezeray, l. 10. Hift. de Fran. tom. 1. *and alfo the Chronicle of* Ademar.

RA-

RAOUL, or *Radulphus*, 31st King of *France*, Son of *Richard* Duke of *Burgundy*, Count of *Autun* and *Hildegarde*, Grand-daughter of *Charlemagne*, having a design on the Throne of *Charles the Simple*, who was detain'd Prisoner in the Castle of *Peronne*, by the Treason and Felony of *Herbert*, Duke of *Vermandois*, caus'd himself to be proclaim'd King, and afterwards crown'd at *Soissons*, in the Church of St. *Medard*, by *Seulphe*, Archbishop of *Rheims*, *July* the 23d, *Anno* 923. tho' he was not of the Royal Family (*c*), which gave him the Name of an Usurper; yet he only govern'd as Regent during the Imprisonment of *Charles the Simple*, in the Tower of *Peronne*, where he dy'd, after a Confinement of six Years, worn away with Sorrow and Misery, *Octob.* 29. 929. But *Charles* leaving no Children, and there being but two Princes that could pretend to the Succession, that is, *Herbert*, Count of *Vermandois* (a Prince legitimated, descended of *Bernard*, King of *Italy*, Son of *Pepin*, second Son of *Charlemagne*, who became odious by the default of Birth from his Great Grandfather, and especially by his Crime of Felony against his Sovereign *Charles the Simple*,) and *Hugo le Grand*, Prince of the Blood, Son of *Robert* (who was kill'd by *Charles the Simple*) but as yet too young to govern; therefore the Crown was entire-

(*c*) Chron. de Verdun, *by* Hugo, *Abbot of* Flavigny.

ly

ly left to *Raoul*, who was the sole Master of it, after the Death of *Charles the Simple*, till his own, which happen'd at *Auxerre*, where he dy'd, eaten up by Vermin, *January* the 15th, 936. after a Reign of fourteen Years (*d*).

(*e*) *LOUIS* IV. called *d'Outremer*, *Ultramarine*, 31st King of *France*, Son of *Charles the Simple*, was anointed and crown'd at *Laon*, by *Artold*, Archbishop of *Rheims*, before above twenty Bishops, *Hugo le Grand*, and the other Lords of *France*, *June* the 20th, 936.

LOTHARIUS, 33d King of *France*, Son of *Louis* IV. ascended the Throne at the Age of twelve or thirteen Years; and was anointed and crowned at *Rheims*, immediately after the death of his Father, by Archbishop *Artold*, *November* the 20th, 954, in the presence of *Hugo le Grand*, Duke of *France*, his Tutor, the Prelates and Lords of the three Kingdoms of *France*, *Burgundy* and *Aquitaine*, which after were all united. It is observed, that immediately

(*d*) Mezeray Hist. de Fr. lib. 10. tom. 1. Chron. Verdun. Labb. tom. 1 pag 125

(*e*) After the Imprisonment of *Charles the Simple* his Father, *Ogine* his Mother, Daughter of *Edward*, King of *England*, carry'd him thither, but *Hugo le Grand*, and the other Lords, brought him back, after the Death of *Raoul*, Usurper of his Father's Crown When *Louis* IV. arriv'd at *Boulogne*, the Nobles of *France*, that went to seek for him, took the Oath of Fealty to him, as their lawful Sovereign, proclaim'd him King, and conducted him to *Laon*, in order to his Anointing and Coronation *See the* Fragm. ex Ant Membran Floriac. ad ann 936 after he kept his Residence at *Laon*; but that five Months after, his Tutor brought him to *Paris*, of which he was Count, and treated him in a splendid manner. It was fourscore Years, since the Kings of the *Carlovingian* Race had enter'd it: the Counts of *Paris* being Masters of that City (*f*).

LOUIS V. called *the Lazy*, 34th King of *France*, was anointed and crown'd the first Time, during the Life of his Father *Lotharius* (*g*), at *Compiegne*, in the Year 978, or, according to others, in the Year 979.

The second time at *Rheims*, by the Archbishop *Adalbero*, in the Year 986, a very little time after the death of his Father, which happened about the end of the Year 985.

This Prince was, as yet, under the Regency of *Enima* his Mother, tho' he was about 18 or 19 Years old, at the time of anointing.

He reign'd only one Year, and some Months; and dying without Children, *June* the 22d, 987, the *Carlovingian* Race, or that of *Charlemagne*, ended with him; and the Kingdom was transferred to the third Line, of which *Hugh Capet* was Chief:

(*f*) *See* Glab. Rad. Hist. de France. Mezer. Hist. Franc. l. 10.

(*g*) *See* the Supplement of the Diplomatique of F. Mabillon, in his Marca Hispanica. Chap. 10, 11, 12. Pag. 42, & 43.

becauſe *Charles* of *France*, Brother of King *Lotharius*, Uncle of King *Louis* V. and the ſole Heir in the Collateral Line, who could pretend to the Crown, had been adjudg'd by the Eſtates General to have forfeited the Right of Succeſſion, by having taken Arms againſt the King his Brother: The Felony of Vaſſals being then puniſhed by the Privation of their Domaine (*b*).

As to the reſt, this ſecond Race laſted 236 Years; and ſaw a Chain of eleven Kings, taking in thoſe of Weſtern *France*, and not accounting *Louis* and *Carloman*, but for one.

All the Hiſtorians agree, that in the Time of this Race, the Kings, when they took the Crown, received alſo the Holy Unction by the Miniſtry of a Biſhop: Their Royal Ornaments were the Sceptre, or Baton of Gold, of their Majeſty, the Hand of Juſtice, the Crown, the Bracelets; and the Mantle, or Long Robe, with an Apparel caſt behind, underneath a Tunicle.

They were almoſt always on Horſeback, and in the Field, lodged in Tents, and took their Wives along with them.

Charles Martel, and *Pepin*, made their abode at *Paris*, and in the neighbouring Country; *Charlemagne* at *Aix la Cha-*

(*b*) F. Daniel, Hiſt de France. Col. 467. t. 1. Bacquet. & Charles du Moulin, in verbo Felonie.

pelle; *Charles the Debonnair*, at the same Place, or at *Thionville*; *Charles the Bald*, at *Soissons* and *Compiegne*; *Eudo* at *Paris*, *Charles the Simple* at *Rheims*; *Louis d'Outremer* at *Laon*, *Lotharius* sometimes there, and sometimes at *Rheims*. Most of these Princes were very pious, and gave large Donations to the Church; till the latter, about the end of this Race, invaded the Rights of it.

The Ruin of this second Race is imputed, 1. To the Division of the Body of the State into several Kingdoms, which occasioned Civil Wars. 2. To the Weakness of most of these Princes. 3. To the too great Power of the Princes of the Blood, and the Illegitimate Issue; and the extravagant Power of the Queens, and their Enormities. 4. And especially to the Ravages of the *Normans*, who made a Desolation in *France* above a hundred Years; and favoured the Attempts of the Factious. To which *Mezeray* adds with reason (speaking of the *Carlovingian* Line) that, as this Tree bore good Fruit no longer, God was pleased to cut it down, and plant another in the stead of it, infinitely more beautiful and fertile, which should last in Glory to the End of the World (*t*).

(*t*) Mezeray Hist de Fran. l. 10. t 1. F. Daniel, Hist. de Fran. t. 1. Dupleix, Annal. de Bellefor. ad An. 987, & 988, &c.

A Table of the Coronation of the Kings of the third Race, called the Capets.

(*k*) *Hugh Capet*, 35th King of *France*, Son of *Hugh the Fair*, Grandson of *Robert*, who was anointed and crown'd King of *France* in 922, and slain by *Charles the Simple* in 923, descended of the Blood of *Clovis*, by *St. Arnoul*; whom *Louis* V. had also declared his Heir by his Will, was chosen King by all the Lords and Prelates, as Prince of the Blood, nearest to the Succession in default of Male Issue, on account of the lawful Exclusion of *Charles* of *France*. The Nobles of the Kingdom gave him a Consent so general and unanimous, that they, the People, and the Soldiery, proclaimed and crowned him King with one Voice, at *Noyon*, where they were assembled for that purpose (*l*).

Afterwards he went to receive the Royal Unction at *Rheims*, from the Hands of Cardinal *Adalberon*, *July* the 3d, in the Year 987 (*m*).

ROBERT,

(*k*) Called so, from the Largeness of his Head.

(*l*) Mezeray Hist. de France, tom. 2 l. 1. Frag. Hist. Franc. ad Lud. II. Carol. Calv. usque ad Hug. Caper. Floriac.

(*m*) It is proper to observe in passing, that *Hugh Capet* was the restorer of regular Discipline in the Abbey of *St. Germain des Prez*, founded by *Childebert* I Son of the Grand *Clovis*. *Hugh Capet* took voluntarily the Title of

 Abbot

ROBERT, called *the Pious*, *the Devout*, and *the Wise*, the 36th King of *France*, Son of *Hugh Capet*, was anointed and crowned in the Life of his Father, who made him Partner in his Kingdom, to secure the Crown to his Race, in the City of *Rheims*, by Cardinal *Adalberon*, his Chancellor, in the Year 987, if we reckon according to the manner of that Time, when the Year ended at *Easter*, or in the Year 988, if you compute by the modern Method. (*n*) Some Authors place this Coronation at *Orleans*, but that opinion is uncertain.

It is pretended by some, that the Peers of *France* were instituted by this Prince: Yet some alledge it was owing to *Charlemagne*, others to *Hugh Capet*, others bring it down to *Louis the younger*. but the most common Opinion, uncertain as it is, ascribes it to *Robert*. This Prince intended to attach the Nobles to him by the magnificent Title of Peers, as if they were his Equals, established them to be Assistants to the King, at his Accession to the Crown; to decide the differences of Vassals, to counsel him in important Affairs, and to

Abbot of *St German*, as many Kings his Predecessors, or Counts of *Paris*, had done before, to re establish the regular Abbots

(*n*) Chron Floriac apud Quercetar. t. 4. Aimoin. l. 5. c. 45.

Glaber Rodolphe, l 2. c 1. Du Tillet, Histoire de France.

serve

ſerve him in the Wars. At this Day, the Peers are Officers of the Crown, and the firſt Counſellors of the Parliament of *Paris*; which, upon that ſcore, is called the Court of Peers. There are in it ſix Eccleſiaſtical, choſen at the Sollicitation of the Popes, that often came into *France* in thoſe Times, and raiſed very much the State and Rank of the Eccleſiaſticks, and ſix Laical, as holding the ſix greateſt Fiefs which depend upon the Crown, of which they were then the proper Lords: that is, *Eudo*, deſcended of *Robert*, had the Poſſeſſion of *Burgundy*, *Henry* of *England* had *Normandy*, *Theobald the Old* had *Champagne*, *William* of *Normandy* had *Flanders*, *Raymond*, Son of *Alphonſo*, had the County of *Tholouſe*; and *William*, Father of *Eleonora*, had *Poitou*.

The ſix Eccleſiaſticks are, the Archbiſhop of *Rheims*, the Biſhops of *Langres* and *Laon*, Dukes and Peers: Thoſe of *Beauvais*, of *Noyon*, and *Chalons* upon the *Maine*, are Counts and Peers. The Laicks, are the Dukes of *Burgundy*, *Normandy*, and *Guyenne*; and the Counts of *Flanders*, *Tholouſe*, and *Champagne*. And though our Kings have ſince erected a great Number of Ducal Peerdoms, yet only the twelve above aſſiſt at the Coronation, as the antient Peers of *France*, and have their Functions at it (*o*). And since the six Lay-Peerdoms are reunited to the Domaine of the Crown, except a Part of *Flanders*, which is in the possession of the Emperor (*), these antient Peers are represented by other Princes and Lords, whom the King may chuse for that purpose. The Ecclesiastical Peers are represented by other Prelates, when they cannot assist, or when their Bishopricks are vacant; as it has been practised on the occasions we shall observe hereafter.

HENRY I. 37th King of *France*, second Son of *Robert*, was crowned at *Rheims* in the Life of his Father, by the Archbishop *Ebalus*, in the Month of *May*,

(*o*) *Louis* VII. regulated the Functions of the Peers for the Coronation of his Son, *Philip the August*, where they all appeared the first time, to discharge them, as we shall observe under that Article. It is one of the most solemn Acts in our Histories.

(*) *Burgundy* was united to the Crown by Letters Patents in *November* 1361.

Normandy was confiscated, under *John*, called *Sans-Terre*, King of *England*, Duke of *Guyenne*, for Felony, by an Arrêt, in 1202. This was the first important Judgment of the Peers, and it was against one of their own Number.

Guyenne was then also confiscated on the same account, for his bearing Arms against the King

Champagne was reunited to the Crown, with *Burgundy*, by Letters Patents, in *November* 1361

Flanders is possess'd at present, part by the King, and part by the Emperor.

Tholouse, was reunited at the time, and in the manner, when *Champagne* was joined to the Crown.

Mezeray Hist. de France, tom. 2. *and* Godefroy, *in his Ceremonial.*

1025,

1025, aged no more than ſeven Years; and immediately after the death of *Hugh*, his elder Brother, whom *Robert* his Father cauſed to be crowned, about the Age of twelve or thirteen Years, at *Compiegne*, in the Year 1017, or, according to *Du Tillet*, 1024.

It was very much the practice, in the beginning of the third Race, for our Kings to order their Sons to be crowned, tho' young, during their Life, to put them in poſſeſſion of the Throne, and prevent all oppoſition by this open Settlement of the Inheritance, as we may obſerve by ſeveral Examples that are mentioned, or will be alledg'd.

PHILIP I. 38th King of *France*, Son of *Robert*, was anointed and crowned at *Rheims* by the Archbiſhop *Gervaſe de Belleſme*, May the 27th, being *Whitſunday*, in 1059. He was then ſeven Years old, and his Father *Henry* I. was living. Hiſtorians remark, that this Ceremony was performed with great Solemnity *Gervaſe*, afterwards Chancellor of *France*, was aſſiſted by three Archbiſhops, and a great Number of Biſhops and Abbots. The Pope's Legates, and all the Nobles and Lords of *France* were preſent; but the preſence or aſſiſtance of the twelve Peers is not mentioned: which is a proof that their Places and Offices were not appointed, and that they did not make their Appearance there the firſt time, till *Philip the Auguſt*, in 1179, as we will remark, when we ſpeak of Him.

After the Royal Oath was taken by the King, before the anointing, *Gervaſe* declared, that from the Baptiſm of *Clovis* by St. *Remy*, Pope *Hormiſdas* had granted to St. *Remy*, and his Succeſſors, Archbiſhops of *Rheims*, the Right of anointing our Kings, and the Primacy over all *France*. But they agree, that he was the firſt who advanced this pretended Conceſſion of that Pope, which has been confuted by the Letter of *Ivo* of *Chartres* (whom we have already mention'd, and ſhall ſpeak of again, under the Head of *Louis* VI.) and that his Diſcourſe is oppoſite to that of Archbiſhop *Hincmar*, his Predeceſſor, two hundred Years before, at the Coronation of *Carolus Calvus*; when, as we ſaid, *Hincmar* declared to the Biſhops of the Province of *Treves*, that he would not have crowned him, if they had not required and ſollicited him, as not deſirous to invade the Right of another.

The Pope's Legates were frequently preſent, but that was only in Friendſhip and Goodwill to our Kings, for the Preſence and Conſent of the Pope was not neceſſary to it, as *Godfrey* affirms: " As it is plain, *ſays he*, " that it may be done without the Pope's " Conſent; yet, in reſpect and kindneſs " only, the Legates were preſent." *Grand Ceremon.* tom. 1. p. 121.

LOUIS

LOUIS VI. call'd the *Fat*, the Warrior and Defender of the Church, the 39th King of *France*, was anointed and crown'd in the Church of the *Holy Cross* at *Orleans*, by *Daimbert* (*p*), Archbishop of *Sens*, on the 3d of *August*, in the Year 1108, five Days after the Death of *Philip* his Father.

He was unwilling to be anointed or crown'd by *Raoul*, whom the Pope had made Archbishop of *Rheims*, without his Consent, and resolv'd to have it perform'd at *Orleans*, to prevent the Intrigues of the King of *England*, and some other Malecontents. The Archbishop of *Rheims* and his Chapter were inform'd of it, and sent their Deputies to oppose it, but when *Raoul* found they came too late, and that the Ceremony was finish'd, he fill'd all the Kingdom with his Complaints, and maintain'd afresh, as *Gervase* had done before, that by a special Privilege granted to the Church and Archbishops of *Rheims*, they only had the Right, exclusive of all other Prelates, to give the first Coronation.

But he was not regarded, and *Ivo*, Bishop of *Chartres*, confuted his Propositions, and prov'd, that *Daimbert*, Archbishop of *Sens*, his Metropolitan, acted nothing against

(*p*) *Mezeray. Hist. de Fran. Tom.* 2. *l.* 1. calls this Archbishop *Giselbert*, and says, that he took off the Sword from the King, which he wore, and gave him that of the Church, to punish the Guilty, and then put the Royal Ornaments upon him, in the presence of the Prelates his Suffragans.

Right,

Right, Cuſtom, or Law, when he crown'd *Louis* VI. ſince the Crown was Hereditary to him, and the Prerogative of the Coronation was not annex'd to any particular Church or Prelate (*q*).

LOUIS VII. call'd *the Younger*, 40th King of *France*, was anointed and crown'd at *Rheims*, in the Life of *Louis the Fat* his Father, by Pope *Innocent* II. who then held a Council at *Rheims*, on the 25th, or, according to others, the 27th of *October*, in the Year 1131; and he aſcended the Throne in the Year 1137, aged 18 Years.

Some Hiſtorians tell us, that this Coronation was of all others the moſt ſolemn; that King *Louis* VI. Queen *Alice* of *Savoy* (*r*), Prince *Louis* VII. their Son, all the Princes, Barons, and Nobles of the Kingdom, arriving at *Rheims*, *Renaud* the Archbiſhop pray'd the Pope to perform the Coronation; he conſented, and enjoin'd all the Fathers of the Council to appear the Day after, being *October* the 25th, 1131, in the Cathedral Church of *Rheims*, in their Pontificals, to aſſiſt at it. Then, attended by a great Number of Archbiſhops and Biſhops, and by his ordinary Court, he went in Proceſſion from the Archiepiſcopal Palace, where he

(*q*) *See* the Grand Ceremonial of *France*, Tom. 1. p. 130. Mezeray Hiſt. de Fran. Tom. 2. l. 1. Epiſt. 70. Ivon. Carnot.

(*r*) Daughter of *Humbert* II. Prince of *Piedmont*, Marquiſs of *Suze*, Count of *Morienne*, or *Savoy*.

lodg'd

lodg'd, to the Abbey of *St. Remy*, where *Louis* VII. had his Reſidence. There with the Pontifical Habit, and the (*s*) Tiara on his Head, he return'd in the ſame Order to the Cathedral Church, leading the King to be crown'd under the Arm (*t*). At the Gate they were met by King *Louis* VI. Queen *Alice* of *Savoy*, the Nobles, Biſhops, and Archbiſhops, who attended and enter'd with them; and after the ordinary Prayers and Ceremonies, the Pope anointed the King with the Oil of the Holy Vial.

We (*u*) find that *Louis* VII. was again not only anointed, but crown'd alſo three other times; firſt at *Bourdeaux*, on the Day of his Marriage with *Alienor*, or *Eleonor*, Daughter of *William* Duke of *Aquitaine*: the (*w*) ſecond by *Sampſon*, Archbiſhop of

(*s*) Or Triple-Crown, *Quære*.

(*t*) Croniq. Morini. Cœnob. La Vie de Louis le Gros, Sug.

Note, the Counil above-mention'd, that was call'd at *Rheims* by Pope *Innocent* II. in the Year 1131. conſiſted of 13 Archbiſhops, 263 Biſhops, and a great Number of Abbots and Monks, that came from all Parts. *See* Suger ibid.

(*u*) *Oderic Vitalis*, who wrote at this time, ſays, This Coronation diſpleas'd many, and the Laicks murmur'd at it, hoping they might aggrandize themſelves, if *Louis* VI. had dy'd, without leaving a Son in poſſeſſion of the Throne, and that the Eccleſiaſticks would have hinder'd it if they could, as intending to aſſume the Right of chuſing Kings againſt the Laws of *the Blood*, and of the Realm: but *Louis* VI. ſwore to revenge it by the Death of the Seditious. This caus'd the Aſſaſſination of *Hugh*, Biſhop Elect of *Orleans*, and of *Thomas*, Sub-Prior of St *Victor*, in pretence that he was of the Number of the Factious.

(*w*) Chroniq. Morimac.

Rheims,

Rheims, under the Pontificate of *Eugene* III. At laſt (*x*) the third in the City of *Orleans*, by the Archbiſhop of *Sens*, in the Year 1152 (*y*), with his ſecond Conſort, nam'd *Conſtance*, Daughter of the King of *Spain* It was this *Louis* that regulated the Functions of the Peers, and who, in the Year 1175, appointed the Form of the Ceremonies and Order to be obſerv'd in the Coronation (*z*).

PHILIP II. call'd *the Auguſt*, 41ſt King of *France*, Son of *Louis* VII. was anointed and conſecrated the firſt time at *Rheims*, in the Life of his Father, by Cardinal *William* of *Champagne*, ſurnam'd *aux Blanches Mains*, or the *Fair-handed*, Archbiſhop of that City, and Uncle, by the Mother's Side, of this *Philip*, on the Day of *All-Saints*, in the Year 1179, aged then fourteen Years and two Months.

This was more ſolemn than the former, all the Peers officiated as Great Officers of the Kingdom, or as Peers, the firſt time, as we have remark'd (*a*).

LOUIS VII. after a Reign of almoſt forty three Years, being advanc'd to the Age of ſeventy, and finding himſelf decline,

(*x*) *See* Epiſt 246. of St *Bernard* for the Archbiſhop of *Rheims* to Pope *Eugenius*.

(*y*) Aimoin l. 5. c. 44.

(*z*) Du Tillet. Hiſt des Rois, pag. 187. Godf. Cerem. Tom. 1 pag. 1.

(*a*) Hiſt Anon. de Louis VII. Mezeray, Tom. 2. lib. 1. Hiſt de Franc. Rigor. Chen. Tom. 4 p 4. & 35.

reſolv'd

resolv'd to order the Coronation of his Son *Philip the August* (or *Philip-Augustus.*) On this he assembled the Nobles in the Episcopal Palace at *Paris*, and declar'd, that he would set his Son on the Throne upon the Day of the Assumption next following, by their Counsel and Consent (*c*).

But *Philip* being very much indispos'd by a Fright he receiv'd in hunting, the Coronation could not be done on the Day of the Assumption appointed, but was deferr'd to the Day of *All Saints* following. *Louis* VII. his Father, could not be present, by reason of a Palsy that seiz'd one Side of his Body, after his Return from *Canterbury* in *England*, whither he went in Pilgrimage, to offer his Prayers to God, on the Tomb of St. *Thomas*, for the Cure of his Son.

Henry, the young King of *England*, assisted at this Ceremony, as representing the Duke of *Burgundy*; he came designedly into *France* to discharge his Function, as Peer, and as such he carry'd the Crown Royal from the Chamber of the young King,

(*c*) M. the Abbot *de Camps*, in his Historical Discourse of the Coronation of Kings, has very judiciously remark'd, that these words, *Cum Consilio & eorum Voluntate*, were only by way of Compliment, and without any Necessity, because the Succession then was sufficiently establish'd it was also done because *Philip* was a Minor, tho he was fourteen Years old, for the Kings of the third Race crown'd their Sons when they pleas'd, whether the Nobles approv'd it or no.

and

and before him, to the Church. The Count of *Flanders*, as Peer, carry'd the Sword Royal; the Duke of *Normandy* bore the first square Banner, the Duke of *Guyenne* the second, the Count *de Tholouse* the Spurs, and the Count of *Champagne* the Streamer, or Flag of War. The Cardinal *William de Champagne*, Archbishop of *Rheims*, anointed the King out of the Holy Vial, assisted by the Bishops of *Bourges*, *Tours*, and *Sens*. The Bishop of *Laon* carry'd the Holy Vial, he of *Beauvais* bore up the Train, he of *Noyon* carry'd the Cincture or Royal Belt, and he of *Chalons* the Ring, according to the Ordinance of *Louis* VII. and the Form appointed by his Order in the Year 1195 (*d*).

He was crown'd a second time at St. *Denys*, with Queen *Isabella*, or *Elizabeth*, his first Wife, Daughter of *Baldwin*, Count of *Hainault*, by the hands of *Guy*, Archbishop of *Sens*, on *Ascension-Day*, in the Year 1180, or, according to others, *May* the 29th the same Year.

It is observable, that this Coronation was not at *Rheims*, because the Queens are not anointed with the Oil of the Holy Vial, or crown'd for the Succession, as Kings are; but with the Holy Chrism, merely for Honour and Ceremony: Besides that *William*, Cardinal and Archbishop of *Rheims*, and Uncle

(*d*) *See* du Tillet's Recueil des Rois, pag 187. *and* Godfr. *in his* Ceremon. Tom. 1. pag. 1.

cle of the young King, did not approve this Marriage, and they add, that *Guy*, Archbishop of *Sens*, protested before the Ceremony, that he did not pretend any Jurisdiction over the Church of St. *Denys* (*e*), in Right of a Metropolitan.

LOUIS VIII. 42d King of *France*, call'd *the Lyon*, for his Courage, the only Son and Successor of *Philip the August*, was anointed and crown'd King at *Rheims*, with Queen *Blanche* his Spouse, Daughter of *Alfonso* VIII. King of *Castile*, by the Archbishop *William de Joinville*, *August* 6. in the Year 1223, in presence of the Princes and Lords of the Kingdom. *John de Brienne*, King of *Jerusalem*, perform'd the Office of Constable, and carry'd the Sword before the King in this Ceremony.

This Prince had already been crown'd King of *England* in the City of *London*, in the Life of his Father, in the Year 1215, aged about 36 Years, in the place of *John*, surnam'd *Sans-Terre*, whom the *English* had depos'd; but that fickle Nation having likewise set him aside, and plac'd the Son of *John* upon the Throne, he return'd into *France*, where he came to the Crown immediately after the Death of his Father,

(*e*) *Mezeray*, *Tom.* 2. *pag* 205. It will not be amiss to observe here, that the City of *Paris* was considerably encreas'd under the Reign of *Philip*, and encompass'd with Walls, Towers, and Ditches, from the Tower of *Philippes Hamelin*, or *Nesle*, now the College *Mazarin*, to the *Tournelle*, or *Porte St. Bernard*. *See* Aimoin. Fortunat.

which

which happen'd at *Nantes*, *July* 14. 1213. where he then held his Parliament (*f*).

St. *LOUIS* IX. of the Name, 43d King of *France*, Son of *Louis* VIII. who dy'd *November* the 8th, 1226. was anointed and crown'd at *Rheims*, aged no more than eleven or twelve Years, by *Jacques Bazoches*, Biſhop of *Soiſſons*, the See being vacant on *November* the 19th, or, according to others, the Day after St. *Andrew*, in the Year 1226.

It was this pious King who introduc'd the Cuſtom of going, after the Coronation, in Pilgrimage to *Corbigny*, to pay a nine day's Devotion to St. *Marcoul*, before the touching for the King's-Evil.

It was alſo this Prince, who, after his Coronation, put into the Treaſury of St. *Denys* (*g*), the Crowns and other Ornaments which *Philip the Auguſt* order'd to be made for the Coronation of our Kings.

(*f*) Mezeray Hiſt de Fran l. 1. tom. 2. Rigordus in Vit. Philip Aug Tillet. in Chron Ann. 1223.

(*g*) *Louis* IX was the Son of *Louis* VIII and of *Blanche*, Daughter of *Alphonſo*, King of *Caſtile*, and of *Alienor* of *England*. *Blanche* was Regent, during his Minority, as *Louis* VIII. had declar'd her by his Will. *Louis* IX. after a glorious Reign of 44 Years, died of the Peſtilence and Famine, in his ſecond Voyage to the *Holy Land*, aged about 55 Years, in the Year 1270 He was interr'd at *St. Denys*, and his Head was put into the Holy Chapel at *Paris*, which he founded, and as his Life was entirely pious, he was canoniz'd by Pope *Boniface* VIII in the Year 1297. and *Louis* XII obtain'd of Pope *Paul* V. that this Feaſt ſhould be obſerv'd throughout all *Chriſtendom* as a Feaſt of the Commandment of the Church.

It

It is pretended to be prov'd by Letters, that are in the Treasury of the King's Charters, that *Louis* VIII. lying on his Death-Bed, summon'd the Archbishops of *Sens* and *Bourges*, the Bishops of *Beauvais*, of *Noyon*, and *Chartres*, *Philip* of *France*, the Count of *Blois*, *Enguerand de Coucy*, *Montfort d'Amauri*, *Jean* Sire *de Neele*, the Count of *Sancerre*, and other Nobles, to attend him; and oblig'd them to swear, that they would crown his eldest Son *Louis* as soon as they could, to prevent the Troubles that threaten'd the Kingdom, by reason of the Minority of the young Prince; and it is said to be in execution of this Oath, that they crown'd *Louis* the Day after St. *Andrew*, twelve Days after the Death of his Father. These same Letters prove the Invitation he made to the Prelates, Princes, and Great Lords, to appear at this Ceremony (*b*).

PHILIP III. call'd *the Hardy*, 44th King of *France*, was saluted King in the Christian Army before *Tunis*, after the Death of St. *Louis* his Father, and immediately after his Return to *Afric*, he was anointed and crown'd King at *Rheims*, by *Milon des Basoches*, Bishop of *Soissons*, the See of *Rheims* being vacant, *August* the 13th, according to the Medal; others say the 15th of that Month, on the Day of the *Assumption*, in the Year 1271.

(*b*) *See* Godefr. Grand Ceremon t. 1. p. 142

None of the antient Lay-Peers aſſiſted at this Ceremony, but the Duke of *Burgundy*, and the Count of *Flanders*. *Robert* Count of *Artois* carry'd the Sword of *Charlemague*, which they call'd *Joyeuſe*, before the King, according to antient Uſage.

Mary of *Brabant*, his ſecond Wife, was anointed and crown'd in the Holy Chapel at *Paris*, by *P. Barbet*, Archbiſhop of *Rheims*, *June* the 23d, 1275. but it does not appear that *Philip* III. was anointed or crown'd a ſecond time with her (*i*).

PHILIP IV. called *the Fair*, 45th King of *France*, Son of *Philip* III. aſcended the Throne immediately after the Death of his Father (*k*), aged about 17 Years. He was anointed and crown'd at *Rheims* by the Archbiſhop *Pierre Barbet*, *January* the 6th, in the Year 1286 (*).

This Prince had already been anointed and crown'd the firſt time, as King of *Navarre*, at *Pampelona*, *Auguſt* 16. 1284. on the Day of his Marriage with *Jane*, his Couſin-Germain, Daughter and Heireſs of *Henry* I. of the Name, King of *Navarre*, who had been crown'd Queen of *Navarre* when about two Years old and an half, in

(*i*) Mezeray, du Tillet, Joinville. Hiſt. de St. Louis and Philip III.

(*k*) *Philip* III call'd *the Hardy*, dy'd at *Perpignan*, *Octob.* 26. 1285 aged 45 Years, 5 Months, and 16 Days, after a Reign of 15 Years, a Month, and 12 Days.

(*) *Jane* of *Navarre* his Wife (on whoſe account he was call'd King of *Navarre*) was crown'd with him. *Mezeray*, *Godefr.*

the

the Life of *Henry* I. her Father, to whom *Philip* IV. ſucceeded.

At his Return to *Paris*, after his Coronation, he was harangu'd, in the Name of the Univerſity, by *Gilles Colomne*, who had been his Preceptor; and declar'd, in his Oration, that we ought to ſpeak to Kings with the ſame Reſpect as to God, who has appointed them his Deputies and Repreſentatives in the World, to govern the People under his Authority; and he exhorted this Prince to merit the Surname of *the Juſt*, which has not been us'd by any King that is known in Hiſtory (*l*).

LOUIS X. called *le Hutin*, or *le Hautin*, 46th King of *France*, Son of *Philip the Fair* (*m*), was anointed and crown'd King, with (*n*) *Clemence* of *Hungary*, his ſecond Wife, in the Church of *Rheims*, on the 3d, or, as others ſay, the 25th of *Auguſt*, in the Year 1315, by *Robert de Courtenay*, then Archbiſhop.

This Prince had been anointed and crowned King of *Navarre* at the Age of five Years, after the Death of Queen *Jane* of *Navarre* his Mother, in the City of *Pampelona*, *Octob.* 1. 1307.

(*l*) *See* the Hiſtorical Diſſertation of M the Abbot *des Camps*, on the Coronations, 1722.

(*m*) *Philip the Fair* reign'd twenty nine Years one Month in *France*, and thirty in *Navarre*. He dy'd *Novemb* 2) 1314, aged 46 Years, at *Fontainbleau*, where he was born

(*n*) Daughter of *Robert* II. King of *Hungary*.

PHILIP V. called *the Long*, 47th King of *France*, ſo nam'd for his Tallneſs, came to the Throne (*o*) *November* 22, or 23. 1316. he was anointed and crown'd at *Rheims*, with Queen *Jane* his Wife, Daughter of *Hugh* Count of *Burgundy*, by *Robert de Courtenay*, then Archbiſhop, *January* the 6th, in the ſame Year.

There happen'd three particular Incidents at this Coronation :

1. The Gates of the City and Church of *Rheims* were ſhut during the time, for two of the moſt powerful Princes of the Blood, the Duke of *Burgundy*, and the Count of *Valois*, would not acknowledge him as King; they oppos'd the Coronation, and would not appear at it.

2. *Mahaut*, Counteſs of *Artois* and *Burgundy*, Mother of *Jane*, Spouſe of the new

(*o*) *Louis* X dy'd *June* the 5th, 1316 aged twenty five Years, having reign'd only eighteen Months in *France*, and ten Years in *Navarre*. He left one Poſthumous Son Heir to the Crown, of whom *Clemence* was deliver'd *November* the 14th following, called *John*. We may reckon him among the Kings of *France*, becauſe the Crown was devolv'd to him by the Death of his Father, and juſt after his Birth he was proclaim'd King, but dying in eight Days, *Philip the Long*, his Brother, ſecond Son of *Philip* the IVth, was called by Right to the Succeſſion

Hiſtory does not take notice that *Philip the Long* was anointed and crown'd as King of *Navarre*, for indeed it was not ſo, *Jane*, Daughter of *Louis* X who had her by his firſt Wife *Margaret* II Daughter of *Robert* II. was Heireſs of *Navarre*, but could not be Heireſs of *France*. She carry'd *Navarre* into the Houſe of *D'Evreux*, by marrying *Philip* Count *D'Evreux*, who left it to *Charles* II called *the Wicked*, ſo that it did not revert to *France* till *Henry* IV. *Mezeray*, *tom.* 2. *Froiſſart. Chron. ad Ann.* 1316, & 1317.

King,

King, assisted in the Rank of Peer of *France*, and bore up the Crown with the other Peers, who murmur'd at it, and maintain'd (but in vain) that these High Offices, any more than the Crown itself, could never belong to the Distaff.

3. When the Bishops of *Langres* and *Beauvais* disputed the Precedence, one being a Duke, and the other only a Count, it was decided in favour of him of *Beauvais*, because his Peerdom was of the most antient Erection (*p*).

CHARLES IV. call'd *the Fair* (from the Beauty both of his Mind and Body) 48th King of *France*, third Son of King *Philip the Fair*, came to the Crown by the Death of the two former Kings, *Louis le Hutin*, and *Philip the Long*, his Brothers, who deceas'd, without Male Issue He was anointed and crown'd at *Rheims* on the 9th, or, according to others, on the 12th of *February*, in 1321. by *Robert de Courtenay*, who in six Years had the Honour to crown three Kings (*q*).

He caus'd *Jane d'Evreux*, his Cousin-Germain, to be anointed and crown'd (whom he marry'd, with a Dispensation, in the Holy Chapel at *Paris*) on his Wedding-Day, which was kept with great Magnificence in the Year 1326.

(*p*) Godfr. Grand Ceremon. Favin. Marlot. Theatr. d'Honneur.

(*q*) *Louis* X. *Philip* V. *Charles* IV. all Brothers.

PHILIP IV. call'd *de Valois, the Catholic, the Happy*, or the *Fortunate*, 49th King of *France* (r), was anointed and crown'd at *Rheims*, with the Queen his Wife, *Jane*, Daughter of *Robert* II. Duke of *Burgundy*, by the Archbishop *William de Trie* his Uncle, on *Trinity-Sunday, May* 29. 1328.

After their Coronation the King and Queen made their Entry into *Paris*, where they were magnificently receiv'd.

Under this Reign *Dauphiné* was united to the Crown of *France*. The Donation of it was made by *Humbert*, last Dauphin of *Viennois*, who, on the unhappy Death of his only Son, by a Fall from his Hands thro' a Window, gave *Dauphiné* to the Kings of *France*, with a Charge, that the eldest Sons of *France* should bear that Name (that of

(r) *Charles the Fair* dying in the Year 1328, in the 7th of his Reign, aged 34 Years, and leaving no Male-Issue, the Estates assembled gave the Crown to *Philip de Valois*, youngest Brother to *Philip the Fair*, preferring him on the foot of the Salique Law, which excludes all Women from the Crown of *France*, to a Daughter of *Charles the Fair*, last King of the Line, that was of the first Branch of the third Race. So that *Philip de Valois* was the first King of the second Branch of the third Race, called the first Branch of the *Valois's*, which comes down to *Charles* VIII. the last of that Branch, it continuing 260 Years upon the Throne. *Edward* III King of *England* disputed the Crown with him, as Son of *Isabella* of *France*, Daughter of *Philip the Fair*, and lawful Wife of *Edward* II King of *England*. Hence the *English* Kings have ever since us'd the Title of Kings of *France*, and great Wars have been occasioned by it between the two Nations. *Arral. d'Angleterre du Tillet. Mezeray.*

Dauphins)

Dauphins) and their Arms should be quarterly of *France*, and of *Dauphiné* (*s*.)

JOHN I. call'd *the Good*, 50th King of *France*, eldest Son of *Philip de Valois*, and of *Jane*, Daughter of *Robert* II. Duke of *Burgundy*, and of *Agnes* of *France*, Daughter of St. *Louis*, ascended the Throne at the Age of forty Years, by the Death of *Philip* VI. his Father, which was *August* 27. 1350, was anointed and crown'd at *Rheims* by *John d'Arcy*, the Archbishop, *September* 26. the same Year, with Queen *Jane*, Countess of *Boulogne*, his second Wife. At (*t*) his Return from *Rheims*, the City of *Paris* made him a very splendid Reception, the Streets were all cover'd with Tapestry, the Companies of Tradesmen were all in their Liveries, and the Bur-

(*s*) Mezeray. Du Tillet.

(*t*) He re-establish'd the Order of the Star, in the Palace of *St. Owen*, near *Paris*, in the Year 1350. This Order of Knighthood was instituted by King *Robert*, in the Year 1022 in Honour of the Blessed Virgin, instead of that of the Bridle, erected in 626, by *Charles Martel*, after a Defeat of the *Saracens*. In this Order the Collar was of Gold, made of three Chains, intermix'd with Roses enamell'd with White and Red, at the end of which was a Golden Star with five Rays It was so considerable, that it was only this of which the Kings of *France* condescended to be Heads and Sovereign Great Masters. *Philip the August*, *Louis* VIII. and St. *Louis*, were made Knights of it, and receiv'd the Collar of their Order on their Coronation-Day But *Charles* VII. having given up this Order, which was only given to Princes and Great Lords, that it might not be restor'd, gave it to the Head of the Night-Watch, whom he call'd *Knight of the Rounds*; all the Princes and Lords quitted the Collar upon it, and at one Stroke the Order was abolish'd. *Favin. Theatr d'Honneur & de Chevalerie.*

ghers under Arms. After this he held his Bed of Justice in Parliament, and gave the Order of Knighthood to his two eldest Sons, and to some other Lords.

CHARLES V. called *the Sage*, and *the Rich* (u), 51st King of *France*, Son of *John* I. and of *Bonne*, Daughter of *John de Luxembourg* King of *Bohemia*, came to the Throne immediately after the Death of his Father, *John* I. which was *April* 8, 1364, aged 65 Years, after having reign'd 13 Years and six Months; and he was anointed and crowned at *Rheims*, with *Jane* of *Bourbon*, his first Wife (x), by the Archbishop, *John* of *Craon*, *May* the 19th, being *Trinity Sunday*, 1364, in presence of the King of *Cyprus*, the Dukes of *Anjou*, and of *Bohemia*, *Luxembourg*, *Brabant*, *Lorrain*, and other his Allies and Subjects.

When he found himself infirm, and would prevent the Inconveniences of that green Age, in which he left his Son and Successor, he abolished the Law of not crowning the Kings, till their full Majority: and ordain'd, that, for the future, they should be *Majors* at fourteen Years of Age, and govern

(u) Because he left at his death seventeen Millions of Crowns, a prodigious Sum in those days. He was the first Dauphin of *France*, after the Donation of *Humbert*.

(x) Daughter of *Pierre*, Duke of *Bourbon*.

then

then by themselves (*y*), as if they were twenty-five.

This was done at *Vinçennes*, in *August*, 1374. It was published and registred in Parliament the Year following, the King holding there his Bed of Justice, *May* the 20th, 1375, in presence of the *Dauphin*, the Duke of *Anjou*, many Archbishops, Bishops, and other Nobles of the Kingdom (*z*).

CHARLES VI. called *the Well-beloved*, and *the Merciful*, 52d King of *France*, Son of *Charles* V. was anointed and crown'd at *Rheims*, aged about twelve or thirteen Years, by the Archbishop *Richard de Piaque*, call'd of *Besançon*, on *All-Saints* Day, *November* the 1st, 1380.

Charles V. on his Death-bed, summoned the Dukes of *Burgundy* and *Berry*, his Brothers, and the Duke of *Bourbon*, his Brother-in-law, to attend him, and after having given them several Orders and Counsels for the Government of the Kingdom, he recommended to them his Son *Charles*, exhorting them to behave themselves towards him, like good Uncles to a Nephew, and to crown him King, just after his decease. He obliged likewise all that were in the Court, to promise him, that, after his death, they

(*y*) Dupuis, Traité de la Majorite de nos Rois, p. 79. & Preuves de ce Traité, p. 155.

(*z*) *See* la Traduction de l'Hist. de Charles V. by le Laboureur, & du Tillet.

would

would faithfully ſerve his eldeſt *Son*, *Charles* the Dauphin (*a*).

And *Charles* V. dying *September* 16. in the Year 1380, after a Reign of 16 Years, and a Life of 42 Years, and ſix Months, *Charles* VI. his Son, was at that Inſtant own'd as his lawful Succeſſor. But there was a Diviſion about his Coronation (*b*); ſome maintaining in Council, that he ought not to be crowned before his Majority, according to the antient Law; and that, in the mean time, the Duke of *Anjou*, the eldeſt Uncle, by the Father's ſide to this young Prince, ſhould have the Regency of the Kingdom. (*c*) Others, on the contrary, urged, that, to avoid all Strife, he ſhould be crowned forthwith, like St. *Louis*, and other Kings of the third Race, who were crowned for theſe, and the like Reaſons, before their Majority. This prevailed, ſo that he was crowned at the Age of twelve

(*a*) Froiſſart vol. 2. c. 56. tom. 1. p. 97. Juvenal. Hiſt. de Charles V. by Godfrey. To which ſome Authors add, That he, not doubting his departure before the Dauphin arrived at the Age of fourteen, reſolved to make him an Aſſociate in his Kingdom, and to crown him King, during his Life, and he cauſed the Royal Veſtments for that purpoſe to be made. But as he was on the point of accompliſhing his Deſign, he fell ſick and died. *Labour. Trad. de l'Hiſt. de* Ch. 5.

(*b*) *Dorgemont*, Chancellor of *France*, and others.

(*c*) *John Deſmaretz*, Advocate-General of the Parliament of *Paris*, one of the moſt learned and wiſe Magiſtrates of that time.

or thirteen (*d*). All the Peers, both of the Clergy and Laity, except the Count of *Flanders*, who was kept away by a Revolt of his Subjects, were present; as also, among a great Number of other Lords, the Dukes of *Anjou*, *Berry*, *Burgundy*, *Bourbon*, *Bar*, and *Lorain*; the Counts of *Savoy*, *Marche*, *d'Eu*, and *William de Namur*.

Here the Duke of *Anjou*, as Regent, contested the Precedency with the Duke of *Burgundy*, as Dean of the Peers. This remarkable Difference was decided expresly by the King in favour of the Duke of *Burgundy*, because this Action was part of the Office of the Peers, in that Capacity.

The King, on the Day of his Coronation, conferred the Honour of Knighthood on (*e*) three young Lords of his own Age; the Son of the King of *Navarre*, of the

(*d*) Dupuy, Trait. de le Major. des Rois. Nic. Gilles. Annal. Mezeray; and many others, remark, That the Duke of *Anjou* was declar'd Regent, during the Minority of *Charles* VI but that he behav'd himself very ill, that he caused a Civil War by his excessive Impositions upon the People, and that there never were in *France* more Divisions among the Princes of the Blood, nor more cruel Wars, than those that befell in this Minority. The Duke of *Anjou* died at *Naples* in 1384.

(*e*) This was the Order of the Star. There was no other at that time more distinguished, and the King was Great Master only of that Order. The military Orders of *St. Michael*, and of the Holy Ghost, were not instituted till *Louis* XI in 1469, and *Henry* III. in 1579. *See* Favin. Theatr. d'Honn. & Cheval.

Hist. de Charles VI. by Juvenal des Ursins. Le Laboureur, & Marlot. Theatr. d'Honn.

Duke

Duke of *Bar*, and of the Sieur *d'Albret*; and ſeated them at his Feet, during the Ceremony.

The Royal Entertainment after it, was particular in one Circumſtance, that a great Scaffold was erected in the Court of the Epiſcopal Palace at *Rheims*, on which the Tables were placed. There was the King, and, at a diſtance below him, were his five Uncles, of *Brabant*, *Anjou*, *Berry*, *Burgundy*, and *Bourbon*; and, oppoſite to them, the Archbiſhop of *Rheims*, with four other Prelates, who aſſiſted at the Ceremony, in performing the Office of Peers. And as the Duke of *Anjou*, without regard to the King's Judgment of Precedence for the Duke of *Burgundy* his Brother, was ſitting down at a Table, near the King, above the Duke, leaving only the Diſtance requiſite between his Majeſty, and himſelf, the Duke of *Burgundy* ſtept (*f*) boldly between them, and took his Seat.

The Conſtable, *Oliver du Cliſſon*, *Coucy*, *la Trimouille*, *John de Vienne*, and many other Lords and Great Officers of the Crown, ſerved at this Feaſt in an extraordinary manner, mounted on great Horſes, richly adorned.

(*f*) This ſhews us, that there was a difference between the manner of diſpoſing the Tables at that time, and the preſent arrangement of them. This Action gave the Name of THE HARDY, to the Duke of *Burgundy*

Froiſſart Paul. Æmil. Nic. Gille, & Marlot. Theatr. d'Honn. l. 1.

It

It was this *Charles* VI. who ordained by an Edict of the Month of *December*, 1407, that his eldeſt Son, and his Succeſſors, Kings of *France*, ſhould be anointed and crowned immediately after the deceaſe of their Fathers; and, in caſe they came to the Crown in their Minority, that they ſhould govern by the Advice and Counſels of the Queens their Mothers (if they were alive) of the neareſt Princes of the Blood Royal, of the Conſtable, the Chancellor, and the Council.

We muſt not here omit to take notice, that this Prince, in the firſt Year of his Reign, reduced the Arms of our Kings to three *Flower-de-luces*, which before were of no ſet Number (*g*). And that, having fallen into a kind of Madneſs, by an Accident that happened to him in 1392, the Regency of the Kingdom was given to the Duke of *Orleans*, to whom it belong'd in full Right, as Brother of the King, and neareſt a-kin to the Blood-Royal.

CHARLES VII. called *the Victorious*, 53d King of *France*, youngeſt Son of *Charles* VI. was in the Caſtle of *Eſpally*, belonging to the Biſhop of *Puy* in *Auvergne*,

(*g*) St Marthe, c 6 tom. 1. p. 498. Mezeray Hiſt. de Fr. in the Reign of *Charles* VI

Some Authors oppoſe this Opinion, and pretend, that the Kings of *France Pariſian*, (or of *Paris*) always bore Saphir, three *Flowers de-Lys*, Topaz, and that the other Kings of *France* had no more, but bore their Coats of ſeveral Colours, otherwiſe called of different Enamels (*Emaux*).

when

when he heard of the death of *Charles* VI. his Father, which happened *October* 22, 1422. He wore Mourning only one day, and the next day, dreſs'd in Scarlet, he went to hear Maſs in the Chapel of that Caſtle; after that was performed, he commanded a Standard of *France* to be ſet up, at the view of which, they that attended cry'd out, *God ſave the King*. And at that time he was recognized and proclaimed as ſuch, by all good *Frenchmen*. Afterwards, having aſſembled at *Poitiers* (which was as it were the Capital of the Country he was then in poſſeſſion of, moſt of the Towns of *France* being under the Power of the *Engliſh*) thoſe of the Parliament and Univerſity, that were of his Party; he was recognized and proclaimed King. But after he had been very ill treated by the *Engliſh*, affairs took a new Face, and the Victory turned on his ſide, and, aſſiſted by the Counſels and Help of *Joan* of *Arc*, ſirnamed the *Maid of Orleans*, he opened a way to *Rheims*, where, maugre the Attempts of the *Engliſh*, *Charles* VII. was anointed and crowned in the Great Church by the Archbiſhop, *Renaud de Chartres*, Chancellor of *France*, *July* 17. 1429 (*h*).

The

(*h*) When the *Engliſh* blocked up this Prince in *Berry*, they called him in deriſion, King of *Bourges*

The Maid of *Orleans* was a Labourer's Daughter, of the Village of *Vaucouleur* in *Lorain*, inſpired by God to take Arms,

The Marshals of *Rieux* and *Boussac* went with a strong Guard to fetch the holy Vial from *St. Remy*, where it was safely kept.

The Duke of *Alençon*, the Count of *Clermont*, the Lords of *Trimouille*, *Beaumanoir* and *Mailly*, represented the Lay-Peers.

Before the Coronation, the King was Knighted by *John* Duke of *Alencon*, and departing from *Rheims*, he went to pay his Nine-days Devotion in the Church of the Priory of *St. Marcou*, and afterwards touch'd many for the King's Evil.

LOUIS XI. 54th King of *France*, eldest Son of *Charles* VII. being come to the Throne, after the Death of his Father, which happened *July* the 22d, 1461. was anointed and crowned at *Rheims* by the Archbishop *John Juvenal des Ursins*, on the day of the Assumption, *August* the 15th, 1461, in presence of the Pope's Legate, the Cardinal of *Constance*, four Archbishops, six Bishops, the Princes of the Blood, and other great Lords of the Kingdom (*i*).

It is observed, that *Louis* XI. when he was on the point of receiving the Unction, drew his Sword, gave it to the Duke of

Arms, and raise the Siege of *Orleans*, expel the *English*, and prepare a way for the King's Coronation at *Rheims*.

See John Chartier, Berry Herault, Hist de Charles VII. St Marthe, & Mezeray, Hist. de France

(*i*) See the History of *Charles* VII. by *Monstrelet*, St *Marthe*, *Mezeray*, the *French* Ceremonial, *Favin* in his Theatre of Honour, *cap.* 1. about the Ceremony of touching for the Evil, after the Coronation.

Bur-

Burgundy, praying to make him Knight. This was done accordingly. And afterwards above Two-hundred Knights were made, as well by the Hand of the King, as by that of the other Princes who were present (*k*).

The Royal Feaſt ſucceeded the Coronation, at which the Twelve Peers aſſiſted.

Afterwards, the King having been at *Corbigny*, to invoke *St. Marcou*, he touch'd for *the Evil*; then paid his Devotions in the Church of *St. Dennis*, at the Tomb of the Martyrs, and offered upon the Altar a hundred Crowns of Gold.

At the ſame time, the City of *Paris* made him a magniſicent Entry, as far as that Age was capable. The great Lords attended, and the Number of Perſons on Horſeback, was computed to be Twelve thouſand.

We muſt not forget here, that it was this *Louis* XI. who inſtituted the military Order of *St. Michael*, when he was at *Amboiſe*, *Auguſt* 1. 1469 (*l*).

CHARLES

(*k*) When *Charles* VII. dy'd, *Louis* XI. was in *Flanders* with the Duke of *Burgundy*, who conducted him back to *France*, and aſſiſted at the Coronation.

(*l*) *See* Philip de Comines, Mem. de Louis XI Leferon, Mezeray, Varillas, Hiſt. de Louis XI. Favin, Theatr. d Hon. He declared himſelf the Head of this Order, and enjoined the Knights to wear daily a Collar of Chains of Gold, made in the faſhion of Shells, mingled one with another, at the end of which hung a Medal of the Arch-angel St. *Michael*, the antient Protector of *France*, and the Device was,

Immenſe

CHARLES VIII. called *the Affable*, and *the Courteous*, 55th King of *France*, Son of *Louis* XI. and of *Charlotte* of *Savoy*, came to the Throne about the Age of 13 Years, by the Death of his Father; it happened *August* 30. 1483. He was anointed and crown'd at *Rheims* by the Archbishop, *Pierre de Laval*, *May* 30. 1484 (*m*), whither he was conducted, with general Consent, by all the Princes and Nobles of the Kingdom, when he arriv'd at the Age of 14, which was the Term of Majority fix'd by the Ordinance of *Charles* V.

Louis XII. his Successor, assisted at this Coronation, and represented the Duke of *Burgundy*.

Charles VIII. paid his nine Days Devotions to St. *Marcou*, before he touched the Sick, and then he went to St. *Dennis* to

Immensi tremor Oceani.
The Terror of the Boundless Main.

This Order was in great Honour under four Kings; but the Women made it a mercenary thing, under the Reign of King *Henry* II. So that, tho it ought to have consisted of no more than 36 Knights, Gentlemen, Queen *Katherine de Medicis* gave it to all the World, so that the Lords would no longer accept of it. At present, all the Knights of the Order of the Holy Ghost, instituted by *Henry* III, in 1579, take the Order of *St. Michael* the Evening before they receive that of the Holy Ghost. Hence their Arms are surrounded with two Collars, and they are called Knights of the Orders of the King. *Favin. Theatr.*

(*m*) The Medal then struck, shews it was done in *July* 1484. But this is, because the Coronation was fixed for that time, and yet performed two Months sooner.

do the ſame, according to Cuſtom, to the firſt Martyrs of *France*.

On *July* the 6th following, he made his Entry into *Paris*, in this Order: The Biſhop and Clergy, the Court of Parliament, the Chamber of Accounts, the *Prevôt des Marchands*, and the Sheriffs, habited each according to his Quality, and keeping their Ranks, went before his Majeſty to the Chapel of the Peers, where the *Prevôt des Marchands*, and the Sheriffs, preſented him with the Keys of the Gate of St. *Dennis*, the Princes of the Blood, and great Lords of the Kingdom attended, in compleat Armour, covered with rich Coats of Arms, and mounted on Horſes, whoſe Capariſon and Equipage was all embroidered, ſet with precious Stones, and adorned with large Bells of Silver.

The King himſelf was in white Armour, except the Head-piece, which was carried before him by a Page; and he wore, inſtead of it, a Cap of State, encompaſſed with a rich Crown of Gold.]

The Streets, thro' which he paſſed, were lined with magnificent Tapeſtry, and embelliſhed with Triumphal Arches, Paintings, and ſeveral Repreſentations of living Perſons. With this Pomp the King was conducted by the Clergy to the Church of *Notre-Dame*; the Rector of the Univerſity having paid his Duty to him in a reſpectful

ſpectful Harangue, at the Corner of the new Street of *St. Mary*.

After *Charles* VIII. had finiſhed his Prayers, he was reconducted to the great Hall of the Palace, where a Royal Feaſt was prepared, followed by a Largeſs to the People, and by publick Rejoicings (*n*).

Then he took the Title and the Arms of King of *Jeruſalem* and *Sicily*, becauſe *Charles* VI. King of the ſame, had given them by Will to *Louis* XI. and to his Succeſſors, Kings of *France*, whom he appointed his Heirs And Pope *Alexander* VI. was obliged to give him the Inveſtiture of the Kingdom of *Naples*, where he entered triumphantly, *May* 12. 1495, as King of *France*, *Jeruſalem*, and *Sicily*.

LOUIS XII. called *the Father of the People, and the Juſt*, 56th King of *France*, Son of *Charles* Duke of *Orleans*, and of *Mary* of *Cleves*. Before he was King, he was Duke of *Orleans*, *Milan*, and *Valois*; Count of *Blois*, *Pavil*, and *Beaumont* upon the *Oiſe*, Lord of *Aſte* and *Coucy*, and firſt Prince of the Blood; deſcended of the third Branch of the *Valois's*, which we call the Branch of the Houſe of *Orleans*, being the Grandſon of *Louis* of *France*, Duke of *Orleans*, Brother of *Charles* VI. aſſaſſinated at *Paris* by the Duke of *Bur-*

(*n*) *See the Memoirs of* Philip de Comines, Bellè-foreſt, Guichardin, Mezeray, & Doublet *in his Hiſtory*.

gundy (*o*): He aſcended the Throne in the Year 1498 (*p*), aged 36 Years, *Charles* the VIIIth having dy'd, without Iſſue, *April* the 6th, in the ſame Year 1498, and he was anointed and crowned at *Rheims* by the Cardinal *William Briçonnet*, then Archbiſhop, *May* the 27th, 1498, after having perform'd the Funeral Obſequies of *Charles* the VIIIth, his Predeceſſor, with more Solemnity, than many other Kings have done to their Fathers.

At the Anointing of *Louis* XII. the Peers of *France* were repreſented thus: The Duke of *Burgundy* by *René*, Duke of *Alençon*; the Duke of *Normandy* by *Pierre*,

(*o*) The Crown was his by the Right of Proximity, for his Father was Son of *Louis*, Brother of King *Charles* V whoſe Poſterity ended in *Charles* VIII So that, tho' his Adverſaries ſaid, he had forfeited his Right, in taking Arms againſt the King deceaſed, and was a Head of the League againſt *Charles* VIII defeated at the Battle of *St. Aubin*, in 1488, yet as we have no ſuch Law, nor Example in *France*, he came to the Throne in 1498, and after a peaceful and happy Reign of 16 Years, 8 Months, 23 Days, he died on New-Year's Day, 1515, aged 53 Years, univerſally regretted by all his Subjects. *See* St. Marthe, Dupleix, Mezeray, Hiſt de France.

(*p*) The Annals of *Aquitaine*, and *Nicholas Gille*, tell us, that *Louis* XII as well as *Francis* I who ſucceeded, after their anointing at *Rheims*, went, as uſual, to take the Crown at *St Denis* But this is an Error, proved by all the Hiſtorians and the crowning of our Kings, ſince *Pepin the Short*, was never divided from their anointing For tho ſome of our Kings have made themſelves to be owned and proclaimed Kings before their anointing in troubleſome times, as it happened under *Charles* VIII. yet we do not find that their Coronation was ſeparate from their Unction.

Duke

Duke of *Bourbon*, the Duke of *Guyenne* by *René*, Duke of *Lorrain*; the Count of *Flanders* by *Philip de Cleves*, Count of *Raveſtan*; the Count of *Champagne* by *Angilbert* of *Cleves*, Count of *Nevers*; the Count de *Tholouſe* by *John de Foix*, Viſcount of *Narbon*, the King's Brother-in-law (*q*).

Marlot, in his *Theatre of Honour*, adds, That Pope *Alexander* VI. granted Indulgences to the King, and thoſe that aſſiſted at the Ceremony.

Louis XII. took alſo the Title of King of *France*, of *Jeruſalem*, and of the two *Sicilys*, by the ſame reaſon that *Charles* the VIIIth, his Predeceſſor, had taken it.

FRANCIS I. called *the Grand King*, and the Father of Learning, 57th King of *France* (*r*), Son of *Charles*, Count of *Angoulême*, whoſe Father was *John*, third Son of *Louis* I. Duke of *Orleans*, Brother of (*s*) King *Charles* V. and Spouſe of *Valentine* of *Milan*, having come to the

(*q*) *See* Dupleix, Mezeray, & St. Marthe, Hiſt. de France.

(*r*) He was called *de Valois*, becauſe he poſſeſſed that Dutchy before he was King. And *Louis* XII having begun and ended the third Branch of the *Valois's*, called the Houſe of *Orleans*, *Francis* I began the fourth Branch, called the ſecond of the *Valois's*.

(*s*) Some Authors pretend, that *Francis* I did not receive the Crown at *Rheims*, but went to receive it at *St Dennis*, after his anointing, which does not appear to be authorized by Uſage, nor ſufficiently prov'd, notwithſtanding what is ſaid by the Annals of *Aquitaire* and *Nicholas Gille*.

Crown by the Law Salique, as first Prince of the Blood, *Louis* XII. dying without Male Issue, *Jan.* 1. 1515; he was anointed and crowned at *Rheims* at the Age of 20 Years, by the Archbishop *Robert de Lenoncourt*, *Jan.* the 25th, the same Year.

After his Coronation he went, as usual, to St. *Dennis*, then made his Entry into *Paris*, where he gave the People pompous Shows and stately Tournaments, but it was this Prince who lost the Kingdom of *Naples* and the Dutchy of *Milan*, which he was oblig'd to yield to the Emperor *Charles* the Vth, by the Treaty of *Cambray*, in 1529. The great Wars and Misfortunes of *Francis* I. did not hinder his living in a very magnificent manner, making his People happy, loving the Sciences and the Learned, building a great part of the Royal Palaces in *France*, adorning them with Pictures, Statues, Arras, an Infinity of rare Furniture and Curiosities, which he purchas'd from all Parts; and notwithstanding all this, he paid all his Debts, and left 400000 Crowns, when he dy'd, in his Coffers, and a Quarter's Revenue untouch'd. He was so great a Lover of his People, that, in the last Moments of his Life, he recommended it expresly to his Son *Henry* II. to lessen the Taxes which he was oblig'd to put upon them, in order to defray the Charges of the War. He dy'd at the Castle of *Rambouillet* on the last Day of *March*, 1541,

after

after a Reign of 32 Years and 2 Months, and a Life of 52 Years, 6 Months, and 19 Days. His Funeral was perform'd with extraordinary Pomp, there were eleven Cardinals, and above forty other Prelates. He was there proclaim'd a Prince, merciful (*t*) in Peace, victorious in War, Father and Restorer of good Learning and of Liberal Arts.

HENRY II. 58th King of *France*, Son of *Francis* I. and of *Claude* of *France*, Daughter of *Louis* XII. began to reign in the Year 1547, aged 28 Years. He was anointed and crown'd at *Rheims*, by *Charles*, Cardinal of *Lorain*, Archbishop of that City, *July* the 28th, in the same Year 1547 (*u*).

To make this Ceremony more pompous, and to shew his Enemies that he took the Sword with the Scepter, he caus'd ten Companies of Foot to be levy'd in *Saxony* by Colonel *Volgesperg*, and two Captains of *Strasbourg*, nam'd *James Mentel* and *Thomas Wolfius* (*w*), who attended at his Colo-

(*t*) *See* the Memoirs of *William du Belly*, *Francis de Beaucaire*, and *Dupleix* and *Mezeray*, sur l'Hist. de Fran.

(*u*) *Henry* II. was second Son of *Francis* I. He first bore the Title of Duke of *Orleans*, then of Dauphin, after the Death of his eldest Brother, and succeeded his Father in 1547.

(*w*) It is said that this *Mentel* descended from *John Mentel*, a *High-Dutch* Gentleman, born at *Strasburg*, to whom the Chronicle of *Strasburg* gives the Invention of Printing in 1440. *James Mentel*, in his Treatise of the Origi-

Coronation, and were, in the Year following, order'd by the Emperor, on this account, to be beheaded, as if it was a Design of a Conspiracy against the Empire.

Henry II. caus'd the Coronation-Ornaments to be made, which are still preserv'd in the Treasury of St. *Dennis*.

This Prince having his Eye wounded by the shivering of a Lance, in a *Joust*, in the Street *St. Antoine*, against *Gabriel* Count of *Montgomery*, during a Tournament appointed for the Nuptials of his Daughter *Isabella*, *June* the 29th, 1559, dy'd eleven Days after. He reign'd twelve Years four Months; he was aged forty Years, three Months, and eleven Days (*x*).

FRANCIS II. 59th King of *France*, Son of *Henry* II. came to the Throne immediately after the Death of his Father, in 1559, aged 16 Years (*y*), and he was anointed and crown'd at *Rheims* by *Charles*

nal of it, brings the Letters Patents of the Emperor *Frederic* III granted in 1466, by which he declares *John Mentel* the sole Inventer of the Art of Printing.

(*x*) *See* Francis Beaucaire, de Thou, du Plessis, & Mezeray, Hist de Henry II.

(*y*) He was called *Monseigneur le Duc*, while the King was living, and then had marryd *Mary Stuart*, Daughter and only Heiress of *James* V. King of *Scotland*, and of *Mary* of *Lorain*, eldest Daughter of *Claude*, Duke of *Guise*, and of *Antoinette* of *Bourbon*. This was the Cause that the Duke of *Guise*, and the Cardinal of *Bourbon*, his Brother, had the Regency of the Kingdom during his Minority; the Duke of *Guise* having the Command of the Army, and the Cardinal the Conduct of the State.

Cardinal

Cardinal of *Lorain*, Archbishop of *Rheims*, *September* 18. 1559 (*z*).

CHARLES IX. 60th King of *France*, third Son of *Henry* II. and Brother of *Francis* II. came to the Throne in 1560, aged only ten Years; *Francis* II. his Brother dying without Issue that same Year, after a Reign of 16 Years and 10 Months: and he was anointed at *Rheims* on *Ascension-Day*, *May* 15. 1561. by the Cardinal who crown'd the two Kings before him.

Catherine de Medicis, his Mother, stept into the Regency during his Minority, she was declar'd Regent in the Assembly of the Estates at *Blois*, in the Year 1560, and made *Anthony* of *Bourbon*, King of *Navarre*, Lieutenant-General of the Kingdom.

At his Coronation it was particular, that there were thirteen Peers. Monsieur *Alexander*, Duke of *Orleans*, assisted at it, and, according to antient Usage, he preceded the King of *Navarre*, because he did not assist as Peer, but as nearest to the Crown. The Duke of *Guise* had place before the Duke *de Montpensier*, and follow'd immediately the King of *Navarre*; because the Duke of *Guise* represented the Duke of *Normandy*, and the Duke of *Montpensier* the Duke of *Guyenne*, who is the third Peer at a Coronation (*a*).

(*z*) The Medal struck for it points out the 17th, but the Ceremony was delay'd one Day. *Dupleix & Mezeray.*

(*a*) *See* de Thou. Pierre Matthieu. Mezeray. Godefr. Grand Ceremon. Marlot. Theat. d'Hon.

Henry

HENRY III. 61ſt King of *France*, 4th Son of *Henry* II. and of *Catherine de Medicis*, came to the Throne by the Death of *Charles* IX. his Brother, who departed *March* 30. 1574. aged 23 Years, 11 Months, and 4 Days, without leaving any Children.

Before, he bore the Title of Duke of *Anjou*, and he was elected King of *Poland*, *May* the 9th, 1573, in a General Aſſembly held near *Warſaw*, and he was anointed and crown'd King of *Poland* at *Cracow*, *February* the 15th, 1574. but having been inform'd three Months after this Coronation of the Death of his Brother *Charles* IX. he retir'd privately from *Poland* to *France* where he was anointed and crown'd King of *France* at *Rheims*, by *Louis* Cardinal of *Lorain*, Biſhop of *Metz*, the See of *Rheims* being then vacant, *Feb.* 15. 1575, the ſame Day that he was crown'd in *Poland* the Year before (*b*).

The Day after he marry'd at *Rheims* *Louiſa* of *Lorain*, Daughter of Prince *Nicholas* of *Lorain*, and of *Margaret* of *Egmond*, with great Magnificence; but ſome note, the People were offended, that neither on the Coronation-Day, nor on that

(*b*) Cardinal *Charles* of *Lorain* was dead, and *Louis* of *Lorain*, his Nephew, nominated to the See of *Rheims*, not being yet even a Prieſt *Charles de Rouſſi*, Biſhop of *Soiſſons*, proteſted, that he ought to crown the King in the Abſence of the Archbiſhop of *Rheims*, whoſe Suffragan he was, yet he receiv'd and complimented the King at the Gate of the Church.

of his Nuptials, the Maſs could be ſaid till Evening, the King and Queen being taken up in adjuſting their Dreſs and Figure; that the Muſicians forgot, in both the Ceremonies, to ſing *Te Deum*, which is a Song of Joy, and that the Crown fell from his Head as he was anointing; to which the Leaguers added, but falſely, that there was no Oil in the Holy Vial, from which they drew an ill Preſage, as well to his Reign as Perſon (*c*).

In this Coronation the Diſpute was renew'd about the Precedence of the Peers and Princes of the Blood: The Duke of *Montpenſier* came Poſt for that purpoſe from *Poitou*, a little after the taking of *Luſignan*, and he was arriv'd within two Leagues of *Rheims*, without asking the Permiſſion of the King, with a deſign to place himſelf above the Duke of *Guiſe*; but not being in favour with the Queen-Mother, and the Duke of *Guiſe* having her Eſteem, the King put a ſtop to him, by an expreſs Prohibition, to come no farther, not to enter *Rheims*; ſo that he was oblig'd to return (*d*).

The Reign of *Henry* III. was very troubleſome, and tho' he was a Prince magnanimous, good, eloquent, religious, and generally well-intention'd, he could not eſcape

(*c*) *See* Davila, de Thou, Dupleix, & Mezeray Hiſt. de Fran. & Marlot Theat. d Hon.

(*d*) Mezeray. Marlot.

the

the Outrage of the League, and the Evening before the Day, when he design'd an Attack upon the City of *Paris*, then besieg'd on the account of her Rebellion, being at *St. Clou*, where he resided, a villainous Monk wounded him with a Knife in the Breast, as he was reading the Letters which he brought to amuse him. He dy'd the Day after, *August* third, 1589, in the 39th Year of his Age, and the 15th of his Reign (*e*).

He leaving no Issue, the Race of *Valois* was extinct, after having given 13 Kings to *France*, in the space of 161 Years.

This Prince instituted the Order of the Holy Ghost, with great Pomp and Solemnity, *January* the 2*d*, 1579 (*f*), in the Church

(*e*) The Monk was call'd *Jacques Clement*, a *Jacobine*, Native of the Village of *Sorbonne*, near *Sens*. *Mezeray*. *Duplеix*.

(*f*) The Order of St. *Michael*, founded by *Louis* XI. having much declin'd under the Regency of *Catherine de Medicis*, and during the Civil Wars, *Henry* III. without annulling that Order, commonly called, *The Order of the King*, appointed that of the *Holy Ghost*, in Memory of his being twice crown'd on *Whitsunday*, as King of *Poland* and of *France*. The Device was,

DUCE & AUSPICE,

Under his Auspicious Guidance,

to express the Protection of the Holy Ghost. He declar'd himself and his Successors Chiefs and Sovereigns of it, and united for ever the Great Mastership of it to the Crown of *France*, with an Injunction, that they, who were to be honour'd with the Collar of this Order, should receive that of St. *Michael* the Evening before. The Number of Knights at present is 100, not including the Sovereign, there are always nine Prelates, and five great Officers

Church of the *Great Augustines* at *Paris*.

HENRY IV. called *the Great*, 62d King of *France*, born at *Pau* in *Bearn*, *December* 13. 1553. He was Son of *Anthony* of *Bourbon* II. Duke of *Vendosme*, Son of *Charles* and *Frances* of *Alençon*, and King of *Navarre*, by his Wife *Jane d'Albret*, Daughter of *Henry*, King of *Navarre*, and of *Margaret*, Daughter of K. *Francis* I (*g*). He descended, in a direct Male Line from St. *Louis*, Father of *Robert*, Count of *Clermont*; and his Right to the Crown was so evident, that they, who disputed the Possession of it with him, could alledge no other Pretext for it, but that of the Reform'd Religion, which he profess'd. This rais'd a considerable Party, call'd *the League*, or the *Holy Union of Catholicks*; their Head was the old Cardinal of *Bourbon*, youngest Brother of *Anthony* of *Bourbon*, Father of *Henry* IV. whom the Duke *de Mayenne*, and the Enemies of *Henry* IV.

Officers of the Crown, with the Title of *Commanders*. The Cross of the Order is of Gold, enamelled with eight, every Ray *Pometty* of Gold, a Flower-de-Lys of Gold at every Angle of the Cross, and in the middle a Dove of Silver, and on the other Side a St *Michael*. This Cross hangs at the Neck by a Sky-blue Riblond the Prelates have not a St. *Michael* on the Reverse, but carry the Dove on both Sides. The Collar of the Order, since 1597. is composed of Flowers-de-Lys, with Flames and Streams of Fire issuing from them *D H* crown'd with Festons and Trophies of Arms *De Thou* *Lefleix* *Mezeray*

(*g*) By this means *Navarre* return'd to the House of *France*, and still belongs to it.

would

would place upon the Throne. They gave him the Title of King, under the Name of *Charles* X. coin'd Money in his Name; and the Duke of *Mayenne* (who, under the Name of this pretended *Charles* X. called by him the only true King of *France*, tho' he was only a Shadow, would in effect reign himſelf) took the Quality of Lieutenant-General of the State and Crown of *France*. The Pope himſelf and the King of *Spain* very warmly eſpous'd this Party, and ſent numerous Forces into *France* to ſupport the Leaguers, and the Pope thunder'd out his Cenſures againſt thoſe who acknowledg'd *Henry* IV. as their King; but they were declar'd null by the Parliament.

Henry IV. ſurmounted, by his Valour, all theſe Obſtacles that oppos'd his Coming to the Throne, and won many Battles; but he did it chiefly by abjuring the Hereſy of *Calvin*, in the Church of the Abbey, between the Hands of *Renaud de Beaune*, Archbiſhop of *Bourges*, of *Charles*, Cardinal of *Bourbon*, and Archbiſhop of *Rouen*; of nine Biſhops, and all the Princes of the Court, *July* 23. 1593.

Then the Catholick Lords recognized him for their King, and he was anointed and crown'd at *Chartres*, in the Church of *Notre-Dame*, by the Biſhop of that City, *Nicholas de Thou*, *Feb.* 27. 1594. and *March* 22. following, *Paris*, and many Cities of the

the Kingdom, own'd him their (*b*) Sovereign.

Here, instead of the Oil of the Holy Vial of *Rheims*, was us'd that which is kept in the Abbey of *Marmoutier* at *Tours*, which *Severus Sulpitius*, *Fortunatus* Bishop of *Poitiers*, and *Alcuin* Preceptor to *Charlemagne*, report, was brought by an Angel to St. *Martin*, to recover him of a great Contusion receiv'd by a Fall. They convey'd this precious Liquor in a Chariot made for the purpose, *Gilles de Souvray*, Governor of *Tours*, having the Charge of it, and it was conducted with great Solemnity. They sent a white Horse for the Sacristan of the Abbey of *Marmoutier*, who carry'd the Sacred Vial from the Entrance of the City of *Chartres*, mounted upon him, under a Covering, damask'd with Golden Flowers-de-Lys, supported by four *Religious*, cloth'd with Albes.

(*b*) He could not enter *Champagne* to be crown'd, because it was in the Power of the League, and the Civil Wars were a Hindrance.

Renaud de Beaune, pretended to represent the Archbishop, Duke of *Rheims*, not only on the score of his Archiepiscopal Dignity, but as he was nominated to the Archbishoprick of *Sens*, which is the Metropolitan of *Chartres*, but he desisted from that Pretension, at the Representation of *Nicholas de Thou*, Bishop of *Chartres*, That, by the Canons, the Archbishops were forbidden to perform any Function in the Churches of the Bishops, who were not their Suffragans, that besides, he was not yet consecrated Archbishop of *Sens*, if he had been so, he had in Honour paid him that Deference *See* Dupleix, Mezeray, Baptist le Grain, *and* Hardouin de Perefixe *Bishop of* Rodez, *in their Histories of this Prince.*

The

The whole Ceremony was full of Splendor and Magnificence, notwithstanding the Division and the Troubles that harassed a great Part of the Kingdom.

The Marshal *de Matignon* perform'd the Function of Constable.

The Count of *St. Paul* that of Great Master.

The Dukes of *Longueville* and *Bellegarde* those of Great Chamberlain, and Master of the Horse.

The Lay-Peers were thus represented.

The Duke of *Burgundy* by the Prince of *Conti*.

The Duke of *Normandy* by the Count of *Soissons*.

The Duke of *Guyenne* by the Duke *de Montpensier*.

The Count *de Tholouse* by the Duke *de Piney*.

The Count of *Flanders* by the Duke *de Retz*.

The Count de *Champagne*, by the Duke *de Vantadour*.

For the Ecclesiastical Peers, since those Dignities were then vacant, or they, who held them, were of the Party of the League:

Philip du Bec, Bishop of *Nantes*, served for the Bishop Duke *de Laon*.

Henry Magnan, Bishop of *Digne*, for the Bishop Duke *de Langres*.

Henry d'Escoubleaux, Bishop of *Maillezais*, for the Bishop Count *de Beauvais*.

Cosme

Cosme de Clausse, who was Bishop of *Chalons*, discharged his Function in Person, and *Claude de l'Aubespine*, Bishop of *Orleans*, served for the Bishop, Count of *Noyon* (*i*).

After the Coronation there was a Royal Feast, with the ordinary Ceremonies, and at Night the King gave an Entertainment to the Ladies, attended by the same Officers that waited upon the King at Dinner.

On the Day following, after Vespers, the King received the Collar of the Order of the Holy Ghost, in the same Church, where he was crown'd, from the same Bishop, taking the usual Oath, which he pronounced after the Chancellor.

May the 13th, 1610. he caused Queen *Mary de Medicis*, his second Wife, to be crowned in the Church of St. *Dennis* with extraordinary Pomp. She was his second Wife, Daughter of *Francis de Medicis*, Great Duke of *Tuscany*, and of *Jane*, Archdutchess of *Austria*, and Queen-born of *Hungary* and *Bohemia*, Daughter, Sister, Aunt, and Niece of Emperors.

The King himself took the Charge, and gave the necessary Orders for this Ceremony, and the Day after, while he was preparing for his Entry into *Paris*, *Henry* IV. was assassinated in his Coach, as he past thro' the Street of *la Feronnerie*, on Friday the 14th of *May*, 1610; so that he died (aged

(*i*) Marlot, Theatr. d'Hon. Mezeray.

fifty seven Years, five Months, one Day, having reigned in *France* twenty Years, ten Months, eighteen Days, and in *Navarre* thirty eight Years) in the time that he was preparing to go in Person to make War with *Spain*, which always (*k*) opposed him, leaving, for his Heirs, two Sons, *Louis* the XIIIth, who succeeded him, and *John Baptist Gaston* of *France*, Duke of *Orleans* and of *Chartres*, Count of *Blois* (*l*), Peer of *France*

LOUIS XIII. called *the Just*, 63d King of *France*, eldest Son of *Henry* and of *Mary de Medicis*, born at *Fontainbleau*, *Septemb*. 27. 1601. came to the Throne at the Age of ten Years. He held his Bed of Justice in his Parliament, which sat in the Great Hall of the *Augustines* at *Paris*, 24 Hours after the Death of his Father, and he caused the Queen, his Mother, to be there declared Regent, during his Minority, *May* 15. 1610. He was anointed and crown'd at *Rheims*, *Octob*. 17. 1610 (*m*), by the Cardinal *de Joyeuse*, Archbishop of *Rouen*, representing the Archbishop of *Rheims*, whose great Age prevented his appearing.

(*k*) He that killed him was *Ravillac*, a Native of *Angoulesme*, who was taken and punished according to his Crime

(*l*) Dupleix, Mezeray, Mailot.

(*m*) *See* la Conference des Ordonnances de Guenois, L. 12. Sect. 11.

On

On (*n*) the Evening of the Coronation the King received, in the Church of *Rheims*, by the Hands of the Cardinal *de Joyeuſe*, the Sacrament of Confirmation; to which he was preſented by Queen (*o*) *Margaret*, and by the Prince of *Condé*.

The ſix Eccleſiaſtical Peers who aſſiſted at this, were,

The Cardinal *de Joyeuſe*, Archbiſhop of *Rouen*, repreſenting the Archbiſhop of *Rheims*.

Geoffroy de Billy, Biſhop, Duke of *Laon*.

Charles des Cars, Biſhop, Duke of *Langres*.

René Poitiers, Biſhop, Count of *Beauvais*.

Coſme Clauſſe, Biſhop, Count of *Chalons*.

Charles de Balſac, Biſhop, Count of *Noyon*.

(*n*) *Louis* XIII. was not crown'd till after the Funeral of his Father. When he made his Entry into *Rheims*, on the Evening of his Coronation, he was in Mourning, plainly dreſs'd, his Robe was only a Violet-coloured Serge, without the leaſt Garniture. He enter'd, mounted on a white Horſe, with a Violet Houſing and Equipage, (which is the mourning Colour of the Kings of *France*) All the Princes and Lords were in Black, even on the Day of the Coronation, and only the Heralds at Arms appear'd in Colours and Embroidery

(*o*) Dutcheſs of *Valois*, Daughter of *Henry* II. and of *Catherine de Medicis*. *Henry* IV. married her in 1572, but having no Children by her, about the end of the Year 1599, this Marriage was declared null by the Conſent of both Parties, and the Proximity of Blood, and the want of a Diſpenſation from the Holy See, ſerved as a Pretence for this Divorce.

The six Lay-Peers:

The Prince of *Condé* for the Duke of *Burgundy*.

The Prince of *Conti* for the Duke of *Normandy*.

The Count of *Soissons* for the Duke of *Aquitaine*.

The Duke *de Nevers* for the Count of *Flanders*.

The Duke *d'Elbeuf* for the Count of *Champagne*.

The Duke *d'Epernon* for the Count of *Tholouse*.

The Constable was represented by the Marquiss *de la Chastre*.

The Chancellor was *Nicolas de Brullard*, Sieur *de Sillery*.

The Grand Master was represented by the Marshal *de Lavardin*.

The Great Chamberlain was the Duke *d'Eguillon*.

The Marquiss *de Bellegarde* held the Place of Master of the Horse, and first Gentleman.

LOUIS XIII. was declar'd *Major* in Parliament in 1614 (*p*), having at that time concluded and accomplished (at the Age of thirteen) a double Alliance between *France* and *Spain*, by his Marriage with *Anne* of *Austria*, Infanta of *Spain*, and that of

(*p*) Till then he reign'd under the Tuition of the Queen his Mother, in the same Year the Estates assembled at *Paris*.

Eliza-

Elizabeth of *France*, Sister to the King, with the Infante *Philip* IV.

He died at *St. Germain en Laye* on *Ascension-Day*, *May* the 14th, 1643, on the same Day that he came to the Throne, after a Reign of 33 Years, and a Life of 42, leaving for his Heirs *Louis* XIV. his Successor, and *Philip* Duke of *Orleans* (*q*).

LOUIS XIV. called *the Great*, 64th King of *France*, eldest Son of *Louis* XIII and of *Anne* of *Austria*, born at *St. Germain en Laye*, *Septemb.* the 5th, 1638, came to the Throne of his Father, *May* the 14th, 1643, aged only four Years and an half (*r*).

May

(*q*) Dupleix & Marolles Hist de France.

(*r*) By the Decease of *Eleonor d' Estampes de Valency*, *Henry de Savoye*, Duke *de Nemours*, nominated to the Archbishoprick of *Rheims*, not having yet received his Bulls, nor being consecrated, nor put in possession of it, could not perform the Ceremony. This makes it proper to quote the Letter of the King, written on this Subject to the Bishop of *Soissons*, of which this is the Tenor, and the Subscription.

To Monsieur the Bishop of Soissons, *Counsellor in my Council of State*

'Monsieur, the Bishop of *Soissons*, whatever Prosperity 'God has given me, I cannot rest satisfy'd that my Coro-'nation has not confirm'd my Reign, and that my Zeal 'for the compleating of this August and Holy Ceremony 'has not surmounted all the Obstacles that have hinder'd 'it till this time.

'On this Account I have resolv'd to be in my City of '*Rheims* on the 28th of this Month, and have appointed 'you to officiate at that Solemnity, and to represent the 'ArchBp Duke of *Rheims*, one of the six Peers of *France*, 'Clerks. As I doubt not, but that to satisfy my Desire, and

 'comply

May the 18th, the same Year, he held his Bed of Justice in Parliament, and caus'd his Mother *Anne* of *Austria* to be declared Regent. and in the 16th Year of his Age he was anointed and crowned at *Rheims*, *June* the 7th, 1654, by *Simon le Gras*, Bishop of *Soissons*, as Dean and first Suffragan of the Archbishoprick of *Rheims*, that See being then vacant.

Thus of 64 Kings of *France*, which we reckon from *Clovis*, we find only sixteen or seventeen who were not crowned in the Church of *Rheims*, or by that Archbishop, and forty seven or forty who were so crowned, by consequence, we may say, that the Church of *Rheims* has the Privilege of the Coronation, and that the Baptism and Anointing of the first Christian King, done within her Walls, has acquired her this Honour. An eminent Right indeed, and a glorious Possession! of which this City and its Prelates only can boast, if it belongs at all to any Particular.

'comply with the Advice I now send you, you will attend me on the Day and in the Place in this Letter prescribed, I will not make it more express to you, and I pray God to have you, Monsieur the Bishop of Soissons, in his Holy Keeping

Written at Paris the 13th Day of May, 1654

LOUIS.

And lower, De *GUENEGAUD.*

See the Verbal Process of the Coronation of this Prince, by M. the Bishop of *Soissons*, printed afterwards at *Paris*, for *J. Chardon* in 1717.

As every thing is perfected by Custom, the Ceremonies of the Coronation of *Louis* the XIVth were the most compleatly pompous that have been known, till the present, both for the Magnificence of the Habits and Ornaments, and for the Quality and Number of the Princes, Princesses, Prelates, and Lords who assisted at it. And since the three first Ecclesiastical Peerdoms were vacant, the King caused them to be represented; as that of *Rheims* by the Bishop of *Soissons*, and those of *Laon* and *Langres* by the Bishops of *Beauvais* and of *Chalons*, who were themselves represented by other Prelates, named by his Majesty.

There still was a Difference about Precedency, between the Archbishops of *Rouen* and of *Bourges* (who would go first) and the Bishops of the Province of *Rheims*. Upon which the King, in his Council, ordained, on the Evening before his Coronation, that the Bishops of the Province of *Rheims* should precede the Archbishops of *Rouen* and *Bourges*, by the following Order; and as they were called by the Chancellor to bear the Crown, and crown the King, with the Bishop of *Soissons*, representing the Archbishop of *Rheims* in his Office.

The Names of the Peers who aſſiſted at the Coronation of Louis *XIV according to the Order of the Call then made.*

The ſix Lay-Peers were all by Repreſentative.

M. the Duke of *Anjou* repreſented the Duke of *Burgundy*.

M. the Duke of *Vendome* was for the Duke of *Normandy*.

M. the Duke *d'Elbœuf* for the Duke of *Aquitaine*, or *Guyenne*.

M. the Duke of *Candale*, or *Eſpernon*, for the Count of *Champagne*.

M. the Duke *de Rouanez* for the Count of *Flanders*.

M. the Duke of *Bournonville* for the Count *de Tholouſe*.

The ſix Eccleſiaſtical Peers were all by Repreſentative.

M. *Simon le Gras*, Biſhop of *Soiſſons*, repreſented the Archbiſhop of *Rheims*.

The Biſhop of *Beauvais* was for the Biſhop of *Laon*.

The Biſhop of *Chalons* was for the Biſhop of *Langres*.

The Biſhop of *Noyon* was for the Biſhop of *Beauvais*.

The Archbiſhop of *Bourges* for the Biſhop of *Chalons*.

The Archbishop of *Rouen* for the Bishop and Count of *Noyon* (s).

The Great Officers of the Crown.

The Constable was represented by the Marshal (t) *d'Estrees*, as antient Marshal of *France*.

Prince

(s) The Chapter of *Rheims*, which pretends, that the Bishops of *Soissons*, and other Suffragans of *Rheims*, have no Right to exercise any Function in that Church, during a Vacancy, without their Consent, has been accustom'd to make a Protest, in opposition even to the Ceremony of the Coronation, so far, that the Bishop, who is preparing for it, has given a Declaration, and an authentick Recognizance, before Notaries, setting forth, That the Coronation which they perform, by the Consent of the Chapter, should not acquire to them any Right, either petitory or possessory, contrary to the Rights of the Chapter, which should still be entire, as if no Coronation had been done. This happened at the crowning of *Louis* the IXth, *Philip the Hardy*, and *Louis* the XIVth. *See* the Verbal Process quoted above

(t) The Constable was the first of the Great Officers of the Crown of *France*. This Post is so antient, that we find Constables in the Reign of *Theodore*, or *Thierry*, in 680, but they were only *Comites Stabuli*, like the Master of the Horse, and after they were set higher to command all the Forces The Person of the Constable was so far privileg'd, that an Offence of Fact against it was an Offence against that of the King. During the Minority of the Kings, they were named after the Princes of the Blood. The keeping of the Royal Sword was committed to him, and he received it unsheathed, being obliged to make Liege-Homage to him for it, without its being Hereditary. The last Constable was *Francis de Bonne*, Duke *de Lesdiguieres*, after whose Death, in 1626, *Louis* XIII suppress'd this Office, the Functions of which are now reunited to the Offices of the Marshals of *France*, and since the Suppression of it, the Constable is represented, at a Coronation,

Prince *Eugene* of *Savoy* bore the Train of the Royal Robe.

The Marſhal *de l'Hôpital* carried the Scepter.

The Marſhal *du Pleſſis Praſlin* carried the Crown.

The Marſhal *d'Aumont* carried the Sword of Juſtice.

The Chancellor *Seguier* performed his own Office.

The Grand-Maſter was repreſented by the Marſhal *de Villeroy*,

The Great Chamberlain was the Duke *de Joyeuſe*, who performed his Office.

The Count *de Vivonne*, firſt Gentleman of the Chamber, the Count *de Noailles*, and the Marquiſs *de Charoſt*, Captains of the Guards, as well as the Sieur *de Rodes*, Great Maſter of the Ceremonies of *France*, performed each their ſeveral Charges.

The Offerings.

The Marquiſſes of *Souvré* and of *Sourdis*, the Count *d'Orval*, and the Duke of *St. Simon*, Knights of the Order of the Holy Ghoſt, carried the Offerings.

tion, by a Lord, named by the King, who is ordinarily the antient Marſhal of *France*. *See* Paſquier's Recherches de la France, l. 2. c. 11, & 12.

The

The Knights and Bearers of the Holy Vial.

The Baron *de Lomercy* was the only Knight of the Holy Vial that discharged his Office, the three others were represented by two Religious, and the Bailiff of the Abbey of St. *Remy*.

The four Lords sent by the King to conduct the Holy Vial, were the Marquisses of *Coislin* and *Richelieu*, the Count of *Biron*, and the Marquiss *de Mancini*, whose Places were appointed by Lot, the last being unwilling to accept the Precedence which each of the other would have given him.

Queen *Anne* of *Austria*, Mother of *Louis* XIV. and Regent during the Minority of her Son, and Monsieur *Philip* Duke of *Orleans*, only Brother of the King, assisted at this August Ceremony, with the Queen of *England*, the Dukes of *York* and *Glocester*, her Sons, the Princess of *England* her Daughter, the Princess *Palatine*, and the Dutchess of *Vendôme*, accompanied with the Ladies of the Court, Prince *Thomas*, and one of his Sons.

The Cardinal *Grimaldi*, the Archbishop of *Tholouse*, and the Bishops of *Bayonne*, *Dol*, *Montauban*, *Toulon*, *Cominges*, *Rodez*, *Leon*, *Saint Paul*, and other Bishops, in their Rochets, and Violet-colour'd *Camails*.

The Count *de Servien*, Sur-intendant of the Finances, the Counsellors and Secretaries

of

of State, the Marſhals *de l'Hôpital, du Pleſſis Praſlin, d'Aumont, d'Albret*, and *Clerembault*, the Pope's Nuncio, the Ambaſſadors of *Portugal, Venice, Savoy, Malta*, the Reſident of *Poland*, and others, who were conducted to their Places by the Maſters of the Ceremonies.

After the Coronation, Maſs, and Communion of the King, his Majeſty returned to the Archiepiſcopal Palace, where a Royal Feaſt was prepared. He dined, ſtill in the ſame Habit, with the Crown on his Head.

The Day after, being the 8th of *June*, the King received the Order of the Holy Ghoſt from the Hands of the ſame Prelate who crown'd him, and afterwards conferred it upon *Monſieur* with the accuſtomed Ceremonies.

On Tueſday the 9th, after hearing Maſs, and communicating by the Hands of one of his Almoners in the Church of St. *Remy*, he went into the Park of that Abbey to touch the Sick, in Number about 2605, having by his Side the Marquiſs *de Charoſt*, Captain of his Guards, followed by Cardinal *Grimaldi*, Great Almoner of *France*, who diſtributed ſome Money to the Sick, as the King touched them.

After a Reign of 73 Years, glorious to the Nation, and ſtill more to its Prince, who made it, during his Life, the Admiration and Aſtoniſhment of all *Europe*; he died at *Verſailles*, *September* the 1ſt, 1715, aged

77

77 Years, leaving the Heir of this great and potent Kingdom,

LOUIS XV. of the Name, now reigning, 65th King of *France* and *Navarre*, born (*u*) at *Versailles*, *February* 15. 1710. When *Louis* XIV. of Glorious Memory, had paid his last Debt to Nature M. the Duke of *Orleans*, first Prince of the Blood, who is always attentive to give an Example of the Respect and Submission due to Royal Majesty, follow'd by the other Princes and Nobles of the Kingdom, went to salute the King, and to kiss his Hand, with one Knee

(*u*) *Louis* XIV had by Queen *Maria-Theresa* of *Austria*, his Wife, one only Son, called *Louis*, *Dauphin of France*, who was born at *Fontainbleau*, *Novemb* 1. 1661, and dy'd at *Meudon*, *April* 14 1711, aged 50 Years. He married in 1680, the Princess *Maria-Anna-Victoria* of *Bavaria*, by whom he had three Princes, I *Louis*, Duke of *Burgundy*, born at *Versailles*, *August* the 6th, 1682. II. *Philip*, Duke of *Anjou*, now King of *Spain*, born at *Versailles*, *Decemb.* 19. 1683. III *Charles de Berry*, born also at *Versailles*, *August* the 31st, 1686, who married *Maria-Louisa-Elizabeth* of *Orleans*, and died, without Male-Issue, *May* the 4th, 1714, aged 28 Years. The Duke of *Burgundy*, who became afterwards Dauphin of *France*, by the Death of Monseigneur, married *Maria-Adelaide*, Princess of *Savoy*, *December* the 7th, 1697, and died at *Marly*, *February* the 18th, 1712, aged thirty Years, surviving Madame the Dauphiness, his Spouse, only six Days. She died the 12th of the same Month, in the same Year He left by her three Princes; the two first were known by the Title of the Duke of *Bretagne* I. who died *April* the 13th, 1705, aged nine Months, and the Duke of *Bretagne* II. who died *March* the 8th, 1712, aged five Years. The youngest is *Louis* the XVth, now reigning He was first Duke of *Anjou*, then Dauphin, and came to the Throne of *Louis* the XIVth, his Great Grandfather, *September* 1. 1715, aged five Years, and six Months.

upon

upon the Ground, as his new Monarch; and at the same time *Louis* XV. was proclaim'd King of *France* and *Navarre* with Drum and Trumpet.

Thus, as Royalty is immortal in *France*, in the moment, that the Greatest King in the World ceased to live, *Louis* XV. by the Right of his Birth, began to reign. Heaven grant that he may equal the Virtues, and exceed the Years of his Great Grandfather! and that among the famous Reigns, which fill our Histories, his may carry an uncommon Lustre! His first Advance is a happy Presage, and already promises whatever we desire.

The first Instant of his Reign was mark'd by an Action full of Religion, Piety, Love for the Memory of the deceas'd King, and an Affection for his People; it is the Letter *de Cachet*, dictated by Wisdom itself, written to the Parliament of *Paris* to continue its Sitting, and the Administration of Justice (*w*).

The Day following M. the Duke of *Orleans*, to whom the Regency belonged of Right by his Birth, and to whom the People had already given it by their Views, was declared Regent of *France*, during the Minority of the King, with the unanimous Consent of all the Princes and Nobles, as-

(*w*) *September* 1. 1715. in the Verbal Process of what passed in Parliament, *September* 2. 1715.

sembled

ſembled in the Parliament of *Paris*, on Monday, *September* 2 1715.

Ten Days after, *Louis* XV. ſhewed himſelf to his Subjects, in his Bed of Juſtice, held in his Parliament, on Thurſday, *September* 12. 1715. where, being with all the Princes and Nobles, he confirm'd the Regency to M. the Duke of *Orleans*, conformably to the Arrêt of the ſecond of that Month.

It was not without Reaſon, that the Choice of a Regent ſo capable was look'd upon as a certain Preſage of Happineſs to the Publick. To judge of Regencies by that of this Minority, we muſt think it a time deſtined to the Peace, Welfare, and Tranquillity of the People, but if we run over the Hiſtory of former Minorities, when we ſee Troubles, Cabals, Intrigues, Diviſions, and Civil Wars, and all the Evils that are unknown to us in this, what ſhall we ſay of a Prince, who, more jealous of the Regulation and Laws of the State, than of his own Power, leſs concern'd for his own Intereſt and Repoſe, than the Publick Good, and the Glory of the King, has not only maintain'd the Union and Tranquillity of the Realm within, but has eſtabliſh'd Peace abroad, by Steps of the moſt wiſe and ſagacious Policy?

What Joy will it be to his Majeſty, at preſent reigning, when he himſelf ſhall take the Helm of the State, to find it all in a

profound

profound Peace? What Satisfaction will this be to a Prince, who is pleas'd to cherish his People, and is the Love and Delight of them? How happy is the Harmony of so perfect a Government, and what Glory is it to a Regent, who has procur'd him all these Advantages?

CHAP. IX.

Whether there be a Necessity of Anointing the Kings of France? *and whether they can receive the Royal Unction before their Majority?*

THO' the Anointing is not the only thing that gives the Kings of *France* the Character of Sovereign, and the Authority over their People, since we own the Rights of our Monarchs, independent of this Ceremony, and revere, even before their Birth, those who, by the Laws of Blood, are destin'd to govern us, the Kingdom being never vacant, and having a Continuation of a King; so that the very Instant that the Reign of the Father ends, that of the

the Son commences, that is, of the nearest Male-Heir to the Crown (*x*).

Yet, till they are crown'd, they seem to want something of their proper Majesty; and History tells us, that our Kings, not content with the first Proclamations and Acknowledgments done to their Persons, at the Head of their Armies, in Funeral Solemnities, in a stated Assembly, or in the Bed of Justice, immediately after the Death of their Predecessors, have also, for near one thousand Years, demanded and received the Royal Unction, persuaded that it is a Symbol of that Grace and Assistance, which is promised them by God for the Government of their People, that the Soul being consecrated (*y*) by the anointing of the Flesh, their Persons are covered with the Shield of the Lord, and become more precious and sacred, according to the Word of God (*z*), *Touch not mine Anointed*; speaking of the Kings of *Israel*. It is likewise a publick Ratification of their Right to succeed to the Crown of their Ancestors, and a Confirmation of the first Act, which put them in possession of the Throne; it is a kind of spiritual Alliance of a King with his Kingdom; which he espouses, if we may

(*x*) The First-born of *France* is called King before his Coronation. *Papin de Her l* 1.

(*y*) *Caro ungitur*, &c. The Flesh is anointed, that the Soul may be consecrated, the Flesh is signed, that the Soul may be fortified. *Tertul. de Resur. Carn.*

(*z*) 1 Sam.

say so, which he engages to maintain, defend, and protect, at the same time that the Kingdom, by the Voice of its People, solemnly promises Fidelity and Obedience to him: so that tho' Birth entitles them to the Throne, Anointing is necessary. Amongst us, till the 12th Age, the succeeding Princes were not acknowledg'd Kings till the Day of their Anointing and Coronation, till then, as our old Chronicles say, the King was dormant, and the Royal Authority was entirely in the Nobles, or in the Regent, whose Name alone was signed in the publick Acts (*a*) Hence till *Charles* the Vth (*b*), call'd the *Sage*, or *the Wise*, the Nobles, whose Interest it was to prolong the Regency and the Minority, laid it down for a Maxim, That the Kings ought not to be crown'd before their Majority, which then was not till the Age of Twenty.

This oblig'd *Charles* V to ordain, That, after his Death, his eldest Son, and his Successors, Kings of *France*, should be esteem'd *Majors* at the Age of Fourteen, so as then to have the Government of the Kingdom, to receive the Homages and Oaths of Fealty, the Consecration, Unction, and Coronation, and make the proper Oath at it.

(*a*) Chron Albert. ad Ann 988, &c. Chron. Viridun. tom. 1, & 2. Chron. Floriac. Chen. Annale de Met 2 Ivo Carnot.

(*b*) He made an Edict about the Minority, dated at *Bois de Vincenres* in *August*, 1374 registred in the Parliament, *March* 20. 1375 *Sancimus ut si r.s, &c.* *See* the Confer. des Ordon. de J. Guenois.

Charles VI. called *the Well-beloved*, confirmed the Edict of his Father as to the Majority; but as to the Anointing, he appointed it to be done at the Age of their coming to the Throne, like the Kings of *Israel* and *Judah*, and many of our first Kings, who were anointed in their Infancy, during the Life of their Fathers, or at the first moment of their Election and Accession to the Crown (*c*).

So that, at present, tho' the Anointing of our Kings comes pretty near the Nature of our Sacraments; yet as it requires no more Capacity than Baptism, it is certain, there is no Point of Age, at which they may not be anointed. We may also observe that Heaven has always visibly protected those Kings that were anointed in their tender Years, in delivering them from the Hands of their Enemies, whom they have conquered by means altogether miraculous, inspiring them with good Sentiments, to maintain their People in Peace and Justice, and make their Reign ever glorious.

(*c*) This Edict was given at *Paris*, *Decemb* 13. 1392.

David, *Solomon*, and *Manasses* were only ten or twelve Years old at that time, *Josiah* and *Joash* no more than six or seven when they were anointed

Clothaius II. was but four Months old when he was proclaimed and crowned, just after the Death of his Father *Pepin* *Louis the Debonnair*, *Philip* I. *Louis* IX and *Louis* XIII were crowned in their Childhood. See Sainte Marthe & Mezeray.

CHAP. X.

Who ought to defray the Expence of the Preparation for this Ceremony, and the Feast that follows it.

THIS was antiently the Charge of the Archbishops of *Rheims* (*d*). *Marlot* observes, that Cardinal *William* of *Champagne*, Archbishop of *Rheims*, Legate of the Holy See in *France*, to shew his Zeal, in the most splendid and magnificent manner, towards the Kings *Louis* VII. and *Philip the August*, his Nephews, and particularly to the latter, was at so excessive an Expence for the Feast and Coronation (all being entirely his private Charge) that he was oblig'd to borrow large Sums, and desir'd his Chapter to assist him in the Payment of them, which he obtain'd, and that this Favour might not be drawn into Consequence, he disavow'd the gaining of any Right over them by this Gratuity, and declar'd it should be (*e*) no Prejudice to them.

(*d*) Theatr. d'Honneur, l. 4 c. 10

(*e*) This is the most antient Proof, that these Archbishops were at the Cost of it. We have still more Proofs in the following Reigns.

At

At the Coronation of *Louis* VIII. and of Queen *Blanche*, his Spouse, *William de Joinville*, Archbishop of *Rheims*, having been oblig'd to this Expence, laid out in it 4000 *Parisis* (*f*).

Louis VIII. ordain'd, that all the Burgesses of *Rheims*, of the Royalty and Seigneury of the Archbishop, should bear their part in his Expence, as we are appris'd by the Letters Patents of that Monarch, dated at *Sens* in *August*, 1223. by which he declares to the Sheriffs and Burgesses of that City, that the Archbishop alone could not support the Charge of the Feast and Coronation of him and his Spouse; that therefore he enjoin'd them to furnish a share of it, that was agreeable to his Majesty, and in order to oblige them to it the sooner, without Contest, he declar'd (when the Archbishop would have eas'd them of this Obligation) he would not suffer it (*g*).

So that, from this time, the Inhabitants of *Rheims* are obliged to it, it is part of the Honour they receive by this great Action. and the King, in acknowledgment of their Expence at his Entry and at the Feast, is accustom'd to relieve them of certain Duties, which are rais'd upon the other Towns of the Province, and to grant them several Franchises and Exemptions.

(*f*) That is 47750 Livres of our Sterling, if we reckon the Crowns at three Livres, a great Sum for that time.

(*g*) Gest. Lud. Chen. VIII. tom. 5. pag. 284, & 291

CHAP. XI.

Whether our Kings may have more than one Coronation.

AS there is no Law that hinders our Kings from being crown'd in their Infancy, so there is none that deprives them of the Liberty to repeat that Ceremony (*b*) But of what Use (you will say) can it be to reiterate this Unction in the same Person for the same Kingdom? The first time they receive it, it not only imprints a sacred Character upon them, so proper to their Greatness, which is never effac'd, but confirms a Respect to them, even after their Decease. We remark likewise, that tho' many of our Kings of the second and third Race were crowned two or three times, and some of the second four times, yet we do not count above two or three who repeated it merely out of Piety. the rest did it, either because they were successively advanced to several Thrones, or put in possession of some other

(*b*) We find in Scripture that *David* was anointed three times, as an Evidence that he was the Type of Christ, the Lord's anointed, who thrice received it, in his Conception, his Baptism, and his Resurrection, as we are told by *Rupertus* on 1 *Sam.* But the Figures of the Old Law being accomplished in the Law of Grace, that antient Usage is not to be followed more without Necessity.

Part

Part of *France*, then divided among different Princes (*i*); so that it was not so much to renew the Unction, as to take it in the Quality of a new King. Thus *Charlemagne*, after he had been crowned at St. *Dennis*, during the Life of his Father *Pepin*, in 754, was again crowned at *Noion*, after his Father's Death, to note his Accession to the Throne of *France* in 768.

He was afterwards crowned at *Milan* as King of *Lombardy* in 774.

At *Rome* in 800, as Emperor of the *West*, with his Son *Lewis* I called *the Debonnair*, who was then crowned King of *Aquitaine*, and again in the Church of St. *Remy* at *Rheims* in 816, after the Decease of his Father, as Emperor of the *West*, and King of *France*.

Charles II. called *the Bald*, received the Unction four times:

1. At *Rome*, as King of the *Romans*, or *Lombards*, in 846.

2. At *Limoges*, as King of *Aquitaine*, in 854.

(*i*) *Pepin the Short* was anointed, in the Cathedral of *Soissons*, with the Holy Oil, by the Archbishop of *Mentz*, in 751 and again, with his Wife and Sons, at *St Dennis*, by Pope *Stephen* III who came into *France* in 754.

Charles VII. was twice crowned King of *France*, because at first *Rheims* was in the *English* Power, so that he was first crowned at *Poitiers* in 1422. till by the Assistance of the Maid of *Orleans* he was anew crowned at *Rheims*, 1429 So *Lewis* V. was first crowned at *Compiegne*, in the Life of *Lothaire* his Father, in 978, and again at *Rheims*, after his Father's Death, in 986.

3. At *Metz*, as King of *Lorrain*, in 869.

4. At *Rome*, or *Pavia*, as Emperor of the *West*, in 876.

Louis VIII. was crowned at *Rheims*, as King of *France* in 1223, after he had been crowned at *London*, as King of *England*, in 1215.

Philip IV. called *the Fair*, and *Louis* X. called *le Hutin*, were crowned at *Pampelona*, in the Years 1284, and 1307, as Kings of *Navarre*, and a second time at *Rheims*, as Kings of *France*, in 1575.

We do not find that any of our Kings, who received the Heavenly Unction at *Rheims*, were a second time anointed elsewhere as Kings of *France*, except *Philip* the IId, who was crowned at *Rheims* in 1179, during the Life of his Father *Louis* the VIIth, and again at *St. Dennis* with the Holy Chrism, together with Queen *Isabel*, his Spouse, in 1180, but rather in point of Honour, and to shew his Elevation to the Throne, of which he was the sole Possessor, by the Death of his Father, than by any Necessity.

For as to *Louis* XI. who, after having been crowned at *Rheims* in 1462, commanded the Holy Vial to be brought to *Plessis les Tours*, where he lay sick; it is well known, this was not with a Design to renew the Ceremony of his Anointing, but out of the Respect and Confidence he placed in that Sacred Balm, hoping that the very

Odour

Odour and Approach of this Celestial Liquor would restore him to his Health; as it appears by Letters, written to that effect to the Chapter of *Rheims*, *April* 17. and *July* 14. 1483, and by the Bull of Pope *Sixtus* the IVth, granted to him for this purpose, at the end of the Month of *June*, in the same Year (*k*).

And indeed if the Royal Unction ought to be looked upon as a Spiritual and Sacramental Marriage of Christian Kings with their Kingdoms, there is no need to repeat it, when it has been once performed in a lawful manner, and with the ordinary Solemnities.

CHAP. XII.

Whether the Sons of our Kings may be anointed and crowned, and as such have the Title of Kings during the Life of their Fathers.

THO' Policy and Maxims of State seem not to admit of two Sovereigns, with equal Authority, in the same Monarchy, yet it has often happened in Hereditary Kingdoms, that Kings have taken in their Sons to a Share of the Crown during their Life, either to confirm it the more to

(*k*) Marlot. Theatr. d'Honn. & Sacre des Rois, l 2 c. 3.

their

their Families, or discharge the Care of Government upon them, when they have found them equal to it. It was upon these Motives that *David* caused his Son (*l*) *Solomon* to be proclaimed and crowned King of *Israel* in his Life-time, knowing his Wisdom, and that the *Persians*, whose Empire was so potent, and the first after that of the *Jews*, often practised this way with good Success. and that among us, in the first and second Race of our Kings, *Childeric*, *Dagobert*, *Theodebert*, *Charlemagne* and *Carloman*, *Louis the Debonnair*, and *Charles the Bald*, who reigned in *Austrasia* and *Neustria*, were all anointed and placed upon the Throne in the Life of their Fathers. But without looking into Examples so remote, and to speak only of those Princes who have borne the Title of Kings of *France*, *Louis* V. was anointed and crowned King in 978, in the Life of his Father *Lotharius*, who thought by that to fix his tottering Scepter, and secure it to his Family (*m*).

But this Precaution was in vain, *Louis* V. died without Issue, and without Glory, and the *Carlovingian* Race ended with him.

Robert, called *the Devout*, and *the Sage*, was made an Associate in the Kingdom, and crown'd at *Rheims*, in the same Year that *Hugh Capet* his Father was declared

(*l*) 1 Kings 1. Justin lib 10 Plutarch. in Artaxerx.
(*m*) Sainte Marthe, Mezeray Cartular. S. Vinc Laudun.

King

King by the Estates. *Robert* bore the Quality of King, and governed jointly with his Father, as appears by the Date of the Council of *Rheims*, assembled in the Year 991, *in the fifth Year of the Reign of our Lord* Hugh *the August, and the most excellent King* Robert (*n*)

This same *Robert* took also his Son *Hugh* into a Share of the Crown, causing him to be crowned in the Church of *St. Cornelius* in *Compiegne*, in the Year 1024, being the 28th of his Father's Reign, but *Hugh* (*o*) dying young, when he just began to make himself beloved by the People, and particularly by the *Romans*, who had already marked him out for the Empire, *Robert* commanded his second Son *Henry* to be crowned at *Rheims*, in the Year 1025.

Henry I. imitated the Politicks of his Fathers, and caused his Son *Philip* to be crowned, in his own Life, at *Rheims*, in 1060.

Louis VII. Son of *Louis the Gross*, and *Philip* II. called *the August*, Son of *Louis* the VIIth, were likewise crowned while their Fathers were living, in the Years 1131, and 1179, by Consent of the Prelates, Barons, and Lords of the Kingdom assembled for that purpose, in Consideration of the Age and Illness of their Father (*p*).

(*n*) Aimoin. l 5 c. 40.
(*o*) Glab Rodulph l 3 Hist. c 9
(*p*) Rigord in Vit Phil. Aug. Tillet. in Chron. Sainte Marthe & Mezeray.

These are all the Sons of *France* who have wore the Crown, and taken the Quality of Kings in the Life of their Fathers, after having been anointed by their Agreement and Approbation (*q*).

CHAP. XIII.

Of the Ceremonies of the Coronation in all Times observed, and especially on the later Occasions.

TIME, which perfects all Things, has ever added some Magnificence to the Pomp of our Coronations. And besides, there is such a Variety of Conjunctures in each Reign, that it is impossible for all to be alike, especially as to the Forms of Preparation and outward Appearance, which are, for the most part, arbitrary. But since what is essential in this August Action does not change, with whatever exterior Pomp it is attended, we may still say, it is ever the same.

(*q*) Some Authors say, these Princes, before they were crowned, had the Title of *Designed Kings*. Marlot du Sacres P. l 2. c. 13.

SECTION I.

Of declaring the Day of the Coronation, and of the Departure of the King for Rheims, *and of his Arrival in that City.*

ANtiently the King having, by his Arrêt, fixed the Day and the Place of his Coronation, he notified and made it publick in all his Parliaments, his Majesty sent likewise Circular Letters to all his Governors of the Provinces, that all the necessary Officers, for the Pomp of it, the Journey, Retinue, and Guard of the King should be ready for their respective Duties, but the Princes of the Blood, Peers, Prelates, and Nobles of the Kingdom, the Ambassadors and Ministers of foreign Princes, always were, and still are, some convened, and others invited to it (*r*).

The Archbishop Duke of *Rheims*, or he who is to represent him, is advertised in a Letter from the King to attend him on the Day, and at the Place appointed, and by a Letter of the same kind, directed to the Lieutenants of the Inhabitants, the Sheriffs and Corporation of *Rheims*, the Inhabitants are advertised to prepare for the Entry and Reception of his Majesty.

(*r*) *See* Marlot's Theat d'Hon. Denys Godefroy's Grand Ceremonial The Publications and Invitations are for the most part abrogated by Disuse, since the Coronation of *Henry* III. when they began to neglect them.

While

While the City is making all its Efforts to adorn her Streets, to enrich her Gates, changing them into Triumphal Arches, and raising Pyramids and Statues, enlivened with proper Devices, the Great Master of the Ceremonies, according to the Orders he has received of the King, marks out the Places where he must be received, and designs the Theatres where he is to be harangued. He fits up the Throne, and prepares the Places that are to be taken by his Majesty in the Church, disposes the Seats and Scaffolds where the Princes, the Ambassadors, the Cardinals, Prelates, Ministers, Lords, and Officers ought to sit, according to their Rank. He orders the finest Furniture of the Crown to be set up in the Apartments of the Archiepiscopal Palace, where the King is to have his Residence, and the Royal Ornaments for the Coronation to be brought from the Treasury of *St. Dennis.* In a word, all the King's Officers of the Guard, Houshold, Chamber, Wardrobe, Stables, and Kitchen, execute and give, in all that concerns them, the necessary Orders, that nothing in the Journey or Stay of his Majesty may be wanting, as to the Security, Convenience, Pomp and Affluence of the Ceremony.

When the King departs from *Paris*, or any other Town, accompanied by the Queen, when there is one, the Princes and Princesses of the Blood, and the Chief Officers of the

Crown,

Crown, and all his Guard, to render himſelf at *Rheims*, he ordinarily paſſes thro' *Fimes* (s) where he is accuſtomed to lodge in his Progreſs thither.

Here the Deputies of the Town of *Rheims* attend him, to receive his Commands, and know the Time of his Entry.

This Entry is always made three or four Days before that of the Coronation.

The King takes his Leave of *Fimes* early in the Morning, and dines ordinarily at *Chateau de Gueux*, two Leagues from *Rheims*, or at *Chateau de Muize*, or *Muiſon*, or ſome other, at the Gate of that Town, if the Caſtle of *Gueux* is not in a Condition to receive him, from whence he takes his Rout towards *Rheims*, by the Suburbs of *Veſle*, or of *St. Eloy*, as it is ordered by the Maſter of the Ceremonies. At his Approach to *Rheims*, he is met by the Companies of the City, as well Arquebuſiers as others, who do the Part of Infantry, and make up the Number uſually of five or ſix Thouſand Foot. The Nobility and moſt conſiderable Inhabitants are on Horſeback, at leaſt to the Number of two Thouſand, all

(s) We ſpeak here only of *Rheims*, as the moſt general Place of the Coronation.

Fiſmes is a ſmall Town in *Champagne*, ſituate on the River *Veſle*, in the Dioceſe of *Rheims*, ſix Leagues from it. It is famous for two Councils held there, one in 881, and the other in 935, in the Church of St. *Macer* the Martyr, and for the Lodging which our Kings make uſe of there in their Paſſage to *Rheims*.

under

under Arms, and ſo diſpoſed, as to line the Ways, thro' which the King paſſes, as far as the Gates of the City.

Is is ordinarily, in theſe firſt Meetings of the King, that they make their Harangues, as the Great Maſter of the Ceremonies has ordered it. They do it all on their Knees, (except the Rector of the Univerſity, if he is a Prieſt) to teſtify the Reſpects and Submiſſion of the Inhabitants to their Sovereign. As ſoon as theſe Speeches are finiſhed, the Companies of the City re-enter, in good Order, along the Street of the Cavalcade, which is lined with Tapeſtry on both Sides, as far as the Great Church. The King's Horſe-Guards follow, in their beſt Equipage, and in the Center of them appear in Order, and their Robes of Ceremony, the Bodies of the Preſidial, of Election, and of the Council of the City. Theſe laſt are placed by their Archers and Sergeants of the Gariſon, with their Coats parted, marching immediately before the Lieutenant of the Inhabitants.

It is a Cuſtom, from all Antiquity, for our Kings, at the Diſtance of a quarter of a League or more from *Rheims* to quit their Coaches, and mount a white Horſe, richly adorned, to make their Entry on (*t*) Horſeback.

The

(*t*) Yet *Louis* XIV. who came to *Rheims* in the Queen's Coach, paſt a-croſs the Town in it, and alighted at the Great

The King advances, surrounded with his *Scotch* Guards, preceded by his Constable, or one that represents him, carrying the Sword-Royal, by his Heralds at Arms, and follow'd by the Princes, Dukes, Marquisses, Barons, Great Officers, and Lords of his Court, with Trumpets sounding, all the Bells of the City ringing, and the Cannon playing, till he comes to the first Gate, where he receives the three Keys of Silver from the Lieutenant. This first Gate is usually graced with Festons, Emblems, and Ornaments, in form of a Triumphal Arch.

At the first Step which the King takes into the Town, he is receiv'd under a rich Canopy, borne up by four of the principal Inhabitants, which are commonly the President and Lieutenant-Criminal (to the Presidial of *Rheims*) and the High Sheriff and Lieutenant of the Town.

The Regiments of *Swiss* and *French* Guards line the Street *St. Dennis*, from the Gate to the Archbishop's Palace, and in the Center of them are, first the University in Procession, then the Minims, the four Orders of Mendicants with their Crosses, and Torches burning, follow'd by an hundred, and sometimes two hundred Men, chosen by the Sheriffs among the

Great Gate of the Cathedral, a Master-piece of Architecture, set off with a Variety of Figures, representing the Baptism and Coronation of *Clovis* I. Antiently, and till *Louis* XIII the Keys were presented by a young Lady, richly dress'd, called *la Pucelle, the Maid*. Godfr. Marlot.

Tradeſmen of the Town, marching two and two, carrying each a large Flambeau, of white Wax, burning, painted on each Side with the City-Arms (*u*). Then march the Curates and Clergy of the thirteen Pariſhes of the Town, with their Croſſes and Reliques, in the Form and Order of their General Proceſſions.

The Preſident, Lieutenant, Officers of Election, and of the Salt-Magazine of the City; the Body of the Preſidial after them, the Notaries, Proctors, and Advocates, all in long Robes and ſquare Caps; in the laſt Rank are the particular Lieutenants, Aſſeſſors, and Counſellors of the King's-Bench, then the fifty Archers of the Guard of the Lieutenant, and after, the City-Counſel; the Bodies both of the Clergy of *Rheims*, and of the Judicatures of the City, each entring in due Rank and Order; then march the Companies of the Ordnance, led by their Colonels, Captains, and Officers.

The great Provoſt, followed by his Archers; the hundred *Swiſs* of the Life-Guard, with Halberds on their Shoulders, and Drums beating, headed by their Captain.

The hundred Gentlemen of the Chamber, richly clothed, the Pages, the Maſter of the Horſe.

(*u*) A Ceremony always obſerved in Memory of the Light of the Faith given to the *French* by the Inſtructions of St. *Remy*, and the Baptiſm of *Clovis*.

The King encompass'd, and follow'd, as aforesaid, continues his March still under the Canopy, along the Street of Triumph, adorned with Pyramids, Trophies, Arches, Festons, Pictures, and other Embellishments, such as we may properly imagine in so great a Pomp, to the Court before the Church-Porch, where he alights from his Horse, before the Great Gate, and is received at the Entrance of the Church by the Archbishop of *Rheims*, or his Deputy, in his Pontifical Habit, preceded by his Cross, assisted by some Ecclesiastical Peers, Suffragans of *Rheims*, or other Prelates, all habited in the same manner, and the Canons of the Cathedral, all in their Copes of Cloth of Gold. The King immediately kneels upon a Cushion with both his Knees; the Archbishop officiating, presents him with the Holy Water, and the Text of the Gospel, carried by a Canon in the Habit of a Deacon. After a short Prayer, the King receives the Compliment of the Archbishop, (who makes a Speech to him in the Name of the Clergy) and presently the Submission of the Chapter, by the Mouth of the Great Archdeacon, or some other Canon deputed for it. Then the Chanter begins the Response, *Ecce, ego mitto*, &c. *Behold, I send*; which is continued by the Musick. The Clergy re-enter, in Order of Procession, into the Quire; and the King advancing the last, after the Bishops, still under the Canopy, is conducted to a Footstool, prepared before the High Altar, accompanied with the Princes of the Kingdom. The Archbishop is upon the Steps of the Altar, and after the Anthem, *Beata Dei Genitrix*, &c. *Blessed Mother of God*; *Te Deum* is sung to Musick with the Organ: the Cannons playing, all the Troops firing their Rounds perpetually, and the People making their Acclamations.

When *Te Deum* is finished, the Archbishop reads some Prayers that are appointed in the Ritual, form'd for that purpose, then gives the Benediction; after, the King retires into the Archiepiscopal Palace, where the Canons forthwith appear in their Habit and Caps, to pay their Duty to him, and make him the ordinary Presents of Bread and Wine.

On the Eve of the Coronation, the King is accustom'd to visit, in the Morning, some Churches, out of Devotion, commonly he hears Mass from his Confessor, or some of his Almoners or Chaplains, in the Church of St. *Remy*, to pay his Vows at the Tomb of that Apostle, and reverence the Oil of the Holy Vial (*x*).

After Dinner, which is usually in the Archbishop's Palace, he goes into the Metropolitan Church of *Rheims*, where he

(*x*) The Holy Vial is preserved at *St Remy*, near the Shrine of that Apostle, in the finest Monument we have in *France*.

assists

affifts at the firft Vefpers that are chanted to the King's Mufick, and that of the Chapter; the Archbifhop officiates at it pontifically, and places himfelf in the firft Seat on the right Hand, and the Ecclefiaftical Peers, and the other Bifhops, in their Rochets and *Camails*, are fome on one Side, and fome on the other, each according to their Ranks. All the Canons place themfelves in the Seats above, the Chaplains and Inhabitants below.

The King approaches before the Altar under his Canopy, of which we fhall fpeak in the Article of the Difpofition of the Church; having on his Right, a little below him, the firft Prince of the Blood, his Governor behind him, when he is a Minor, and lower ftill the Cardinals, that are prefent in their Rochets and Scarlet Robes; and after, two of the Ecclefiaftical Peers, and the other Bifhops, who affift here, all in their Rochets and Violet-colour'd *Camails*.

The High Altar ought to be beautified with fuch Ornaments, as the King is accuftom'd to prefent on that Day to the Church, which are commonly of Satin, or white Damask, rais'd with Golden Embroidery, like the reft of the Chapel.

There is alfo placed on the Altar a rich Chapel of maffy Gold, all covered with Diamonds and precious Stones, belonging to the Crown, and brought hither, for the

Occaſion, from the Roal Wardrobe, where it is preſerved (*y*).

We muſt not forget, that if the King has not yet received the Sacrament of Confirmation, he takes it this ſame Day, before or after Veſpers, from the Prelate that is to crown him . and he is preſented for it by a Prince and Princeſs of the Blood-Royal, who ſtand as his Godfather and Godmother, as it was practis'd at the Coronation of *Louis* XIII.

During the Veſpers a Canon of the Church of *Rheims*, conducted by the Maſter of the Ceremonies, takes to the Sacriſty the ſecond Preſent which the King makes to the Church, which is commonly a *Reliquary*, or (*z*) Shrine, richly adorn'd; he carries it, cover'd with a golden embroider'd Mantle, ſuiting the other Ornaments, as far as the Canopy, puts it in the Hand of one of the Peers, or principal Lords, near the King, who preſents it to the firſt Prince of the Blood; they having born it up on each Side to the King, carry it to the Altar, where it is placed ready for him, in order to preſent it to the Church of *Rheims*.

When the Veſpers are finiſhed, the King hears the Sermon, which is deliver'd by a Biſhop, or ſome other Eccleſiaſtick, as the King pleaſes to pitch upon him.

At

(*y*) This Chapel was given to King *Louis* XIII. by the Cardinal *de Richelieu*.

(*z*) *Louis* XIII offered the Head of *St Louis*, ſupported by two Angels, weighing 64 Marks of Silver.

Lo

At the Coronation of *Louis* XIII. the Reverend F. *Coton* was the Preacher; and at that of *Louis* XIV. the Bishop of *Dôl* made a very pathetick Sermon, on this Text, very suitable to the Victories of the King before his crowning, and to the Ceremony itself, *His Enemies shall be clothed with Shame, but upon himself shall his Crown flourish.*

When the Vespers and Sermon are ended, the King returns to the Archbishop's Palace, to repose till the Morrow, being his Coronation-Day: But the Piety of our Princes engages them to prepare for that important Action, in which they are to receive the precious Body and Blood of our Lord, under both kinds; and for this purpose they usually retire under a Pavilion of Crimson and Purple Velvet, embroider'd, and lin'd with a Silver Stuff, in one of the most proper Places of the Quire, to make their Confession.

Antiently our Kings, and all who were to be knighted on the Coronation-Day, passed the Night in the Church, this was called *the Eve of Arms*, in the Term of Chivalry. *Froissart*, in the Life of *Charles* the VIth, *Tom.* 2. *chap.* 60. speaking of that King, says, *And on Saturday the King*

Louis XIV. gave the Head of St. *Remy*, supported by two Angels, on a Pedestal, with the Figure of the King on one Side, and on the other an Inscription, signifying the Time and Circumstances of presenting it, it weigh'd 100 Marks of Silver, and was gilt.

heard Vespers in the Church of Notre-Dame *at* Rheims, *and kept his Vigil in the Church, as the Usage is, the greatest part of the Night, and all the young Gentlemen who were to be knighted with him* (*a*).

SECTION II.

Of the Disposition of the Seats, Galleries, and Scaffolds, and the Decoration of the Cathedral of Rheims, *for the Day and Ceremony of the Coronation* (*b*).

THE Church, from the Upper Galleries to the Bottom, both in the Quire and Body of it, and both the Isles, is lined with the richest Tapestry of the Crown; the Pavement and Steps of the Altar, and all the Floor of the Quire, are covered with fine *Turkey* Carpets, and the High Altar, besides the Marble and the Gilding, is graced with antique Figures, enriched with an infinite Number of precious Stones, and set off with all the magnificent Presents given by the King, on the Eve of his Coronation, with the rest of the Chapel.

On the same Altar is placed the Golden Chapel we spoke of, with two Shrines of

(*a*) These were the King's Cousins, *de Navarre*, *d'Albret*, *de Bar*, and *d'Harcourt*, and a great Number of other Sons of the Great Lords of the Kingdom.

(*b*) Taken from the Grand Ceremony of *Denis Godefroy*, printed in 1649. The *Theat. d'Honn.* of *Will. Marlot*, and his Coronation of *Louis* XIV. of *France*, printed at *Paris* in 1717

Re-

Relicks, very large, one given to this Church by the last King that was crowned here, and the other by the Prince reigning, on the Eve above-mentioned.

At the lowest Step, before the High Altar, is set the Chair for the Archbishop, or his Deputy, covered like all the other Benches and Seats, which we shall speak of hereafter, with Violet-coloured Velvet, all seeded with Golden Flower-de-Luces; and opposite, eight Feet or thereabouts from the Chair, is planted a Stand, eight Feet square, and a Foot high, covered with a Carpet of Purple Velvet, embroidered with Flower-de-Luces, and upon it the Foot of an Oratory, covered with another Carpet, an Arm-Chair, and two Cushions, with a broad Canopy above, set ready for the King, all of the same Velvet. In the middle, between the Archbishop's Chair and the Oratory, is a great Cushion an Ell long, of the same Velvet, for the King to prostrate himself upon with the Archbishop, while they sing the Litany.

Five Feet behind the King's Chair is a Seat for the Constable, or his Representative; another, three Feet farther, for the Chancellor or his Deputy; and farther yet behind, another for the Grand-Master, the Chamberlain, and the first Gentleman of the Chamber.

On the right Side of the Altar is a Bench for the Ecclesiastical Peers, behind which is another

another for the Cardinals, and farther ſtill two others for the Prelates, who do not officiate, and lower yet, beneath the Eccleſiaſtical Peers and the Prelates are Benches for the Counſellors of State, the Maſters of Requeſts, and the King's Secretaries; above the Bench of the Eccleſiaſtical (*c*) Peers, is one on the Side of the Altar for the Biſhops, who are deſired to chant the Litany, and behind two other Benches for the twelve Deacons and Archdeacons, Canons of the Church of *Rheims*, who are to go out and aſſiſt occaſionally.

On the ſame Side, between two Pillars, twelve Feet in height, is fitted up a Gallery, in the form of an Oratory, for the Queen (when there is one) and the other Princeſſes, who are to accompany her; and adjoining to this a Scaffold for the Daughters of the Queen, and the Ladies of Condition.

On the left Side of the Altar, over againſt the Bench of the Eccleſiaſtical Peers, is a Seat, with a Footſtool half a foot high, for the firſt Prince of the Blood, who is to repreſent the Duke of *Burgundy*, and againſt that a Bench for the other Lay-Peers, behind whom are Benches for the Marſhals of *France*, and other Great Lords, and lower for the Secretaries of State; and lower yet behind, for the Officers of the King's Houſhold.

(*c*) The chanting Biſhops are commonly very few, named out of thoſe preſent, by the King or the Chancellor.

On

On the ſame Side, between two Pillars, is raiſed a Scaffold, twelve Feet high, for the Pope's Nuncio, the Ambaſſadors and Reſidents of foreign Princes.

The higher Seats of the Quire are kept for the Canons, except the four firſt on the right Side, which are reſerved for the four Knights of the Holy Ghoſt, who are to carry the Offerings, and the four on the left Side for the four Barons, who are to conduct the Holy Vial.

From the Entrance, in the middle of the Seats of the Canons, on either hand, are two large Stair-Caſes, up to the Lobbey, between the Quire and the Nave, with fifty Stairs in each, covered at the Bottom with a Carpet of three Breadths, two of Cloth of Gold, and that in the middle of Purple Velvet, ſeeded with Flower-de-Luces of Gold, and the Rails on each hand covered with the ſame Velvet.

The Chairs of the Chanter and Sub-chanter are ſet on each Side between theſe Stair-Caſes, and the Seats of the Canons; the Space between the two Stair-Caſes, being free, for the Ingreſs or Egreſs of the Choir.

On the midſt of the Lobbey aforeſaid, whoſe Baluſtres on the Side of the Quire are demoliſhed, is a Throne, where the King is to ſit after the Coronation, upon a Platform, that has three Steps in height, eight Foot long, and five broad. On this Platform is placed a Stand of an Oratory, in the

the fore part, an Arm-Chair behind it, and a large Canopy above, all of Crimſon Velvet, ſeeded with Golden Flower-de-Luces; ſo that the King, ſitting there, may be ſeen, as well as in the Body of the Church, by the opening below the Crucifix, in form of an Arch, as in the Quire, having his Face to the Altar.

Before the Royal Throne, on the Floor of the Lobby, is a Seat for the Conſtable; to the right, on the ſecond Step of the Throne, is the Place of the Great Chamberlain; and at his left, upon the laſt and loweſt Step, is that of the firſt Gentleman of the Chamber; on a little Scaffold, between the two Stair-Caſes, advancing a little into the Quire, a full Foot from the ſaid Lobbey, is a Seat for the Chancellor to the right, and another for the Grand Maſter to the left. Againſt the Rails of the Lobbey, that look to the Quire, to the Right of the King, is a Bench for the Eccleſiaſtical Peers, and to the left a Seat, with a ſmall Footſtool, for the firſt Prince of the Blood, repreſenting the Duke of *Burgundy*, and after that a Bench ſet againſt that, on the ſame Line, for the other Lay-Peers.

At the Extremity of the Lobbey, on the right Side of the Throne, is an Altar, with a Canopy over it, where one of the King's Almoners is to ſay Low-Maſs, as ſoon as ever High-Maſs begins.

From

From the Lobbey, to the leſſer Doors of the Quire, on either hand, above the Seats of the Canons, are Galleries, like Amphitheatres, for Perſons of Quality, as likewiſe a Scaffold behind the high Altar, taking up the whole Breadth of the Church for the King's Muſick, where if they be not commodiouſly enough placed for the View of them, they are ſet in a Gallery above the firſt Seats of the Canons, on the left Hand, as it happened at the Coronation of *Louis* the XIVth.

In the hindermoſt part of the Quire, between the High Altar, and that which they call at *Rheims*, *The Altar of the Cardinal of* Lorain, are Tables for the Ornaments of the Biſhops, and Canons officiating.

SECTION III.

Of the Royal Robes and Ornaments.

SOME (*d*) Authors have endeavoured to prove, that the Royal Robes and Ornaments, for the Coronation, were depoſited at St. *Dennis*, to be kept there, ever ſince the Reign of *Pepin*; but it is certain, that they have been formerly kept in the King's Cabinet, as appears by ſeveral Inſtances, during the ſecond Race of Kings, who, on the point of dying, ſent or gave, with their own Hands, theſe Ornaments to their Son,

(*d*) F. Doublet's Chronicles.

to

to invest them in the Kingdom, by that Token, and that St. *Louis* was the first, who, in Veneration to the Holy Martyrs, whose Relicks are in this Monastery, sent thither the Royal Robes and Ornaments to be kept, with a Charge to the Abbots and Religious of *St. Dennis*, to return them to him, and the Kings his Successors, when they were demanded for the Coronation of a King or Queen, or for any other Occasion (*c*), which they promised, as it is expresly signified by the Charter of St. *Lovis*, in *May*, 1621. all reported entire by *Marlot. Theat. d' Hon. l.* 4. *c.* 1.

In consequence of this Charter, they, on the King's Order to bring the Ornaments aforesaid, depart on the Day assigned for *Rheims*, where they are lodged by the Harbingers, and entertained at the Expence of his Majesty.

On the Day of the Coronation they are introduced into the Church early in the Morning, and placed at the Extremity of the Altar, where they dispose the Ornaments they have brought on rich Cushions of Cloth of Gold; they are,

1. The Great Imperial Crown, received by *Charlemagne* from the Hands of Pope *Leo* III. in *Rome*, when he was crowned the Emperor of the *West*.

(*c*) Du Tillet, Recueil des Offic. de la Cour. Aimoin, l. 5 c. 29.

This

This Crown is all of Gold, enriched with large Rubies, Saphires, and Emeralds; and as it is of great Magnitude, Weight, and Circumference, the Peers bear it up, on the King's Head, at the Ceremony of the Coronation.

Formerly they brought also the Crown of the Emperor *Charles the Bald*, of an inestimable Price, and since it has been often taken by those of the League, they have sometimes brought in the room of it that of St. *Louis*, yet since these Crowns are too bulky and heavy to be supported by our Kings, who are commonly crowned very young, it has occasioned two to be made for them, the one of Gold, the other of Silver gilt, proportioned to their Age and Size, and fit to be worn, with Ease, during the Mass, the Feast, and Day of the Ceremony. This has been often practised, and particularly at the crowning of *Louis* XIII. and XIV. and our Kings often present these Crowns, after the Coronation, to the Treasury of St. *Dennis*, or to some other Church, according to their Devotion.

Louis XII. gave his Crown to the Church of the sacred Host of *Dijon*, *Henry* IV. *Louis* XIII. and *Louis* XIV. gave theirs to St. *Dennis*.

2. The Sword is also that which was received from Pope *Leo* III. by *Charlemagne*, therefore called *the Sword of St.* Peter, but most commonly *Joyeuse*, because it is used only

only on Days of Rejoicing. The Handle, the Hilt, and the Top of the Scabbard, are of maſſy Gold, enriched with precious Stones; the Scabbard is covered with Purple Velvet, garniſhed with Pearls. The Conſtable holds it in his Hand, with the Point erected, during part of the Coronation, at his Return from the Church, and during the Feaſt (*f*).

3. The Scepter is likewiſe that of *Charlemagne*; it is ſix Foot high, and at the Top, *in Relief*, is the Figure of that Emperor ſitting in a Chair, garniſhed with two Lions and two Eagles. He is repreſented holding a Scepter and Globe in his Hands, with the Imperial Crown on his Head, all of maſſy Gold, enamelled and enriched with Oriental Pearls. This is the moſt antient of the Regalia, and is thought to be much older than the Crown.

The Scepter of *Artaxerxes* is mentioned in Scripture; *Xenophon* tells us, that *Cyrus* reſigned his to his Sons. The Coins, Seals, and Medals of our firſt Kings repreſent them with a Scepter in their Hands, and without a Crown.

4. The Hand of Juſtice is that of *Charlemagne*, from the ſame Pope. It is a Verge or Truncheon of Gold, a Cubit long, at

(*f*) This Cuſtom was before *Charlemagne*, they uſed to carry before the Emperors of *Conſtantinople* the Sword, which was the Symbol of their Power, and a Lamp, to ſignify the good Works they have done. *See* Curopalat. des Offic de la Cour Imper.

the

the end is the Figure of an Hand of Ivory, with a Ring on the fourth Finger, enriched with a beautiful Saphir. Under the Hand is a Circle of Foliage, set with Grenats, Saphires and Pearls; in the middle, and at the lower End, are the like Circles of Foliage, with Pearls and precious Stones; this is called, *The Rod of Virtue and Equity* (*).

The Time is not agreed upon when our Kings began to use it, some Authors pretend it was in use from the earliest Date of the Monarchy; others, after the first Race. The Opinion most followed is, that *Charlemagne* first bore it, and after him *Hugh Capet*, St. *Louis*, and the succeeding Princes.

5. The Spurs are those of *Charlemagne*; they are of Gold and Azure enamelled, seeded with Flowers-de-Lys of Gold, and adorn'd with Grenats. The two Buckles are likewise of Gold, shaped like the Head of a Lion.

6. The Clasp of the Royal Robe is a Lozenge of Gold, garnished within with Golden Flower-de-Luces, enriched with precious Stones, Diamonds, and Pearls of inestimable Value.

7. The Coronation Prayer-Book is plated over with Silver gilt, and set with Pearls and Jewels.

These seven Ornaments are never changed, but are used in all the Coronations of our Kings; as to the rest, as the Buskins, or

(*) *See* Aimoin. l. 5 c. 5 and the Coronation Prayers

Sandals, the Tunic, the Dalmatic, and the Royal Robe, ſometimes they are of a Sky-blue Sattin, as in the Coronation of *Henry* the IId, ſometimes of a Purple Velvet, as in thoſe of *Louis* XIII, and XIV; yet they are always ſeeded with Flowers de-Lys, embroidered with Gold, very thick, lined with Crimſon Taffeta, and the Tunic is enriched with Embroidery of Gold, or Pearls, in all the Openings of it.

The Robe of *Henry* II. was of Blue Sattin, lined with Crimſon Taffeta, with a large Embroidery of Pearls, on a Ground of Gold-Wire.

That of *Henry* IV. was lined with white Sattin, with a large Border of Ermines; the Cape likewiſe of Ermines. Thoſe of *Louis* the XIIIth and XIVth were of Purple Velvet, bordered with Ermines, the Cape of Ermines, ſeeded with Flowers-de-Lys of Gold, doubled with Purple Taffeta, and edged with Gold Lace. But theſe Habits are made new almoſt at every Coronation, to ſuit them to the Make and Age of the Prince, and they are done, as far as poſſible, in imitation of the Antients.

In the Liſt of the Ornaments of *Henry* II. that are in the Treaſury of St. *Dennis*, we find a Purſe of Blue Sattin, ſprinkled with ſmall Flowers-de-Lys of Gold, with Pendants, Strings, and Ties of Gold and Blue Silk, worn antiently at ſuch a time by our

Kings,

Kings, but now it is out of fashion, and it is thought that *Henry* II. was the last that wore it.

SECTION IV.

The Morning of the Coronation-Day.

EARLY (*g*) on the Day of the Coronation, four Lords, named by the King to fetch the Holy Vial, set out, from the Archbishop's Palace for the Abbey of St. *Remy*, where it has been kept since the Coronation of *Clovis*, with their Gentlemen before them, each carrying before his Master the Banner of his Arms, and at the Head of them a led white Horse, richly adorned, for the Great Prior of the Abbey, who is accustomed to bring the Holy Vial (*h*).

At

(*g*) Commonly about five a-clock.

(*h*) Our Kings have always deputed four Barons, or Lords, of the most antient Nobility of the Kingdom, to go to *St. Remy* for the Holy Vial, attend it to the Cathedral, where the Ceremony is performed, and conduct it back to the said Abbey, not only out of Honour and Respect for this Gift of Heaven, but to guard it on the way, and that this precious Treasure may not be taken out of the Kingdom, or from the Abbey of *St Remy*, where it has been lodged for so many Ages. Many have believed, that these Lords stay in the Abbey by way of Hostage, till the Holy Vial is returned. But the Terms of a Charter, made under *Charles* VIII in 1484, reported by *Marlot*, in his *Theatre of Honour*, Book IV. prove, that when they are at the Abbey, by the express Order of the King, to demand the Vial, that he may be anointed with it like his Predecessors, they are to swear, on the Holy Gospels, to conduct it, as they are ordered, for the Coronation, and

reconduct

At the ſame time the Archbiſhop of *Rheims*, or he that repreſents him, in his Rochet and Camail, with the Stole and Cope, Mitre and Croſs, aſſiſted with two Canons in their Copes, named by the Chapter, appears in the Church, preceded by the Biſhops that are to aſſiſt him, and the Canons and Reſidentiaries of the Church of *Rheims*, in their Copes of Cloth of Gold, and other neceſſary Ornaments. As to the Aſſiſtant-Biſhops, one is habited like a Deacon, the other like a Sub-Deacon, to chant the Epiſtle and Goſpel, with their Mitres, and the four other Biſhops, that are deſired to ſing the Litanies, are with their Mitres and Copes, without a Stole, the Chanters in their Copes, with their Verges of Silver.

Thus the Archbiſhop, preceded, as uſual, in the Order of a Proceſſion, having made

reconduct it thither, when that is ended After this Oath the Abbot of St *Remy*, or, in his Abſence, the Prior, faſtens at his Neck the Shrine of Silver gilt, enriched with precious Stones, where the Holy Vial is incloſed, and mounts the white Horſe ſent by the King, and thus goes, in form of Proceſſion, under a Canopy of white Sattin, embroidered with Silver, as far as the Steps of the Great Church of *Rheims*, the four Lords preceding him, each with a Flag of Arms of his Family before him, as above, both as he goes and returns but when they come from the Abbey, they hang their Banners, as the Cuſtom is, about the Tomb of St. *Remy*, where ſtill a Number of them may be ſeen All this is the Practice to the preſent Time. *Marlot*, in his *Theatre of Honour*, Book IV. tells us the Names of the Lords that waited thus at the Coronations of *Charles* VII *Charles* VIII *Henry* II *Francis* II. *Charles* IX *Henry* III *Henry* IV and *Louis* XIII We have already mentioned the Lords that attended it under *Louis* the XIVth.

a Reverence to the Altar, goes to place himſelf in the Chair that is ſet ready for him, at the foot of the loweſt Step, before the great Altar, which is covered with Purple Velvet, ſeeded with Flowers-de-Lys of Gold, with his Face towards the Altar. The Canons take their ordinary Places in the higher Chairs, and the reſiding Prieſts in the lower, on each Side of the Chair, and the Biſhops that are to ſing the Litany, as well as the twelve Aſſiſtants, preceding the Deacons and Subdeacons, place themſelves upon three Benches, ranged on the right Side of the Altar, higher than that of the Eccleſiaſtical Peers, and the Chanter and Subchanter are in their Chairs in the Choir.

At the ſame time come the Eccleſiaſtical Peers, in their Pontifical Habits, according to the following Order:

M. the Biſhop,
- Duke of *Laon*,
- Duke of *Langres*,
- Count of *Beauvais*, *Chalons*, *Noyon*.

Then come the Lay-Peers, that is,

M. the
- Duke of *Burgundy*, *Normandy*, *Aquitaine*.
- Count of *Tholouſe*, *Flanders*, *Champagne*

All in Vests or Tunicks of Cloth of Gold and Silver (*1*), and *Aurora* Silk, hanging down to the Mid-Leg, with a Ducal Man-

(*1*) These Peers are here in Person, or by Proxy We do not pretend that the Rank, in which we here place the Peers, is absolutely that which they ought to hold, and the Variations we meet with in former Solemnities of this kind (in all our Historians, and in the Grand Ceremonial of *Fran*[illegible]) plainly shew, that their Rank has not been fixed from their Original, and that there have been many Changes among them in relation to Precedence.

Mutt[illegible] *P*[illegible]*rs*, and some other Historians, say, That the Duke of *Normandy* was acknowledged the first Peer in 1257, that the Duke of *Guyenne* was the second, and the Duke of *Burgundy* the third, that after them come the Counts of *Flanders*, *Champagne*, and *Toulouse*, and that it was not till the 13th Century, under *Philip the Fair*, that the Duke of *Burgundy* became the first of the Peers, the Ducal Peerdoms of *Normandy* and *Guyenne* having been reunited to the Crown, by the Confiscation made in 1202, upon *John Sans terre*, King of *England*, of all his Possessions in *France*.

The Ranks of the antient Lay Peers are marked in the following Order, in the Register of the Process of *Robert of Artois* in 133[illegible], which is in the Repository of the Charters of the Crown

The Dukes of { *Burgundy*, *Normandy*, *Aquitaine*, or *Guyenne* } The Counts of { *Toulouse*, *Flanders*, *Champagne*. }

But this Order has not been always followed, and is not conformable to that of their Erection, as it appears by the last Coronation, and by the *St*[illegible]*e of* France, printed in 1[illegible]18.

The Order of the Ecclesiastical Peers is as unfixed, it is hard to meet with Records sufficient to explain the Changes that have happened in it Their present Rank, according to S[illegible] France, and that printed at *Paris* in 1[illegible]8, [illegible] thus

Ducal Peers, { ArchBp of *Rheims*, Bp of [illegible]*r*, Bp of *Langres*. } Count-Peers, { B[illegible]*is*, Bp of *Chalons*, *Noy*[illegible]. }

the

tle, of a Crimson-Velvet, open on the right, and adorned at the Opening with Diamond-Buttons, lined with Ermins, with a round Collar of spotted Ermins, a Ducal Coronet gilt with Gold, over a Cap of Purple Sattin. They are conducted by the Master of the Ceremonies to the Seats prepared for them, that is, the Ecclesiastical Peers to a Bench of Purple Velvet, seeded with Flowers de-Lys of Gold, on the right Side of the Altar, and the Lay Peers, opposite to them, on the left Side, with this Distinction, that the first Prince of the Blood, who represents the Duke of *Burgundy*, is commonly upon a Seat with a Footstool, half a foot higher than the Bench of the other Peers.

The Queen, when there is one, the Princesses, and all the Ladies of the Court, come at the same time to a Gallery, raised on the right Side of the Altar, thro' a Lobbey made for the purpose, from the Hall of the Archbishop's Palace.

The Cardinals, if any be present, are in their Rochets and Copes of Crimson Tabby, the Archbishops and Bishops in their Rochets and Purple Camails; the four Knights of the Holy Ghost, who are to carry the Offerings, with the great Collar of the Order over their Robes; the Sur-Intendant, or Comptroller-General of the Finances, the Secretaries and Counsellors of State, the Pope's Nuncio, if there be one, the Ambaſſadors of foreign Courts, and other Lords and Miniſters, are conducted by the Maſter of the Ceremonies, to the Places appointed for them.

When every Perſon is ſeated, the Archbiſhop of *Rheims*, with the Peers, as well Eccleſiaſtical as Laical, unanimouſly depute the Biſhops of *Laon* and *Beauvais*, to whom the Privilege belongs, to ſeek the King. They, in their Pontifical Veſtments, with Relicks of Saints hanging at their Necks, depart from the Church, in order of Proceſſion, thro' a great Gallery, reaching to the Hall of the Palace within a foot, four or five foot high, and fourteen broad, with Supports to it, winding about half of the Church, and carried on from the Great Gate of it, to the Great Hall of the Archbiſhop's Palace, in the following Order. Firſt, two Clerks bearing the two Croſſes, then the reſiding Clergy of the Church of *Rheims*, after the Canons, in their Copes, the Chanter and Subchanter, with the Muſick and Singing-Boys of the Choir in the middle of the Proceſſion, the Great Maſter of the Ceremonies by himſelf, and two Biſhops come laſt, preceded by three Singing-Boys, in Copes, one carrying the Holy-Water-Pot, each of the two others a Candleſtick, with a lighted Wax-Taper.

The two Biſhops of *Laon* and *Beauvais*, preceded by the Chanter and Subchanter, come to the Chamber-Door, and finding it ſhut,

ſhut, the Chanter (*k*) knocks at it with his Silver Verge, the Great Chamberlain, without opening the Door, ſays, *Whom do you want?* The Biſhop of *Laon* anſwers, *The King*; the other replies, *The King is aſleep*. After the Chanter's knocking, and the Biſhop's enquiring for the King a ſecond time, the ſame Anſwer is given. The third time the Biſhop replies, *We ſeek for* Louis . . . . *whom God has given us for our King*. At that Inſtant the Door is open'd, the two Biſhops, preceded by the Chanter and Subchanter (*l*), and a Singing-Boy with the Holy-water Pot, enter his Majeſty's Chamber (*m*), and approach a Bed, richly adorned, where the King lies, in a Holland Shirt, a Waiſtcoat of Crimſon Sattin, in form of a Tunick, trimmed with Gold, both open at the Back, before, and at the Sleeves, in the Places where he is to be anointed, and over them a long Robe of Cloth of Silver, and a Cap of black Velvet, with a String of Diamonds round it, a Plume and a double white Tuft of Feathers, faſten'd with a Knot of Diamonds.

(*k*) At the Coronation of *Louis* XIII. it was the Biſhop of *Laon* who knocked at the Door, but this has been altered, and at that of *Louis* XIV. it was the Chanter

(*l*) At the Coronation of *Louis* XIII. the great Chanter entered alone, but at that of *Louis* XIV. both entered.

(*m*) There are only the Conſtable, Chancellor, Great Maſter, Great Chamberlain, firſt Gentleman of the Chamber, and other firſt Officers and Lords, whom the King permits to be there.

The

The Bishop of *Laon* presents the Holy Water to the King, and says the Prayer, *Omnipotens*, &c. *Almighty and Eternal God*, &c. which being ended, the two Bishops, kissing their Hands, raise the King from off his Bed, one on the right, the other on the left, and conduct him in Procession to the Church, thro' the same Gallery, in the following Order, singing the Responses, *Ecce ego mitto*, &c. *Behold I send*, &c. and the Versicle, *Israel*, begun by the Chanter, to the Great Gate of the Church.

SECTION V.

The Order of Procession in conducting the King to the Church.

THE Clergy return as they came; before them is the Great Provost of the Houshold (*n*), with his Archers on both Sides of the Clergy, the hundred *Switzers* of the Guard, headed by their Captain (*o*), who, with his Lieutenant and Ensign, is dressed in white Tabbey, with a Cloke of Black Cloth, turned up with Cloth of Silver, all preceded by ten or twelve Trumpets, Drums,

(*n*) He is M *Louis de Bouschet*, Knight, Lord, and Count of *Montsoreau*, Marquiss *de Sources* and *du Bellay*, Lieutenant-General of the King's Forces, Counsellor of State, and Great Provost of *France*.

(*o*) At present M. ——— *le Tellier*, Marquiss *de Louvois* and *Courtenvaux*, Captain Colonel of the hundred *Swiss* Guards.

Fifes,

Fifes, Hautbois, Flutes, and other Wind-Musick, *&c* all in white Taffeta, after the Heralds at Arms in white Velvet, their Under-dress of Silk of the same Colour, with a Coat of Arms above, being after the Banner of *France* On the Forepart of it, their Names written in Golden Embroidery, with a Cap of white Velvet, and their Tipstaves in their Hands, the hundred Gentlemen-Pensioners, with their Halberds, headed by their Captain (*p*). In the midst of them is the Nobility of the Court, and of the King's Retinue (*), the Great Master of the Ceremonies of *France* in a Vest of Cloth of Silver, his Under-Dress and the Fastening of Silk, a Cloke of black Cloth, faced with Cloth of Silver, all laced with Silver Galloon, and a Cap of white Velvet. The Knights and Officers of the Order of the Holy Ghost, in their Habits of Ceremony, and great Collars of the Order. Just before the King is M. the Constable, or his Representative (*q*), with his naked Sword in his Hand, in a Tunick and Robe, and a Coronet upon his Head, like the Lay-Peers, having on each Side the two Gentlemen-

(*p*) M. the Duke of *Lauzun*

(*) Messire *Thomas Dreux* Kt Marquiss *de Brere*, &c. is Grand Master of the Ceremonies, the Master of the Ceremonies is *Michael-Ancel Desgranges*, and the Assistant of the Ceremonies is *Charles-Ancel Desgranges* Both these, as well as the Grand Master, carry the Truncheon of Command, covered with black Velvet at the end, and headed with Ivory.

(*q*) Who ought to be the eldest Marshal of *France*.

Ushers

Ushers of the King's Chamber, in white Sattin, carrying their Maces.

The King walks alone, between the two Bishops aforesaid, a Lord of Distinction, (chosen by the King) bearing the Train of the Royal Robe; M. the Chancellor (*r*), or the Keeper of the Seals of *France*, when the Chancellor is absent, immediately follows the King in a Cassock of Crimson Sattin, his Robe and Collar of Scarlet, turned up and furred with Ermines, having on his Head his Cap of Cloth of Gold, bordered and lined with Ermines. After him the Great Master of the King's Houshold, or his Proxy, when the Prince, who is actually Great Master, represents one of the Lay-Peers, holding his Staff upright in his Hand, at his Right is the Great Chamberlain, at his Left the Master of the Horse, and then the first Gentleman of the Chamber, all dressed like the Lay-Peers that are Counts. The first Captain of the Life-Guard (he who commands the *Scotch* Guards) being on the Right, and the Captain of the Quarter-Guards (those in present Attendance) on the Left, behind the King, and on each Side the six *Scotch* Guards, otherwise called, *Guards of the Sleeve*, in white Taffeta, with their Coats of white Velvet, all embroidered with Gold and Silver.

(*r*) M. *Daguesseau*, and the Keeper of the Seals is M. *Fleuriau d'Armenonville.*

The King's Entrance into the Church.

When the King is come to the Royal Gate of the Church, the Clergy ſtop at the Entrance into the Body of it, the Biſhop of *Beauvais* chants the Prayer, *Deus, qui, &c. O God, who,* &c. after which the Chanter begins the Pſalm, *Domine, in Virtute tua, &c. O Lord, the King ſhall rejoice in thy Strength,* &c. which is continu'd by the Muſick, in a lower Strain, while the King, preceded by the Clergy, in the Order above-mentioned, goes on to the Quire, and ſix Silver Trumpets play before him.

When he comes near the high Altar, he is preſented by the Biſhops of *Beauvais* and *Chalons* to the Archbiſhop of *Rheims*, who, riſing from his Chair, (the King falling on his Knees before him) ſings the Prayer, *Omnipotens Deus, Cœleſtium, &c. Allmighty God,* &c.

When this Prayer is ended, the King is conducted by the two Biſhops to his Seat and Canopy, over againſt the Archbiſhop's Chair, with the Conſtable, holding the Sword behind him; the Chancellor on a Seat a little farther; behind, on a like Bench, the Grand Maſter, with the Great Chamberlain on his Right (*s*), and the firſt Gentleman

(*s*) The preſent is *Geofroy Maurice de la Tour*, Prince de *Bouillon*, the four Gentlemen of the Chamber are M. the Duke

tleman of the Chamber on his Left. On each Side the King are the two Captains of the Guards, with the six *Scotch* Guards, and those of the *Manche* (Sleeve) and the Captain of the hundred Gentlemen Pensioners, (the Company staying in the Body of the Church with the hundred *Swiss*) standing about two Paces before the King on his Left. When they have thus taken their Seats, the Archbishop presents the Holy Water to the King, and to all the Assembly, and immediately the King's Musick sings, *Veni Creator*, *&c.* *Come Holy Ghost*, &c.

SECTION VI.

The Coming of the Holy Vial.

WHEN the *Veni Creator* is chanted, the Canon, officiating for the Week, begins the third Canonical Hour, and in the mean time the Holy Vial is brought to the Church-Gate, with Drums beating, Trumpets playing, and all the Streets thro which it passes lined with Tapestry, from the Abbey of St. *Remy*, to the Cathedral.

The Abbot of that Place, or, in his Absence, the Grand Prior, in his Alb, Stole, and Cope of Cloth of Gold, with his Horse

Duke of *Tremes*, the Duke *d'Aumont* or *Villequiers*, the Duke *de la Tremouille*, and the Duke *de Mortemar*, who serve throout the Year. The Duke of *Trêmes*, *Francis Bernard Potier*, Duke of *Trêmes*, Peer of *France*, Marquiss *de Gêvres*, was in Service the Year 1722.

led

led at the Reins by two principal Officers of Horse to the King, covered with a Housing of Cloth of Silver, under a Canopy of the same, born up by the four Barons of the Holy Vial, or, in their Absence, by Religious in Albes, and Officers of Justice of the Abbey (*t*).

At the four Corners of the Canopy, are, on horseback, the four Lords, sent by the King, with a Gentleman to each, carrying a *Guidon*, charged with the Arms of *France* and *Navarre* on one Side, and those of his Lord on the other. All the Religious of St. *Remy* go before the Vial processionally, in white Albes, preceded by an hundred of the Inhabitants of *Chesne*, under Arms, for the Safeguard of the Holy Vial, followed by an equal Number, carrying each a Flambeau of white Wax, painted with the Arms of the Abbey.

The Archbishop, informed of its Arrival, leaves the Altar, and goes with the assistant Bishops, preceded by the Canons and residing Clergy of the Church, to the End of the Nave, for the Reception of it, near the great Gate, where the Abbot, or his Proxy, waits for him, under his Canopy; and in presenting it, says, " My Lord, I " put into your Hands this precious Trea- " sure, sent from Heaven to the great St.

(*t*) At the Crowning of *Louis* XIV they were the Baron *de Louvercy*, two Religious of the Abbey, and its Bailiff, who bore the Canopy.

" *Remy*,

" *Remy*, for the Coronation of *Clovis*, and
" of the Kings his Succeſſors ; but I intreat
" you before, according to the antient Cuſ-
" tom, to engage the Return of it into my
" Hands, after the Coronation of our . .
" . . . . King *Louis* . . . .
" ſhall be performed."

This is promiſed by the Archbiſhop on the word of a Prelate ; then he takes it from the Abbot, and the Chanter begins the Anthem, *O precious Gift!* &c. *O pretioſum Munus, &c* which is carried on by the Church-Muſick , then the Clergy re-enter the Choir in the ſame Order they came from it ; the four Lords, who conducted the Holy Vial, take place in the four firſt higher Seats of the Canons, on the left Side, their Gentlemen with the Banners in the lower Chairs before them ; the Archbiſhop openly carries the Holy Vial to the Altar, the King and all the Aſſiſtants give a reſpectful Salute to it. The Abbot and Grand Prior, or, in Abſence of the Abbot, the Grand Prior and Treaſurer of St. *Remy*, (as it was in the Coronation of *Louis* XIV.) take place on the right ſide of the Altar, to make ready the Holy Vial; the others ſtay in the Nave, to attend it after the Coronation. On the left Side of the Altar, againſt the Abbot and Prior, are the Religious, deputed from St. *Dennis*, to make ready the Crown, Scepter, Hand of Juſtice, Sword, Spurs, and Royal Habits brought from their Treaſury. The

The aforesaid Anthem being ended, the Archbishop putting off his Mitre, says the Prayer, *Omnipotens sempiterne Deus, &c. Almighty Everlasting God,* &c.

After the Prayer, the Canon for the Week begins the sixth Canonical Hour, while the Archbishop goes into the Sacristy, behind the high Altar, to put on a Chasuble; and the twelve Canons, the Deacons, and Sub-Deacons, both *proceeding* and *assisting*, put on their Dalmaticks and Tunicks, and return to the Altar in this Order.

First, the six Canons, and Sub-Deacons in their Tunicks; that is, four assisting, and two proceeding; then six Deacons, four assisting, and two proceeding, in Dalmaticks, by two and two; then the Archbishop, with his Cross before him, assisted by two Canons in their Copes.

The proceeding and assisting Canons ordinarily take their Place on two Benches, behind the four Bishops, who are to sing the Litany; and the Archbishop, after a Reverence to the Altar and the King, takes his Chair before the Altar, and the two Bishops seat themselves on each Side of him.

SECTION VII.

The Promises and Oaths of the King, as King and Knight.

AFTER this the Archbishop, assisted by the Bishops of *Laon* and *Beauvais*, approaching the King, makes the following

 Request

Requeſt for all the Churches of *France* that are ſubject to him.

A vobis perdonari petimus, &c.

We pray you to grant us the Preſervation of Canonical Privilege, and due Law and Juſtice to every of us, and the Churches committed to our Charge; and ſuch Defence as a King in his Kingdom owes to every Biſhop, and Church committed to him. To which the King ſtill ſitting, with his Head covered, anſwers,

Promitto vobis, & perdono, &c.

I promiſe and grant to you, that I will preſerve Canonical Privilege, and due Law and Juſtice to every of you, and the Churches committed to you; and ſuch Defence (to my Power, by the help of God) as a King in his Kingdom owes to every Biſhop and Church committed to him, according to Right.

After this the Biſhops of *Laon* and *Beauvais* raiſe the King from his Chair; and ſtanding up, they demand of the Lords and People, according to antient Cuſtom, *Whether they accept* Louis . . . . *for their King*, and after their Conſent is given in a reſpectful Silence, the Archbiſhop tenders the King the Oath of the Realm, which he takes aloud, ſitting with his Head covered, and laying his Hands upon the Goſpel, in theſe Terms:

Hæc

Hæc Populo Christiano, &c.

I make this Promise to the Christian People, and my Subjects, in the Name of Christ first of all, that all Christian People shall maintain the true Peace of the Church of God, at all times, by our Government.

Also that I will prohibit all Violence and Acts of Injustice in all Ranks of Men.

Also that I will enjoin Equity and Mercy to be used in all Judgments, that the merciful and gracious God may indulge his Favour to me and you.

Also I will seriously endeavour to extirpate all Heretick, so branded by the Church, out of my Land, and the Government subject to me. All the above-mentioned Things I confirm with an Oath, so help me God, and these his Holy Gospels.

After this Oath is pronounced, the King kisses the Gospels.

After this Oath *Louis* XIV. likewise pronounced that of the Head and Sovereign Grand Master of the Order of the Holy Ghost, in these Terms:

" We *Louis*, by the Grace of God, King " of *France* and *Navarre*, swear and vow " solemnly, in your Hands, to God the " Creator, to live and die in his holy Faith " and Religion, Catholick, Apostolick, and " *Roman*, as to a good and most Christian " King appertains, and sooner to die than " to fall from it; to maintain always the

" Order of the Holy Ghoſt, founded and in-
" ſtituted by King *Henry* III. without ever
" ſuffering it to fail, decreaſe, or be dimi-
" niſhed, as far as it ſhall be in our Power,
" entirely to obſerve the Statutes and Or-
" dinances of the ſaid Order, according to
" their Form and Tenor, and cauſe them
" to be exactly obſerved by all thoſe, that
" are, or ſhall be hereafter received into
" the ſaid Order ; and never to contradict,
" diſpenſe with, or attempt to change or
" innovate the irrevocable Statutes of it.

" That is to ſay, the Statute which ſpeaks
" of the Union of the Great Maſterſhip to
" the Crown of *France* ; that which con-
" tains the Number of Cardinals, Prelates,
" Commanders, and Officers ; that of not
" transferring the Proviſion made for the
" Commands, in whole or in part, to any
" other, under the Colour of Appanage, or
" any Grant or Conceſſion poſſible ; alſo
" that by which we oblige ourſelves, as far
" as in us lies,never to give a Diſpenſation to
" the Commanders and Officers of the Order,
" from communicating and receiving the
" precious Body of our Lord Jeſus Chriſt on
" the appointed Days ; as alſo that in which
" it is ſaid, that we,and all Commanders and
" Officers, ſhall be no other than Catho-
" licks, Gentlemen by three Deſcents on
" the Father's Side, ſuch as are ſo lawfully
" and duly. Alſo that, by which we put
" it out of our Power to employ, in other

" Uſes,

" Uses, the Monies belonging to the Reve-
" nue, and Entertainment of the said Com-
" manders and Officers, for any Cause or
" Occasion whatever; and likewise that in
" which is contained the Form of the Vows
" and Obligation, always to wear the Cross
" in our ordinary Habits, with that of
" Gold at the Neck, hanging by a Sky-co-
" loured Silken Ribband, and the particular
" Habit on Days appointed. This we swear,
" vow, and promise, touching the Holy
" true Cross, and the Holy Gospel."

In the mean time the Habits and Ornaments of the King, for the Coronation, are laid upon the Altar; that is, the Great Imperial Crown of *Charlemagne*, the middle Crown, the Sword, the Scepter, the Rod of Justice, the Spurs, and the Book of the Ceremony. The Royal Habits for the Occasion, are a Waistcoat of Crimson Sattin trimmed with Gold, a Tunick, and a Dalmatick, which represent the Orders of Deacon and Sub-Deacon, and a large Royal Robe of Blue Velvet, seeded with Flower-de-Luces of Gold, turned up with Ermines.

SECTION VIII.

The Benediction of the Sword.

THE Archbishop sitting in his Chair before the Altar, the King is conducted before him by the Bishops of *Laon* and

Beauvais, and there ſtanding, the firſt Gentleman of the Chamber takes off his long Robe of Cloth of Silver, leaving only upon him the Waiſtcoat of Crimſon Sattin; and after this the Archbiſhop ſays the following Prayers, *Adjutorium, &c. Sit Nomen Domini, &c. Dominus vobiſcum; Deus, &c.* After theſe the King ſeats himſelf in an Arm-Chair, placed before the Chair of the Archbiſhop, and the Great Chamberlain draws on his Buskins (*a*). The Duke of *Burgundy*, as firſt Peer, puts on his Spurs brought from St. *Dennis*, and inſtantly takes them off again; afterwards, the King ſtanding up, the Archbiſhop of *Rheims* bleſſes the Sword of *Charlemagne* in the Scabbard, with the Form *Exaudi quæſumus, Domine.*

After the Benediction he puts it upon the King, over his Waiſtcoat, and immediately takes it off again; then unſheathing it, and leaving the Scabbard upon the Altar, he puts it naked into the hands of the King, ſaying, *Accipe hunc Gladium, &c.*

In the mean time the Choir ſings the Anthem, *Confortare & eſto Vir, &c.*

The King, having received the Sword, kiſſes it, offers it to God, by laying it upon the Altar; from whence the Archbiſhop takes it, and returns it to the King, who

(*a*) After he has received them from the Abbot of St. *Dennis* they may likewiſe be called Sandals, they are of Purple Velvet, embroidered with Golden Flower-de-Luces.

receives

receives it upon his Knees, and gives it to the Conſtable, who holds and carries it naked in all the Acts of the Coronation, and the Feaſt that follows, and while the King is upon his Knees, the Archbiſhop ſays the following Prayers:

Proſpice, Omnipotens Deus, &c.
Benedic Domine, &c.
Deus, Pater æterne, &c.

SECTION IX.

The Preparation of the Holy Oil.

WHEN theſe Prayers are concluded, the Archbiſhop places the Golden Paten of the Chalice of St. *Remy* on the middle of the Altar, and the Abbot (or Grand Prior of St. *Remy*) having received from the Treaſurer of that Abbey, aſſiſting here, the Silver Key of the Shrine, of Silver gilt, ſet with Jewels, in which the Holy Vial is incloſed, produces it, puts it into the Hands of the Biſhop, who officiates as Deacon, who gives it to the Archbiſhop; who making uſe of a Golden Bodkin, preſented him by the Abbot, takes ſome Oil from the Holy Vial, about the Quantity of a Grain of Corn, and puts it upon the Paten: then returning the Vial to the Abbot, in order to his replacing it on the Shrine, he takes ſome of the Holy Chriſm, with a Bodkin, and mixes it with his Fingers on the Paten.

In the mean while the Choir sings the Responses, and the following Versicle, begun by the Chanter, *Gentem Francorum, &c.* After this the Archbishop turns to the Altar, and, without his Mitre, says the Versicle and Prayer of St. *Remy, Ora pro nobis, Beate Remigi, &c. Oremus; Deus, qui Populo, &c.* and during this, with the Bishops of *Laon* and *Beauvais*, loosen the Openings made in the Vestments of the King, to receive the Holy Unction.

After this Prayer the King prostrates himself before the Altar, upon a large Cushion, an Ell long, of Purple Velvet, embroidered with Flower-de-Luces of Gold, and the Archbishop with him at his right Hand, while the four Bishops sing the Litanies; to which the Choir makes the Responses, as far as the Versicle, *Ut obsequium*, inclusively, *&c.* After that the Archbishop standing up, with the Mitre on his Head, and the Cross in his left Hand, says the three following Versicles, with his Face to the King, who lies prostrate before him, which the Choir repeats entire.

Ut hunc præsentem Famulum tuum Ludovicum, &c. bene+dicere digneris; te rogamus audi nos.

Ut, &c. bene+dicere, & sublimare, &c.

Ut, &c. bene+dicere, subli+mare, & conse+crare, &c.

1. *That it may please thee—to bless—this thy Servant* Lewis, *here before thee, who*

who is to be crowned King; we beseech thee to hear us.

2. *That*, &c.—*to bless and exalt*—&c.

3. *That*, &c.—*to bless, exalt, and consecrate*—&c.

After the Versicles, the Archbishop prostrates himself on the right Side of the King, as before, to the end of the Litany, which is continued by the Bishops above-mentioned.

At the end of the Litany the King and the four Bishops, who chanted it, remain prostrate, while the Archbishop, standing up without his Mitre, with his Face towards the King, says the following Prayers.

Pater noster, &c.
Pretende, quæsumus, &c.
Te invocamus, &c.
Deus, qui Populis, &c.
In Diebus ejus, &c.

SECTION X.

The Consecration and Anointing of the King.

THE Archbishop sitting down, with his Mitre, and raising his Voice a little, goes on with the Prayer,

Omnipotens sempiterne Deus, &c.

After this the King, continually kneeling, the Archbishop sitting, as in the Consecration of a Bishop, holds in his Hand the Golden Paten of the Chalice of St. *Remy*, on which

which is the sacred Oil, takes some of it up with his right Thumb, and begins to anoint the King:

1. On the Top of the Head with the Sign of the Cross, and saying,

Ungo te in Regem de Oleo sanctificato, in Nomine, &c.

I anoint thee King, with the sanctified Oil, in the Name of the Fa+ther, of the + Son, and of the Ho+ly Ghost.

Repeating the same Words and Signs of the Cross in the six following Unctions, all the Assistants answering, at the end of each, *Amen.*

2. On the Breast, the Bishops of *Laon* and *Beauvais* opening his Shirt and Waistcoat at each of the Places where he is to be anointed.

3. Between the Shoulders.

4. On the Right Shoulder.

5. On the Left Shoulder.

6. At the Bending and Joints of the Right Arm.

7. At the like Places of the Left Arm.

During the Unction the Church-Musick performs the Anthem, *Unxerunt Salomonem . . . . & læti dixerunt, Vivat Rex in æternum, They anointed* Salomon, *and said with Joy, God save the King.* After which the Archbishop, still sitting as before, with the King kneeling before him, says the Prayers,

Christe,

Christe, perunge hunc Regem, &c.
Deus, Electorum Fortitudo, &c.
Deus, Dei Filius, &c.

Then the Archbishop, assisted by the Bishops of *Laon* and *Beauvais*, and sometimes with a third, who is either that of *Soissons*, of *Amiens*, or of *Senlis*, close the Openings of the King's Shirt and Waistcoat, with Ties of Gold Lace; and then the King standing up, the Great Chamberlain gives him the three accustomed Vestments;

The Tunick,
The Dalmatick, and
The Royal Robe.

Representing the Habits of the three Orders of Subdeacon, Deacon, and of Priest, all of Purple Velvet, sprinkled over with Flowers-de-Lys in Golden Embroidery.

Thus the King, having his Royal Habit on again, kneels down before the Archbishop, who, sitting with his Mitre, takes up the Paten, and makes the eighth Unction on the Palm of the Right Hand, and the ninth on that of the Left, saying,

Ungantur Manus istæ, &c.

Be these Hands anointed with the sanctified Oil, with which Kings and Prophets have been anointed, and as Samuel *anointed* David *to be King, that thou mayst be blessed, and appointed King in that Kingdom,*

dom, which thy Lord hath given thee to direct and to govern, &c.

Then the King being ſtill on his Knees, and holding his Hands joined before his Breaſt, the Archbiſhop ſtanding without his Mitre, ſays the following Prayer;

Deus, qui es Juſtorum Gloria, &c.
O God, who art the Glory of the Juſt, &c.

SECTION XI.

The Bleſſing of the Gloves.

THE Archbiſhop, ſtanding without his Mitre, bleſſes the Gloves, by ſprinkling them with Holy Water, and ſaying the Prayer, *Omnipotens Creator, &c.* Then, with his Mitre on, he puts them on the King's Hands, with the Prayer, *Circunda, Domine, Manus Famuli tui Ludovici, &c.*

SECTION XII.

The Benediction of the Ring.

THE Archbiſhop, ſtanding without his Mitre, bleſſes the Royal Ring, preſented to him by the firſt Groom of the Bed-chamber, and ſays, *Deus, totius Creaturæ, &c.* *O God, the Beginning and End of the whole Creation . . . . ſend forth thy Benediction upon this Ring,* &c. then, ſitting with his Mitre, he puts it on the fourth Finger of his Right Hand, pronouncing theſe

these words, *Accipe Annulum, &c. Take the Ring*, &c. Then putting off his Mitre, he says the Prayer, *Deus, cujus est omnis, &c. O God, to whom all Power and Dignity belongs, give unto thy Servant* Lewis *a prosperous Event of his Greatness*, &c.

SECTION XIII.

The Delivery of the Scepter.

THE Archbishop, resuming his Mitre, puts the Scepter into the King's Right Hand, saying, *Accipe Sceptrum, &c. Take the Scepter of Kingly Power*, &c.

Then putting off his Mitre, he says the Prayer *Omnipotens Domine, &c.* and putting it on again, he puts the Hand of Justice into the King's Left Hand, saying, *Accipe Virgam Virtutis, &c. Take the Rod of Power*, &c.

SECTION XIV.

The Call of the Peers for the Coronation.

THE Chancellor of *France* goes up to the Altar (*b*), on the Gospel-Side, and with his Face to the King and the Choir, calls the Peers according to their Rank; first the Laicks, then the Ecclesiasticks, in this manner:

(*b*) The Archbishop has often made this Call in the Absence of the Chancellor. *Godefr. Gr. Ceremon. Marlot. Theat d' Hon.*

Monsieur

Monsieur the Prince, or M. the Duke, *N* . . . . . who represent the Duke of *Burgundy*, present yourself at this Act, ... Always observing the same Form in calling the rest of them.

SECTION XV.

The Coronation of the King.

AFter the Call, the Chancellor returns to his Place, and the Archbishop, with his Mitre, takes from off the Altar the great Crown of *Charlemagne*, brought for that Purpose from St. *Dennis*, and bears it up alone, with both his Hands on the King's Head, without touching him. Immediately all the other Peers, Lay and Clergy, put their Hands to support it; and the Archbishop, still holding it with his Left Hand, says,

Coronet te Deus Corona, &c.

May God crown thee with the Crown of Glory and Justice, with Honour, &c.

After this, he puts the Crown alone on the King's Head, saying,

Accipe Coronam, &c.

Take the Crown of the Kingdom, in the Name of the Father +, and of the Son +, and of the Holy + Ghost, &c. Then, still holding his Hands upon the Crown, he says standing, without his Mitre, these Prayers:

Deus

Deus Perpetuitatis, &c.
Extendat Omnipotens Deus, &c.
Benedic, Domine, Regem, &c.
Omnipotens Deus, &c.
Benedic, Domine, Fortitudinem, &c.

SECTION XVI.

The Enthroning of the King.

THE Archbiſhop takes the King, after this, by his Right Arm, to conduct him to the Throne, raiſed on the Lobby aforeſaid, in this Order.

Firſt, The Six Heralds; and after, the Peers: the Eccleſiaſtical preceded by the Maſter of the Ceremonies, go up the Stair-Caſe, on the Epiſtle-ſide, and the Lay Peers, with the Grand Maſter of the Ceremonies at the Head of them, go up by the oppoſite Stair-Caſe, on the Side of the Goſpel. The Conſtable bears the Sword naked in his Hand before the King, having the Gentlemen Uſhers, with their Maces, on each ſide, dreſſed in Tunicks, or Veſts of white Sattin; their Maces of Silver gilt: The King, in his Royal Robes, with a leſſer Crown on his Head, made for his Coronation, all ſet with Precious Stones, and holding in his Hands the Sceptre, and the Hand of Juſtice, walks after the Conſtable, led by the Archbiſhop (preceded by his Croſs, and aſſiſted by two Canons in Copes) by the

the Right Arm; The two Captains of the Quarter Guards, with six Guards *of the Sleeve* before them, are on each side of the King; and the Train of the Royal Robe is born up by a Prince, or great Lord, nominated by the King for that Purpose. The Chancellor walks single behind the King; after him the Great Master; between the Great Chamberlain on his Right, and the first Gentleman of the Chamber at his Left.

The King ascends up to his Throne by the Stair-Case on the side of the Gospel; and when he is come to the Pew that is made ready for him, the Peers and other Lords, being each in their Places according to Rank, the Archbishop, holding the King as he stands, with his Face to the Altar, says,

Sta & Retine, &c. Stand and keep from henceforth the Station which thou hast preserved hitherto by Paternal Succession, as it has been conveyed down to thee by Hereditary Right, thro' the Authority of Almighty God, and our present Delivery of it; namely, that of all the Bishops, and the other Servants of God: *and by how much the nearer to the Holy Altars thou viewest the Clergy, by so much the greater Honour thou should remember to confer upon them in the Places that are suitable to them*, &c.

Then, seating the King in his Throne, and holding him by the Hand, he adds, *In hoc Regni, &c. May God confirm thee in in this Throne of thy Kingdom*, &c. After, he puts off his Mitre, makes a profound Reverence to the King as he ſits on his Throne, kiſſes it, and ſays aloud three times, *Vivat Rex in Æternum: Let the King live for ever*; *or*, *God ſave the King*. And while all the Peers, firſt the Eccleſiaſtical, then the Laical, do the ſame, with the ſame Acclamation, each in his turn; and then forthwith re-ſeat themſelves in their Places: The Church-Doors are ſet open to give entrance to the People, who preſs to ſee their King in his Throne of Glory, and teſtify their Joy in him, by repeated Voices of *Vive le Roy*, (*God ſave the King*,) to the Sound of Trumpets, Drums, and other Inſtruments in the Choir. The Regiment of Guards drawn up in Battalia in the Church-yard, anſwers theſe Acclamations by three Vollies of their Fire-Arms; during which, the Chancellor, the Great Chamberlain, and the Heralds, give a Largeſs, both in the Choir and Body of the Church, of Silver Medals, purpoſely ſtruck for the Coronation-Day: They have on one ſide the Effigies and Name of the King, and, on the other, a Hand extended from Heaven with the Holy Vial; with theſe Words in the Exergue, or Part of the Field divided, *Sacratus ac Salutatus Remis*, *Anointed and Saluted King at* Rheims, with the Date of the Day, Month, and Year; and the Officers of the Aviary let fly a multitude of little Singing-Birds from the Lobby into the Church.

Then the Archbishop goes back by the Epistle-side to the Altar, where he begins the *Te Deum*, given out by the Chanter of the Church of *Rheims*, and continued by the King's Musick

SECTION XVII.

The Celebration of the Mass.

AFter this, the Chanter and Sub-Chanter, begin the *Introit* of the Mass in the Middle of the Choir, and it is carried on by the Church-Musick: During which the Archbishop, assisted by two Bishops, and two Canons, in Copes, begins Mass at the High Altar, and the Chanter gives out to him the whole Canon of the Mass, as it is practised on great Festivals. The *Gloria in Excelsis* is sung by the King's Musick. (*c*)

Then the Archbishop chants the Prayer of the Mass for the Day, with that, *Quæsumus Omnipotens, &c. We beseech thee Almighty God, that thy Servant* Louis; and doing the same at the Private and the Post-Communion. One of the officiating Bishops chants the Epistle without his Mitre near the Altar, assisted by two Canons, Sub-Deacons.

( ) At the Crowning of *Louis* XIV. while the *Gloria in Excelsis* was performing, an Almoner begun the Ordinary Mass of the King on the Altar raised in the Lobby on the Epistle-side.

After

After the Prose another Bishop chants the Gospel near the Altar, assisted by another Bishop, and two Deacons, Canons.

During the Gospel, the King stands up; and the Prince, or Duke, who represents the Duke of *Burgundy*, takes off the Crown from his Head, and lays it on the Cushion upon the Stand of the Oratory, (or Pew) and after the Gospel, he sets it again on the Head of the King.

The Archbishop, having kissed the Text of the Gospel, presented to him by the Bishop who chanted it, begins the *Credo*; which is carry'd on by the King's Musick. During which, the Gospel is brought to the King in this Order. First, Six Heralds at Arms, after the Master, and his Assistants; then, the Great Master of the Ceremonies; the Great Almoner of *France* follows, in his Habit of Ceremony, that is, if he be a Cardinal, in a Cope of Crimson Tabby, with a (*d*) Train behind him, if a Bishop, it is of Purple Tabby. Then a Canon, Deacon, carrying the Book of the Gospels, beneath a Covering of white Sattin, embroidered with Gold. The Bishop, who chanted the Gospel, walks after him, followed by another Canon and Deacon assistant, paying the usual Reverences to the Altar when they leave it, before the Queen's

(*d*) The Great Almoner is now M *Armand Gaston de Rohan, de Soubize*, Bishop and Prince of *Strasburg*, Cardinal of *Rohan*.

Gallery (if there be a Queen) to the Ambaſſadors: Then, at the Foot of the Stair-Caſe of the Lobby, towards the Altar; and after, towards the King. When he is at the Middle of the Stair-Caſe, he makes another Reverence to the King, and a third when he comes before the Throne. Here he takes the Book from the Canon, Deacon, after having uncovered it, and puts it again in the Hands of the Great Almoner, who preſents it to the King to kiſs, and after reſtores it to the ſaid Canon, who brought it, and re-conveys it, covered as before, in the Order they preſerved as they came, by the other Stair-Caſe on the ſide of the Epiſtle.

SECTION XVIII.

The Ceremonies of the Offering.

WHILE the Archbiſhop makes the Oblation, and the King's Muſick ſings the Offertory, the Heralds go to take the accuſtomed Offerings in the Sacriſty behind the High Altar, and preſent them on Cloths of Crimſon Damask, fringed with Gold, to four Lords, who are to carry them for the King. On receiving them, they remove inſtantly from their Places, which are the four firſt high Chairs on the right Side, to go up to the Throne, preceded by the Heralds, the Aſſiſtant, the Maſter and Grand Maſter of the Ceremonies.

At

At the Coronation of *Louis* XIV. the Duke of *St. Simon* walked the firſt after the Great Maſter of the Ceremonies, carrying the Wine in a large Veſſel of Vermillion gilt, then the Count *d'Orval*, with the Silver Loaf, on a rich Cuſhion, with Golden Fringe; after, the Marquiſs *de Sourdis*, with the Golden Bread, and the Marquiſs *de Souvre* with the Purſe of Crimſon Velvet, embroidered with Gold, on the like Cuſhion. In this are thirteen Pieces of Gold, each of the Weight of five Piſtoles and an half, ſtamped with the Effigies of the King crowned on one Side, with this Inſcription;

Ludovicus XIV. Franc. & Navar, Rex Chriſtianiſſimus.

Louis XIV. *moſt Chriſtian King of* France *and* Navarre.

And on the other Side the City of *Rheims*, with a Dove over it, bearing the Holy Vial, and around the Field,

Sacratus ac Salutatus Remis 31 Maii, 1654.

Crowned and Saluted King at Rheims, May 31. 1654.

For that Coronation was fixed to that Day, but was deferred to the 7th of *June*.

When theſe four Lords, carrying the Offerings, come to the foot of the Throne, by the Stair-Caſe, on the Goſpel-Side, they make the accuſtomed Reverences to it, and deſcend, in the ſame Order, by the other Stair-Caſe, on the Side of the Epiſtle; and

 after

after them the Grand Maſter, then the Chancellor, the Conſtable with the naked Sword in his Hand, having on each Side the two Gentlemen-Uſhers of the Chamber, with their Maces of Silver gilt. The King follows them to go to the Offering, bearing his Scepter and Hand of Juſtice, preceded by the Eccleſiaſtical Peers on his Right, and the Lay-Peers on his Left, having on each Side the two Captains of the Guards, with the ſix Guards of the Sleeve. The Great Chamberlain and firſt Gentleman of the Chamber ſtay near the Throne to guard it, in the Abſence of the King

When the King comes before the Altar, the Heralds and Uſhers, the Great Maſter, the Chancellor, Conſtable, and Peers range themſelves on each Side, to make way for two Dukes or Marſhals of *France*, who are to hold, one the Scepter, the other the Hand of Juſtice, while the King makes the Offering (*a*).

The Archbiſhop ſitting in his Chair at the middle of the Altar, with the King kneeling on a Cuſhion before him, the four Lords carry the Offerings, and put them, one after the other into the King's Hand, who preſents them in this Order

I The Purſe. III. The Loaf of Silver. II. The Loaf of Gold. IV. The Wine, in the

(*a*) At the Coronation of *Lewis* XIII the Dukes of *Rouannois* and *Crequy* bore the Scepter and Hand of Juſtice, at that of *Lewis* XIV. it was the Marſhals *du Pleſſis Praſlin* and *d'Aumont*.

Silver

Silver Veſſel, kiſſing the Hand of the ſaid Archbiſhop at each Offering. As ſoon as the Archbiſhop receives them, he puts them into a Silver Baſon, held by the Veſtry-Keeper or Warden of the Church of *Rheims*, at his Left Hand, as Things belonging to his Church, that are to be kept in his Repoſitory.

Then the King takes his Scepter and Hand of Juſtice, and reaſcends his Throne by the Goſpel-Side, in the ſame Order as he came down, and each Perſon reſumes his Place.

The Maſs is continued to the *Pax Domini* excluſively, and then a Biſhop performing the Office of a Deacon, with his Mitre, turns to the Choir, having the Archbiſhop's Croſs in his Left Hand, to give notice of the Benediction, chanting, *Humiliate vos ad Benedictionem, Humble yourſelves for the Bleſſing*, the Choir anſwers, *Amen.* At the ſame time the Archbiſhop turns to the Choir, with his Croſs in his Left Hand, and ſays the Benedictions, addreſſing firſt to the King, then to the Clergy and People, as they are in the Ritual of the Coronation-Prayers, to each of which the Aſſiſtants anſwer *Amen.* After this, putting off his Mitre, he gives the general Bleſſing that is uſual at the end of the ſolemn Maſſes.

Then having chanted the *Pax Domini*, the Great Almoner goes to the Altar to receive the *Pax* of the Archbiſhop, kiſſing him on the Cheek, and immediately returns to the Lobbey in the ſame Order and Ceremony that is obſerved for the Text of the Goſpel, and gives the King the *Pax* for him to kiſs it; then all the Peers, firſt the Clergy, then the Lay-Peers, give the Kiſs of Peace to the King, in ſign of mutual Union and Chriſtian Charity.

Obſerve, the Archbiſhop (or, which is all along meant here, the Perſon officiating for him) does not give now, as formerly, the Benediction of the Royal Banner.

SECTION XIX.

The Communicating of the King.

WHEN the Maſs is ended, the King with the Peers, Eccleſiaſtical and Secular, and the Great Officers of the Crown, deſcends from his Throne for the Communion, in the ſame Order as he went up to it before Maſs, he goes down the Stair-Caſe on the Epiſtle ſide, and is attended as before to the Altar, where, after a proper Reverence, he gives the Scepter and the Hand of Juſtice to the two Lords, who carried them at the time of the Offering. The firſt Prince of the Blood that is preſent, or (*f*) he who repreſents the Duke of

(*f*) At the Coronation of *Louis* XIII. the Prince of *Conde* was for the Duke of *Burgundy*, and took off the Crown, at that of *Louis* XIV. it was Monſieur the King's only Brother, who took it off, tho' he did not repreſent the Duke of *Burgundy*, for he was repreſented by the Duke of *Anjou*.

Bur-

Burgundy, takes off his Great Crown, as also the Lay-Peers take off their Coronets. Then the King enters his Oratory, or Pavilion, made up of Pieces of Cloth of Gold, and Purple Velvet, seeded with Flowers-de-Lys of Gold, raised against the large Pillar, on the Gospel-Side, where his Confessor waits in his Surplice to shrive him.

After this the King prostrates himself on a Cushion before the High Altar, and after having said the *Confiteor* on his Knees, the Archbishop absolves him in the Form of the Church, and communicates him in both kinds; that is, with a small *Host*, that was expresly consecrated for the King, and likewise with the precious Blood of our Lord, which he reserved in the same Chalice of St. *Remy* that he used at Mass. As soon as the King has communicated, the Archbishop replaces the Great Crown upon his Head, he is still for some time on his Knees, saying his Eucharistical Prayers, while the Archbishop purifies the Chalice, after which the King rises up. The Archbishop takes off the great Crown, and puts a lesser upon him, made for the purpose, much lighter, but extremely more adorned with Pearls, Diamonds, and pretious Stones, that are part of the aforesaid Jewels of the Crown. Then the Great (*g*) Crown of *Charlemagne* is put into the Hands of a

(*g*) At the crowning of *Louis* XIII. the Duke *de Montbazon* bore it, and at that of *Lewis* XIV. the Marshal *de l'Hôpital*.

Lord

Lord, that is to carry it before his Majesty on a rich Cushion.

SECTION XX.

The Return of the King to the Archiepiscopal Palace.

HIS Majesty resumes the Scepter and the Hand of Justice, and, after a profound Reverence to the Altar, returns to the Archbishop's Palace thro' the Gallery, extending from the great Gate of the Church to the Palace Hall, amidst the joyful Acclamations of the People, in the following Order.

1. The King's Guard of an hundred *Switzers*, with Drums beating

2. The Trumpets, Hautbois, and other Musick.

3. The hundred Gentlemen Pensioners with their Halberds, headed by their Captain.

4. The Heralds at Arms.

5. The Master, Assistant, and Great Master of the Ceremonies.

6. The Duke or Marshal of *France*, who bears the Great Crown of *Charlemagne*.

7. The Constable, bearing the Royal Sword in his Hand, in a Scabbard of blue Velvet, powdered with Flower-de-Luces of Gold, with the Belt of the same, in the midst of the Gentlemen Ushers with their Maces.

8. The

8. The King, with the lesser Crown on his Head, in his Robes of State, holding the Scepter and Hand of Justice a little before him, on his Right all the Ecclesiastical Peers, in their Pontifical Habits and Copes, with their Mitres, and on a parallel Line to them, on his Left, all the Lay-Peers, in their Ducal Robes and Coronets. At his Side, the Archbishop of *Rheims* supporting the King by the Right Arm, preceded by his Cross and Mitre, and assisted by two Canons in their Copes.

9. Next the King follow the Chancellor, and the Prince or Lord that bears up the Train of the Royal Robe (*h*).

10. The Grand Master between the Great Chamberlain at his Right, and the Master of the Horse at his Left.

11 On each Side of the King, the two Captains of the Guards, with the six Guards of the Sleeve, or the *Scotch* Guards.

In the mean time the other Prelates, with all the Clergy, stay in the Choir, till the Abbot, or the Grand Prior of St. *Remy* depart, to reconvey the Holy Vial into their Abbey, in the same Order and Ceremony as it was brought to the Cathedral; and the four Lords, who attended it, fix the Standard of their Arms, that was carried before them by their Gentlemen, at the Tomb of St. *Remy*, in Memory of the Coronation,

(*h*) At the Coronation of *Louis* XIV. Prince *Eugene* of *Savoy* was the Train-Bearer.

and

and the Office they have discharged in so celebrated a Journey.

The King re-entring the Archbishop's Palace, goes into his Chamber, to put off his Gloves and Shirt, which he gives to his first Almoner to burn; since, having touch'd the Holy Oil, they ought not to be profan'd by other Uses (*i*).

SECTION XXI.

The Royal Entertainment, or Coronation-Feast.

AS soon as the King has changed his Linen, he goes out of his Apartment, still in the same Robes, with the Crown on his Head, and the Scepter and Hand of Justice in his Hands, preceded by the Peers, and followed by the other Great Officers of the Kingdom, in the same Order as he came back from the Church, and is conducted to his Table by the Archbishop of *Rheims*.

The Coronation-Feast is always in the Hall of the Archiepiscopal Palace at *Rheims*, made by the Care and at the Expence of the Inhabitants of that City.

The King's Table is ordinarily placed before the Chimney, on a raised Platform of four Steps, about two foot in height, with a Balustrade all round it, and a large Canopy above.

(*i*) Yet at the Coronation of *Louis* XIII. Queen *Mary de Medicis*, his Mother, had the Piety to desire them, in order to preserve them carefully in her Cabinet, which was granted. *Marlot. Theatr. d'Hon.*

When

When the King is ſeated, Grace is ſaid by the Archbiſhop of *Rheims*, the Great Crown of *Charlemagne*, the Scepter, and the Hand of Juſtice are laid upon the Table, where they remain all Dinner-Time, and the Conſtable, with the naked Sword in his Hand ſtands at the upper End of it. The Steward of the Houſhold in his Turn, or of the Day, takes the Napkin, for the King's waſhing his Hands, and delivers it to the Great Maſter of the Houſhold, or his Proxy, who, in his Coronation-Habit, preſents it to the King, and then goes to perform his Office in the Entertainment.

His Majeſty's Table is ſerved by his own Officers, and before each Service, go,

1. The Drums beating, and Trumpets playing.

2. The Heralds.

3. The Stewards of the Houſhold in waiting, the eldeſt coming up the laſt of them.

4. The Great Maſter, or Lord High Steward of the Houſhold, carrying his Staff erect, with the Gentlemen Uſhers of the Chamber on each Side, bearing their Maces.

5. The Great Maſter of the Pantry of *France* carrying the firſt Diſh.

6. The reſt are brought by the Gentlemen of the Bed-Chamber, aſſiſted by the principal Burgeſſes of *Rheims*.

7. The Grand Cup-Bearer and Maſter-Carver perform their reſpective Offices.

In the ſame Hall are many other Tables.

1. That

1. That of the Ecclesiastical Peers on the Right of the King's Table, five or six Paces beneath it, and about two foot lower.

When the Archbishop has said Grace, he places himself at this Table, these Peers, like him, are in their Pontifical Habits and Copes, with their Mitres, all sitting on the same Side. near the Archbishop is his Cross, and two Canons assistant in Copes.

2. That of the Lay-Peers on the Left of the King's Table, over against the former, and of an equal Height, they likewise sit all on the same Side, in their Ducal Robes and Coronets.

3. The Table of Ambassadors, beneath that of the Peers, where the Pope's Nuncio takes the first Place (*k*); and on either Side are the Ambassadors who were at the Coronation, according to their Rank. Here also sits the Chancellor of *France*, and the Introductor of Ambassadors.

4. Opposite to this is a fourth, called the *Table of Honours*, where the Great Chamberlain, habited like the Lay-Peers, takes the first Place, then the first Gentleman of the Chamber, in the same Habit, with the four Knights of the Order of the Holy Ghost, who carried the Offerings, and the four Lords who conducted the Holy Vial, all sitting, on each Side, like the Ambassadors. These four Tables are served by the Lieutenants and principal Burgesses of *Rheims*.

(*k*) At the Coronation of *Louis* XIII. and XIV. the Ambassador of *Venice* was on his Right.

The

The King ſits alone at his Table, unleſs he has a Brother, in which caſe the Prince places himſelf at the Left of the King, as it was obſerved at the Coronation of *Louis* the XIVth, when Monſieur the King's only Brother had that Place.

When there is a Queen, a kind of Gallery, or raiſed Balcony, is fitted up in the Hall for a commodious View of the King at Table, appointed for her, the Princeſſes and Ladies of the Court, as it was obſerved at many Coronations, and the moſt lately at that of *Louis* XIV. over the Table of the Lay-Peers.

When the King has dined, the Archbiſhop advances towards the Table, and ſays Grace. Then his Majeſty takes again the Scepter, and the Hand of Juſtice, and withdraws into his Apartment, conducted and preceded by the Peers, and other Great Officers, in the ſame Order and Ceremony as he came to his Table. Then he gives them leave to retire, and ſtays the remaining part of the Day in his Cloſet, to take his neceſſary Repoſe, after the Length and Fatigue of all theſe Great Ceremonies.

The Archbiſhop of *Rheims*, and the Eccleſiaſtical Peers, return to the Church, to put off their Pontifical Habits.

The Conſtable, the Grand Maſter, the Lords who bore the Scepter and the Hand of Juſtice, the Captains of the Guards, the Grand Maſter of the Ceremonies, the Maſter and his Assistant, and other Officers and Persons of Condition, repair to the Town-House, where they are magnificently treated, and served, at several Tables, at the Expence of the City.

SECTION XXII.

The Cavalcade to St. Remy *on the Day after the Coronation.*

ON the Day following our Kings are accustomed to make a Cavalcade to St. *Remy*, to hear Mass, and implore the Assistance of that Glorious Apostle. His Majesty was attended thither by all the Princes, Dukes, and Peers Laical, Lords and Officers of his Court, who omitted nothing that might render it as stately as possible.

On this Occasion the King is usually dress'd in a Habit of Cloth of Silver, after the *Antique* Mode, with a Cloke of Silver Embroidery, and a Cap of black Velvet, adorn'd with a white Plume of Feathers; he is mounted on a white Horse (*l*) covered with a

(*l*) The old Term is *Haquenée Blanche*, not *Cheval*, I think, in this Case, the former is the most proper. This Custom is not abolished in *Spain*, nor *Italy*, and we read in the *Journeaux du Temps* (*Journals of the Times*) that on *June* 9 1722, the Pope gave the Emperor *Charles-Francis-Joseph* of *Austria*, at present upon the Throne, the Investiture of the Kingdom of *Naples*, on condition of the Tribute which his Imperial Majesty should pay to his Holiness for it, according to antient Usage, which was, a Present of a white Horse, richly caparisoned, and a Purse of 5000 Ducats, or Scudi of Gold, and that the same Pope *Innocent* a rich Housing of Silver Embroidery, preceded by the Company of Light Horse-Guards, the Great Provost of the Houshold, and his Lieutenants at the Head of his Archers, the Guard of an hundred *Switzers*, with their Captain at the Head of them; the twelve Pages of the Chamber on horseback, and the twenty-four Valets on foot. Immediately after the King, was the Great Chamberlain, the Captains of the Guards; and the hundred Gens-d'Arms, at the Rear of the whole Body. Mass is sung by the King's Musick, after which the King returns to the Archiepiscopal Palace, in the same Order as he parted from it in the Morning.

SECTION XXIII.

The Ceremony of conferring the Order of Knighthood of the Holy Ghost.

THE same Day, after Dinner, the King habited, as in the Morning, goes to the Great Church of *Notre-Dame* of *Rheims*, thro' the same Gallery which he past thro' on his Coronation-Day, preceded immediately by the Princes, Knights, and Officers of the several Orders, in their Habits of Ceremony, by the hundred Gentlemen-Pensioners, Trumpets, Hautbois, and other Instruments, with the two Captains of the Guards on each Side, and the six *Scotch* Guards.

Innocent XIII. having been elected into the Pontificate, *May* the 8th, 1721 rode on a white Horse in that great and magnificent Cavalcade, which he made some Days after, when he went to take possession of St. *John* of *Lateran*.

The King takes his Place in the first high Chair of the Choir, on the right Side, upon a spacious Carpet of Green Velvet, powder'd with Flowers-de Lys of Gold, under a Canopy of the same, raised against the Lobbey, in the Partition.

The Great Chamberlain places himself next to his Majesty, the Cardinals and Prelates in their Camails and Rochets; the Princes, Dukes, Chancellor, Counsellors, and Secretaries of State; the Ambassadors and Residents of foreign Princes, the Knights and Officers of the several Orders, all in their Habits of Ceremony, are placed in the Choir on Benches and Scaffolds, fitly disposed, for the Occasion, by the Order and Direction of the Great Master of the Ceremonies.

The Queen, if there be one, the Princesses and Ladies of Condition, are also placed in a Gallery on the right Side of the Altar, as they were on the Day of the Coronation.

The King's Musick sings the Vespers, after which his Majesty, preceded by all the Officers of the Order of the Holy Ghost, advances to the Altar, and takes his Place on a Footstool of Green Velvet, embroidered with Flames of Gold, over which is a Canopy of the same. Then the Archbishop of *Rheims*, or the Prelate who represented him at the Coronation, puts the Great Collar of the Order on his Shoulders, and creates him Knight of the Order of the Holy Ghost, saying the Prayers that are proper to the Ceremony, and

and gives him likewise a Croſs of white Enamel, faſtened to a blue Ribband, according to Cuſtom.

After that the Great Chamberlain of *France* having taken off his Majeſty's Cloke, the Provoſt, and Maſter of the Ceremonies of the Order, put on him the Royal Mantle, or Robe of the Holy Ghoſt. In the mean time the King's Muſick ſings the *Veni Creator*. The Provoſt and Maſter of the Ceremonies of the Order conduct the Princes and Lords that are to be knighted to the King, who inveſts them with the Collar and Mantle of the Order.

Then the King returns to his Place, with all the other Knights and Officers, wearing the Collar of the Order, and after the *Compline*, which is ſung by the King's Muſick, he goes back to the Archbiſhop's Palace, in the ſame Order and Ceremony as he left it, when he came to the Cathedral (*m*).

SECTION XXIV.

Of touching for the Evil, the (*n*) *Pilgrimage to* Corbigny, *and the nine Days Devotion to St.* Marcoul.

THE third Day, after the Coronation, our Kings, whoſe Piety does not in the leaſt degenerate, are accuſtomed to go, according

(*m*) At the Coronation of *Louis* XIV. the Marquiſs of *Mancini* bore the Train of the Royal Robe.

(*n*) *Corbigny* is a Priory, in the Dioceſe of *Laon*, depending upon the Abbey of St. *Remy* in *Champagne*, where the Relicks

cording to antient Uſage, from *Rheims* to *Corbigny*, to viſit the Church of St. *Marcoul*, and there to touch thoſe that are afflicted with the King's-Evil, who always appear, in that Place, very numerous, on ſuch an Occaſion.

This miraculous Power of the Kings of *France*, to cure by their Touch a Malady, almoſt incurable by human Remedies, is a Gift of Heaven, that has no Cauſe but the Will of the Almighty, expreſſing thus, by ſenſible Wonders, his extraordinary Love for the eldeſt Sons of his Church, and giving them the Admiration and Reſpect of all Nations of the Univerſe, above all the Kings of the World.

Hiſtory, and St. *Remy* himſelf aſſures us, that *Clovis* was the firſt who received this Power from Heaven, in favour to his Con-

Relicks of St *Marcoul* (or *Marculfe*, *Marcou*, *Marculphus*) are preſerved

That Saint was born at *Bayeux* in *Normandy*, of noble Parents. After he had given all his Fortune to the Poor, he led a very retired Life to the Age of thirty, when he was ordained Prieſt, in the Dioceſs of *Coûtance*, afterwards he obtained of *Childebert*, King of *France*, Son of *Clovis* I a ſmall Place, called *Nanteuil*, near the Town of *Coûtance*, for the building of a Monaſtery there. He followed the Rule of St. *Benedict*, and coming to be the Head of a great Number of Religious, he was obliged to erect many Monaſteries He performed a great Number of Miracles, while he lived, in the Cure of the King's-Evil He died at *Nanteuil*, in the Year 558, *May* 1. Part of his Bones was carried from the Abbey of *Nanteuil* to *Martes*, and the other Relicks of this Saint are preſerved in the Church of *Corbigny*, which is dedicated to him The King's-Evil is called by ſome *the Evil of St.* Marcoul. *See* the Manuſcript of St. *Remy*. Hiſtoire de France.

verſion;

version, that he made an Experiment of it on the Person of *Lanicet* his Favourite (*o*), who, despairing of his Cure of this Disease, retired from Court. A few Days after, the King having it revealed to him by Vision, that he had touched *Lanicet* for the Evil, and that his Sores were dried up, without the least Scar remaining, discoursed with St. *Remy* about it, who persuaded him to enquire for *Lanicet*, and touch him. This he did, invoking the Name of God, and at once his Pains were eased, and his Ulcers miraculously cured. From this time *Clovis* ever exercised this Power with Success during the Remainder of his Life, and his Successors have been favoured with the same, so that it is perpetuated to this Day.

Yet it is observed, that these Cures have been more frequent under the third Race of our Kings, than under the two former, whether the Kings of the third Line excelled the rest in Piety and Righteousness, or the Distemper is now more universal.

However, the Custom of our Kings performing a nine-days Devotion to St. *Marcoul*, soon after their Coronation, before they touch for the Evil, was introduced by St. *Louis* in 1226, and ever since this devout Pilgrimage has been continued suc-

(*o*) Some Historians pretend, that the antient and illustrious House of *Montmorency* descends from this *Lanicet*, and that this Lord being the first who went down into the Baptismal Font after *Clovis*, he took, for that reason, for the Device and Motto of his Arms, *Dieu aide au premier Chretien, God assists the first Christian.*

cessively by our Kings, who never touch for the Evil before they have accomplished it, either at *Corbigny*, when they can go thither, or in some other Church, when some Disturbances prevent their passing into *Champagne*; as *Henry* IV. performed the nine-days Devotion at *St. Clou*.

The Journey to *Corbigny*, or of *St. Marcoul*, is made on horseback, in the Order of the Cavalcade to the Church of St. *Remy*, on the Day after the Coronation.

Formerly the King stopped at the Monastery of St. *Thierry*, which is two small Leagues distant from *Rheims*, where he was entertained at the Expence of the Abbey, but this Custom has been abolished, on account of the Charge it occasioned.

The King, on his Approach to the Town of *Corbigny*, is received and complimented by the principal Inhabitants of the Place; and when he alights from his Horse, he is conducted into the Church by the Prior and the Religious of St *Marcoul*, then passes under the Shrine of that Saint to the High Altar He is there placed under a Canopy that is prepared for him, where he says his Prayers, and hears Vespers; after which he confesses under a Pavilion, near the Altar, then retires into a Palace, made ready for him in the Monastery, till the next Morning, when he enters the Church, in his Royal Robes, to hear Mass, which is sung by his own Musick, and he receives the Communion from one of his Almoners with the

the uſual Ceremonies. Then he approaches the Diſeaſed (*o*), who are ranged on both Sides of the Body of the Church ; or when there is too great a Number, in the Cloiſter, or Park of the Priory, giving the firſt Rank to the *Spaniards*, and the laſt to the *French*. His Majeſty's Head, during the time, is uncovered; on his Right is the Captain of his Guards, aſſiſted by his Great Almoner (who, diſtributes his Alms to the Diſeaſed as ſoon as they are touched) and by his chief Phyſician, who holds the Head of the Sick behind, while the King, extending his right Hand over their Faces, from the Forehead to the Chin, and from one Cheek to the other, making the Sign of the Croſs, touches them, and pronounces theſe Words.

Dieu te gueriſſe, le Roy te touche, *God cure thee, the King touches thee.*

If the King's important Affairs do not permit him to ſtay nine Days at St. *Marcoul*, he commits this pious Office to one of his Almoners.

Louis XIV. taken up with the Cares of a War, he was obliged to carry on, could not go to St. *Marcoul*, but he diſcharged this Work of Piety in the Church of St. *Remy* at *Rheims*, *June* 9. 1654, three Days after his Coronation (in which he performed his Devotions) he touched the Sick, who were ranged in the Park of the Great Abbey, to about

(*o*) Who have all been viſited by the chief Phyſician and Surgeon of the King.

the Number of 2600. He was preceded by the Company of the hundred *Swiss*, thirty Archers of the Great Provost, and the Life-Guard, attended by Cardinal *de Grimaldi*, Great Almoner of *France*, and by many Lords and Officers of the Court.

SECTION XXV.

Of the Goal-Delivery and General Amnesty to Criminals.

ALL these Ceremonies are finished with an Act of Clemency, worthy of the Majesty and Power of our Kings, which is the Indemnity and General Pardon they grant to Delinquents, whatever they be (*p*), a Custom of equal Antiquity with Monarchy itself (*q*).

Since the time of *Francis* I. it is the Great Almoner of *France* who is charged with the Release of Prisoners and Criminals.

(*p*) At the Coronation of *Henry* II. *Philbert de Cossé*, Great Almoner of *France*, by the Order of his Majesty, released all that were imprisoned at *Rheims*, among whom were Murderers, Robbers, Coiners, and others, to the Number of 445.

(*q*) *Saul*, the first King of *Israel* and *Judah*, pardoned all capital Offenders on the Day that he obliged the King of the *Ammonites* to raise the Siege of *Jabesh-Gilead*, 1 Sam 2 The *Roman* Emperors, according to the Account of *Suetonius*, were likewise accustomed to release the Prisoners when they came to the Empire, or made their Entry into a City. And, among us, St *Remy* obtained of the Sons of *Clovis*, that when the Kings of *France* went to *Rheims* to be crowned, or only passed within the Sight of it, the Prisons should be set open for all Criminals, which has been ever since observed.

The King's Council has the Cognizance of these Affairs at present, and a Master of Requests is made the King's Procurator-General on this Subject.

He goes, by the King's Order, to all the Prisons of the Town of *Rheims*, and causes them to be opened, for the Discharge of all those who are detained there, upon any Crime or Delinquency whatever, but they who are Prisoners for Debt, are, in a certain time, to satisfy their Creditors.

And as this general Pardon is known throout all *France*, an infinite Number of Criminals never fail to get into the Prisons of *Rheims*, some Days before the Coronation, to secure the Benefit of it.

At the Coronation of *Louis* XIV. M. the Cardinal *Grimaldi*, Great Almoner of *France*, computed about ten thousand Prisoners, whom he enlarged, in consequence of this General Act of Oblivion.

CHAP. XIV.

Of the Anointing and Coronation of other Christian Kings, who have been anointed after the Example of the Kings of France.

THE Kings of *France* have not only the Happiness of being the first Converts to the Christian Faith, but they have likewise the Advantage to derive only from God himself the Institution of the Ceremony of their Anointing, which has been conveyed down to other Christian Princes, many Ages after, from their Pattern. And as the

the Kings of *Europe* give the firſt Rank to the Emperor, by reaſon of his Dignity (tho at preſent by the Term Emperor we only underſtand him who is Head of the Empire of *Germany*) yet, as ſince the Diviſion of the Empire of *Conſtantine the Great*, about 339 Years after Chriſt, the *Eaſt* has been governed by the *Greek* Emperors, who have been Chriſtians, and the *Weſt* by the *Latin* Emperors; it is neceſſary to ſpeak of both of them, to prove that even the firſt Emperors of the *Eaſt* were not anointed till after the Kings of *France*, whoſe Ceremonies they have for the moſt part imitated.

SECTION I.

Of the Emperors of Conſtantinople, *and when they were anointed.*

AFTER the Succeſſors of *Conſtantius*, (the youngeſt Son of *Conſtantine*, who had, for his Diviſion, *Greece*, *Aſia*, and *Egypt*) had extinguiſhed the Remains of Paganiſm, deſtroyed the Idols, taken the Name of Emperors of the *Eaſt*, and merited the Title of *Moſt Chriſtian*, by their entire Obedience to the Church: *Theodoſius the Younger* (r) is the firſt that is held to have been bleſſed, and to have received the Crown and Sword of the Empire from the Hands of *Proculus*, Patriarch of *Conſtantinople*, where thoſe Emperors preſided.

(r) He lived in 409. Marcellin le Comte en la Chron. Zonaras, Tom 3. Ann. Theophanes, lib. 16.

But

But Anointing was not yet in Practice, and it does not appear that the Emperors of the *East* were anointed before the Reign of (*s*) *Andronicus* Junior, that is, towards the 13th Century.

They who have written on the Anointing and Coronation of these Emperors, tell us (*t*), that the Day being fixed on which the Emperor was to be anointed, all Persons of Dignity were to render themselves at the Palace by Sun-Rising, that the new Elect was first of all placed upon a Shield (*u*), the forepart of which was supported by the Father, if alive; the hinder-part by the Patriarch and the Princes; and thus they raised him aloft to the View of the People, who made their Acclamations.

Afterwards, when he was set upon the Ground, they conducted him to the Church of St *Sophia*, in order to his solemn Coronation. Here was set an Oratory, or Pew, for the Emperor, where he was arrayed in Purple, and invested with the Diadem, and other Marks of the Imperial Dignity, after they had been blessed by the Bishops

This done, they begun the Mass, which the Emperor heard on a Theatre, raised in the middle of the Church, where his Throne was placed. After Mass, the Emperor approaching the Altar, and uncovering himself at the proper Places, was anointed and

(*s*) He was elected in the Year 1327.

(*t*) Joannes Cantacuzenus in Andron. Juniorem. Georgius Codinus, lib. de Officiis Aulæ Constantini.

(*u*) After the manner of the antient *Gauls*.

conse-confecrated by the Patriarch with the Sign of the Crofs on the Top of his Head, faying *Sanctus* at each Unction, which the Affiftants repeat three times, and the People after them the fame.

Then the Deacons bring the Crown, which is born up, and fet on the Head of the Emperor by his Father, or the neareft a-kin to him, and by the Patriarch, who, during the time, loudly pronounces *Dignus*, which the Affiftants and People likewife repeat three times (*x*). If the Emperor was married, his Spoufe was immediately crowned after him, not by the Patriarch, or any other Bifhop after him, but by the Emperor himfelf, who having received the Crown from the Hands of his Eunuchs, put it on the Head of the Emprefs, after the manner of the *Perfians* (*y*), and then fhe proftrated herfelf before him as his Subject.

If the Emperor was crowned before his Marriage, the Coronation of the Emprefs was on her Wedding-Day.

After Mafs, and the Offerings of Bread and Wine, which were carried to the Altar before the Coronation, the Emperor in the Choir put off his Crown, and the Deacon received from the Hand of the Patriarch the Body of Chrift, which he gave to the Emperor,

(*x*) *Imperator*, &c The Emperor of *Conftantinople* was not confecrated with common fimple Oil, but an Ointment, which was the Holy Chrifm.

(*y*) The Kings of *Perfia* crowned their Wives with their own Hands *Efther*, c. 11. *Jofeph.* l. 11. c 6. *Sulpit. Sever. Sacr. Hift.* m. 11.

peror, and then the precious Blood in the Chalice, which the Emperor took into his Hands to communicate himſelf, as the Prieſt does at Maſs.

This done, the Emperor aſcends a kind of Gallery, raiſed on high, at the Gate of the Church, to be viewed and acknowledged by the People, who teſtified their Approbation by Shouts of Joy, mingled with the Sound of Drums and Trumpets, while one of the Great Lords of the Court orders a great Number of Gold and Silver (*z*) Medals, ſtruck for the purpoſe, to be thrown among the People.

Then the Emperor deſcends from the Gallery, and mounts on horſeback with the Empreſs his Wife, and returns to the Palace, where a Royal Feaſt is prepared for the Occaſion (*a*).

Theſe Ceremonies were obſerved till the Year 1448, that is, till the laſt of the *Conſtantines*, ſince whom the *Ottoman* Princes having made themſelves Maſters of *Conſtantinople*, and of the Empire of the *Eaſt*, went into the Practice of others, more agreeable to their Religion.

(z) Theſe Medals were commonly fine, and in Number above Ten Thouſand, and, to preſerve them, they were diſtributed, wrapt up in Pieces of Cloth. This was repeated the next Day to the Courtiers and Soldiers.

(a) Georg Codinus, lib. de Offic. Aul. Conſtant

SEC-

SECTION II.

Of the Emperors of the West, *and King of the* Romans, *and of their Anointing and Coronation.*

THE two eldest Sons of *Constantine the Great*, *Constantius* and *Constantinus*, having, for their Division, *Italy*, *Afric*, and *Illyricum* to the former, and *Gaul*, *Spain*, and *Great Britain*, with all on this Side the *Alps* to the latter, were saluted Emperors of the *West*; *Rome* being the Seat of this Empire, as *Constantinople* was that of the *Eastern* Empire.

This Empire of the *West* continued to *Augustus Romulus*, surnamed (*b*) *Augustulus*, who lost it in the Year 476. *Odoacer*, King of the *Heruli*, the *Goths*, and *Lombards*, having reduced it, they were in possession of it 300 Years. This Division of the Empire gave rise to that of the *Eastern* and *Western* Church: and towards the 5th Century, under *Honorius* and *Valentinian* the IIId, the *Roman* Empire entirely decayed, and the Barbarians, who had been often repulsed into their Countries beyond the *Danube* and the *Rhine*, which served, as it were, for the two Barriers of the Empire, passed those two Rivers, and made themselves Masters of several *Roman* Provinces. The *Cimbri* were the first who penetrated thro' all *Germany*, and settled themselves on the Lands of the *Romans*, the

(*b*) On the Account of his Minority.

the old *Saxons* made themselves formidable on both Sides of the *Elbe*, as well as *Didier* King of the *Lombards*, and an Infinity of other People; so far, that Pope *Adrian* III. in fear of the Church, whose Countries were overflown by the Barbarians, implored the Succour of *Charlemagne* King of *France*, who, after many Victories over the Enemies of the Church, obliged them for the most part to be Christians, and dispersed them. In acknowledgment of so great a Service, Pope *Leo* III. anointed and crowned *Charlemagne* Emperor of the *West* at *Rome*, by the Consent of *Nicephorus*, Emperor of the *East*; he invested him and his Successors Kings of *France* in this Empire, declaring Anathema's against those who would remove it into another Family. Thus *Charlemagne* is the first Emperor of the *West*, whom we find to have been anointed, and it was on *Christmas-Day*, in the Year 800 (*c*) in like manner as *Clovis* was

(*c*) *Charlemagne* had been anointed and crowned before King of *Lombardy*, in the Town of *Medicia*, by the Archbishop of *Milan*, in the Year 774, in this manner. The Archbishop of *Milan*, with the other Prelates and Nobles of that Nation, attended *Charlemagne* from his Apartment to the Altar, where the King falling on his Knees, the Archbishop demanded of the People, whether they would have him for their King and then he anointed him with the Holy Oil, on the Top of the Head, on the Shoulders, the Breast, and Joints of the Arms. This done, he puts the Sword by his Side, the Bracelets about his Arms, and the Ring on his Finger, the Scepter in his Hand, and the Crown of Iron upon his Head It is so called, because indeed it is an Iron Ring, plated over with Gold. They say that *Tendelane*, who, about the Year 593, drew the *Lombards* from *Arianism*, caused it to be so made, in order

was the first King who was anointed in *France.*

Many other Kings of *France*, Successors of *Charlemagne*, have also, like him, been anointed Emperors, that is, *Louis* I. called *the Debonnair*, *Lotharius* I. *Louis* II. *Charles the Bald*, *Louis le Begue*, and *Charles the Gross*. But the *Germans* having expelled him, and chosen in his Place, on *November* 11. 887. *Arnold*, the Bastard Son of *Carloman*, *Charles* III. was the last King of *France* who possessed the Empire, to the great Dissatisfaction of the *French*, who had acquired it at the Price of so much Blood: for after this Change, which was the first Foundation-Stone of the *German* Empire, the Emperors were elected by the Deputies of the Imperial Cities, whose Title of Elector, at last, remains to the Chief Prelates and Lords of this Empire (*d*).

As

order to crown her Husband King *Agilulfus*, implying, that a Crown is a Weight that has much Inconvenience concealed beneath its deceitful Lustre. *Mezer. Hist. de Fran. l* 9.

(*d*) This Right of electing the Emperors did not come from Pope *Gregory* V. nor from the Emperor *Otho* III. for we find nothing of it in the Archives of the Popes, nor those of the Emperors, yet it is certain, that all the Emperors from the Pontificate of *Gregory* V. and the Reign of *Otho* III. have been elected, in the General Diets or Assemblies of the Princes of *Germany*. Nor is it Pope *Innocent* IV. who instituted the seven Electors, as some Authors imagine. The Right of the *German* Princes to elect and crown whom they pleased as Emperor, seems to be derived from three Popes (1.) *John* XII who crowned *Otco* III. called *The Great*, in 962 It was then that the Imperial Dignity being united to that of King of *German,*

As to the Coronation and Anointing of the Emperors, after having spoken of that of *Charlemagne*, we will pass to the present Practice. On *Christmas-Day*, in the Year 800, *Charles* being at Prayers in the Church of St *Peter* in *Rome*, Pope *Leo* III. declar'd to him the Resolution of the *Romans*, and put the Purple Robe on his Shoulders, and a Crown, set with precious Stones upon his Head, which the People (*e*) immediately approved by this Acclamation, *To* Charles

many, the Right of electing the Emperor became inseparable from that of electing the King. (2.) From *Leo* the Third, who, by a Decree which he made, by Consent of the Senate and People of *Rome*, gave to this same Emperor, and to his Successors, the Right of chusing a Successor, not to the *German* Monarchy, which *Otho* had independent of the Holy See, but to the Imperial Dignity. Then as *Otho* III died without Issue in 1002, his Right of electing was devolved on the States, who afterwards resigned it to three Electors. (3.) From *Sylvester* II. who succeeded *Gregory* V. in 999, who by a Decree gave this Right of Election to the *Germans*.

There were at first but seven Electors, three Ecclesiasticks, the Archbishops of *Mentz*, *Treves*, and *Cologne*, and four Secular; the King of *Bohemia*, the Duke of *Bavaria*, the Duke of *Saxony*, and the Marquiss of *Brandenburg*.

In 1648, an eighth Electorate was created, with the Charge of Great Treasurer of the Empire, to replace the Elector *Palatine*, who had been deposed, without depriving the Elector of *Bavaria*, who had been invested in his Electorate. In 1692, a ninth was established in favour of the Duke of *Hannover*, of the House of *Brunswick*.

Among the Electors, the Succession follows the Order of Blood, only the Electoral Dignity, and the Lands annexed to it, cannot be divided by any Partition.

The Ecclesiastical Electors are made by Election or Collation, as the other Princes of *Germany*, but the Electoral Dignity being Secular, the Ecclesiastical Electors may assist at an Election before the Pope's Confirmation is granted. *See* Joan. Naucl. Chron l'Etat. Pref. de l'Emp. d'Allem.

(*e*) He was anointed after the manner of the Kings of *Judah*, and the first Christian Kings.

the August, the Crowned of God, the Great and Pacifick Emperor of the Romans, *Life and Victory.*

This done, he consecrated and anointed him from Head to Foot.

When this Ceremony was over, the Pope *adored* the new Emperor, that is, he fell on his Knees before him, and recognized him for his Sovereign; then he caused his Picture to be exposed in publick, that all the *Romans* might pay him the same Duty.

Since *Charlemagne* (*f*) the Anointing and Coronation of the Emperors has been attended with greater Magnificence and Preparation, as we shall speak of it hereafter.

How the Ceremony of Anointing the Emperor is performed, and what Prelate has a Right to anoint him.

The Ceremony is usually performed at *Aix la Chapelle*; *Louis the Debonnair* was the first who was crowned there (*g*), and in imitation of him many of his Successors were crowned in the same Place. *Charles* IV. made a Law about it, ordaining, by the Golden Bull, that the Coronation of the King of the *Romans*, that is, the Emperor, should be there for the future (*h*). *Charles* V. was likewise resolved to be crowned there, tho' the Pestilence raged in the Place (*i*): But *Ferdinand* I (*k*). and his Successors, were crowned at *Frankfort*, or at *Ratisbon*, till

(*f*) *See* le Moine's Vie de Charlem. Mezeray. l. 9. t. 1.

(*g*) Jan. 28. 814.

(*h*) Tho he himself had been anointed at *Bonn*, beyond *Cologne*, *Octob.* 11. 1347.

(*i*) June 28. 1519.

(*k*) March. 18. 1558.

Henry

Henry II. who being at *Aix la Chapelle*, would be there anointed and crowned by the Archbishop of *Cologne*, the Diocesan of that District (*l*).

The Electors pretend to have a Right of agreeing to the Place of the Emperor's Coronation; and the Elector of *Mentz*, as first Archbishop of *Germany*, did pretend a Right to anoint and crown him, after the Example of his Predecessors; but the Archbishop of *Cologne* having contested that Privilege with him, they have adjusted the Dispute between them, and have agreed, that each should do it in his respective Diocess, and that if it were transacted out of it, they should do it alternately.

Of the Election of the Emperor.

Since the Golden Bull (which is a Regulation made by *Charles* IV. the Emperor, in the Year 1356, for the Election of the Emperors) and the Treaties of 1648, and 1692, it is at present made at *Frankfort*, in the Church of St. *Bartholomew*, by the Electors; the Ecclesiastick are, the Archbishops of *Mentz*, *Treves*, and *Cologne*; and the Secular are, the King of *Bohemia*, the Duke of *Bavaria*, the Duke of *Saxony*, the Marquiss of *Brandenburg*, the Prince *Palatine*, who was added to them at the last Peace with *Germany*, and the Duke of *Hannover* of the House of *Brunswick*.

The Successor to the Empire ought to be a Native of *Germany*, and by Extraction a Lay-Person, not a Clergyman, of illustrious

(*l*) June 4. 1039.

Birth, and a Count or Baron at least, rich, and capable of sustaining the Imperial Dignity. The Age of his Election and Coronation is not settled by the Constitutions of the Empire.

Otho was elected at the Age of 11 Years, *Henry* III. at 12, *Henry* IV. at 5, *Wenceslaus* at 15, and *Frederic* II. in the Cradle.

The Elector of *Mentz* presides in this Electoral Assembly as Great Chancellor of *Germany*, and Director of that College. When the Election is concluded, by a Plurality of Suffrages, if the new Emperor is of the Assembly, the Electors go from the Conclave, or Place of Meeting, to the High Altar of the Church, and seat him upon it; and here the Archbishop of *Mentz* makes him sign the Capitulation.

When he departs from the Altar, he is conducted to a Gallery over the Entrance of the Choir, where seating himself with his Electors, he hears the Proclamation made of his Election.

As soon as the Election is over, he dispatches an Envoy Extraordinary to *Rome*, to notify it to the Pope, and obtain his Consent and Confirmation of it (*m*).

(*m*) The Emperors, since *Charles* V. have always been invited to be anointed and crowned by the Popes, but almost all of them have been content with his Offers of Confirmation, and the States of the Empire assembled at *Frankfort*, in the Year 1338, and at *Cologne* in 1339, have concluded, that Election alone confers upon a Prince the full Imperial Power, after he has taken the Oath to the Empire, and they have declared the two Coronations made afterwards, one at *Rome*, and the other at *Milan*, to be not at all necessary. Yet the Popes have not thought

Of the Ceremonies of the Coronation and Anointing of the Emperor, and likewise of the Imperial Robes, Crowns, and Ornaments.

When they have fixed the Day and Place for the Coronation, and the Elector of *Mentz* has given Advice of it, to the Magistrates of *Aix la Chapelle* and *Nuremberg*, these Officers send by their Deputies, to the Church appointed for it, the Imperial Ornaments, of which they are the Guardians; that is, those of *Nuremberg* the Golden Crown of *Charlemagne* (of the weight of fourteen Pounds) the Ring, the Scepter, the Globe, the Shoes, and Sword (given, as it is pretended, by an Angel to *Charlemagne*) a long Alb, a Stole, a Cope, with a Cincture, or Girdle.

They of *Aix le Chapelle* send a Shrine set with Diamonds, where is preserved some of the Blood of St. *Stephen*, the ordinary Sword of *Charlemagne*, with its Belt, and a Book of the Gospels, in Golden Letters, used by that Emperor.

These things being thus disposed, the Emperor goes to the Church in the Morning, attended with the Princes and Lords of *Germany*, and the Deputies of the Imperial Cities.

Here, after the preparatory Ceremonies and Prayers, the Archbishop officiating, who

themselves obliged by these Regulations, and have ever refused to recognize the Emperor, if he did not come to *Rome* to receive the Imperial Crown, or if he did not obtain of them a Brief to dispense with it, and confirm their Election. *L'Hist. de l'Emp.* by the Sieur *Heiss*, and *l'Hist. d'Allem.* by *R. de Prade.*

 is

is always one of the Electors, consecrates and anoints the Emperor on the Top of the Head, between the Shoulders, on the Nape of the Neck, on the Breast, on the Right Arm, between the Hand and the Elbow, and within both his Hands; saying at each Unction, *Ungo te in Regem de Oleo sanctissimo, in Nomine Patris, & Filii, & Spiritus Sancti; I anoint thee to be King, with the most Holy Oil, in the Name of the Father, and of the Son, and of the Holy Ghost.*

After which the Emperor is clothed with the Imperial and Pontifical Vestments brought from *Nuremberg*; that is, the Buskins, the long Alb, and the Stole, which is put over his Breast, in the Form of a Cross, and thrown behind upon his Shoulders.

The Elector Archbishop officiating, puts into his Hand the Sword of *Charlemagne*, pronouncing these words, *Accipe Virgam Virtutis, Take the Rod of Power*; and then he takes the Crown from off the Altar, and with the two other ArchBps, Electors, puts it on the Head of his Imperial Majesty.

In the mean time a solemn Mass is sung, in which when they come to the *Per omnia* of the Preface to the Consecration, the Princes, Electors, and Ambassadors, who are Protestants, withdraw till the end of it; and in the mean time the Emperor communicates, in one kind, from the Hand of the Archbishop officiating.

After Mass he is conducted by the three Ecclesiastical Electors, preceded by the Secular, to a Gallery, where he places himself in a Seat that is prepared for him. If

If the Ceremony is done at *Aix la Chapelle*, they set there the Seat of *Charlemagne*, which is always preserved in that Church; then the ABp says to the Emperor; *Take and preserve the Possession of the Place that is given you, not by Right of Inheritance, or Paternal Succession, but by the Votes of the Electors of the* German *Empire, and particularly, by the Providence of Almighty God.*

Then the Emperor, attended by the Secular Electors, confers the Order of Knighthood on some Persons, by touching them with the Sword of *Charlemagne*. After which a Canon of the Collegiate Church of *Aix la Chapelle* remonstrates to him, that by antient Usage every Emperor is received there as a Canon, and desires him to take the Oath, which he does in *Latin*.

After all these Ceremonies, the Emperor departs from the Church, preceded by an Herald, who makes a Largess to the People of Gold and Silver Money, stamped with the Effigies of the Emperor, and the Date of his Coronation (*n*).

SECTION III.

Of the Anointing and Coronation of the Kings of Spain.

THO *Spain* was converted to the Christian Faith, from the first Ages, by the

(*n*) See l'Hist. de l'Emp. *by the Sieur* Heiss, *printed at* Paris *in* 1684. L'Hist. d'Allem. anc. & nouveau, &c. *by the Sieur* Royer de Prade, *printed in* 1683. Disc sur le Bulle Dorée de l'Emp chap. 4. *printed at* Paris *in* 1612 *and* le Disc Hist. de l'El. de l'Emp. & des El. *by M.* Wicquefort, *Resident of* Brandenbourg, *printed at* Paris *in* 1658

Preaching of the Apostles and of St *Eleutherus*, sent thither by St. *Dennis*; yet we do not find that her Kings were anointed till the end of the sixth Century: for tho' this Monarchy has been formerly divided into fourteen Kingdoms, who had each their particular Kings and Princes, not united till the Reign of *Ferdinand* V. King of *Arragon*, in the Year 1474, yet the first King of *Spain*, whom we find to have been anointed, is *Vamba*, King of *Toledo*, who, after a magnificent Entry into that City, was there anointed by *Quiriac*, then Archbishop of it, in the Church of St. *Peter* and St. *Paul*, in the Year 673.

The Oath he took between the Hands of the Archbishop, was to keep the Laws of the Realm, and to have a great care of the People, after which the Nobles paid Homage to him, and swore Fealty to him as their Sovereign. and *Vamba*, in favour of his Anointing, declared *Toledo* to have the Primacy of both *Spains*.

Since that time, all the Kings of *Spain* have been anointed when they came to the Throne, or as soon as possible after it: and the Ceremony has been done almost always at *Toledo*, and sometimes in the Church of St. *Jerom* at *Madrid*, since the Catholick Kings have resided there.

But it is not very pompous: The Coronation Robes are white, furr'd with Ermines; the Royal Ornaments are the Sword, the Crown of Gold set with Jewels, the Scepter, and the Apple of Gold.

When

When the King has been anointed by the Archbiſhop of *Toledo*, or any Prelate appointed for it, he clothes himſelf in his Royal Ornaments, with the Crown on his Head, the Scepter in his Right, and the Apple in his Left Hand: and thus is elevated and ſhown to the People, almoſt after the old *Gauliſh* Manner. After which, the Archbiſhop and other Prelates conduct him to a Throne in the Church, where he is ſurrounded by the Princes, the Knights of his Orders (*a*), and all his Nobles, in their Robes of State: each in his proper Rank.

When the King is enthroned, the Archbiſhop begins *Te Deum*; then he celebrates the Maſs, and after the Offerings, he deſcends from his Throne, and goes in Proceſſion to the Altar, where he receives the Body of our Lord; Largeſſes are made to the People, and the King returns in Cavalcade to the Palace, where a Royal Feaſt is prepared. When there is a Queen, ſhe is ordinarily crown'd and anointed with the King.

Formerly this Crown was Elective, and the Royal Iſſue could not ſucceed to it, without the Suffrages and unanimous Conſent of the Prelates, Nobles, and People, lawfully aſſembled in a full Body of the States: but as the Number of Pretenders to it grew very conſiderable, and each form'd his Party; to avoid the Frequency and

(*a*) There are three Orders of Knighthood in *Spain*, which are Military, and very antient, of *St James*, called the Noble, of *Callatrava*, the Gallant of *Alcantara*, the Rich To which ſome add that of the Golden Fleece, which has no Commandery, and is only a Title of Honour.

Danger

Danger of Divisions, it was made a fundamental Law; that, while there was Royal Issue surviving, the People should not chuse a King; and that the Crown should be Hereditary and Successive, from Father to Son. So that from King *Pelagius*, who reign'd about the end of the eighth Century, the eldest Sons of the Kings succeeded to the Throne, unless this Disposition has been alter'd and interrupted by Violence, Oppression or Tyranny (*b*.)

At first, the Name of *Infantes* was given to the eldest Sons of the Kings of *Spain*; but in 1388, on occasion of the Marriage of the *Infante*, Don *Henriquez*, eldest Son of *Henry* III. with the Princess *Catharine* of *England*, the *Asturia's* were erected into a Principality, with the perpetual Title of Heir Presumptive of the Crown of *Castille* annexed to it. (*c*) Don *Henriquez*, first Prince of the *Asturia's*, was proclaim'd King, under the Name of *Henry* III. He had a Son, named *John*, who was proclaim'd Prince of the *Asturia's* in 1405, and recognized King, after the Death of his Father, under the Name of *John* II. This Prince at first having only Daughters by his Spouse, Donna *Maria*, Infante of *Arragon*, declared the eldest, Princess of the *Asturia's*, to succeed him in the Crown of *Spain*. The

(*b*) *See* Molina, Covarruvias, Camille, Borel.

(*c*) In imitation of the *English*, who call the eldest Son of the King of *England*, Prince of *Wales*, since the Year 1256; and of the *French*, who call the eldest Sons of *France* DAUPHINS, since the Reign of *Philip* of *Valois*, when *Dauphine* was united to the Crown of *France*, about the Year 1347.

Cere-

Ceremony was perform'd in the Church of *Toledo*, in *January*, 1423. But he dying, in the following Year, the youngeſt was declared Infante in the Metropolitan Church of *Burgos*: and the Queen, her Mother, having a Son call'd Don *Henriquez*, that Prince was proclaimed Prince of the *Aſturia's* in 1427; and by his Proclamation, the Title of Princeſs, which had been given to his Siſter, became extinct; and ſhe reaſſumed that of Infante, which ſhe bore before. In 1432, he was proclaim'd the ſecond time, and from that time it became a Cuſtom, with regard to all the Firſt-born Princes and Princeſſes of the Royal Houſe of *Spain*; and Don *Louis*, Son of *Philip* V. the preſent King, and of Donna *Maria Louiſa Gabriella* of *Savoy*, was proclaimed Prince of *Aſturia's* in the Church of St. *Jerom* at *Madrid*, in *February* 1710, in the Aſſembly of the States-General, conven'd for that purpoſe; conſiſting of the Prelates, of the Nobles, the Titulado's of *Caſtille*, of the ſeveral Cortes, and Procuradors of the Cities, who all had a place at this Ceremony. It was diſcharged with greater Magnificence than, to that time, was ever known.

But this Proclamation of Prince of the *Aſturia's* does not give any Rights to him, but what he has by his Birth, and that of being call'd the Prince deſign'd for the Crown of *Spain*; for he can neither do nor enterprize any thing during the Life of his Father, (*d*) without his Permiſſion.

(*d*) *See* Les Chroniques Generales d'Eſpagne, *printed in* 1534 and 1586. Les Memoirs Curieux, *ſent from* Madrid, *con-*

SECTION IV.

Of the Anointing and Coronation of the Kings of England.

THE *English*, or Antient *Britons*, whose Religion before the Birth of Christ was the same with that of the *Gauls*, pretend they receiv'd the Faith from the first Century, and that *Lucius*, having desired some Missionaries of Pope *Eleutherius*, to instruct his Subjects in the Truths of the Gospel, he was baptiz'd, with many of his *Britons*, about the Year 156. Yet the most antient Writers of the *English* Story do not mention any Kings to have been anointed before *Ergar*, or *Edgar*; who receiv'd the holy Unction from Archbishop *Eudo*, about the Year 959 (*e*.) From this time, the Kings of *England* have been anointed in a manner nearly resembling that of *France*. The Anointing of *John Sans-Terre*, was celebrated in the City of *London*, in the Year 1195, by the Archbishop of *Canterbury*, who claims the single Right of Anointing and Crowning the Kings of *England*.

concerning the Manners, Maxims, Ceremonies, and Country of Spain, *printed at* Paris *in* 1670 *and the* Journal Historique de Verdun, *for the Month of* May, 1710.

(*e*) Edgar, call'd *The Peaceable*, the Darling of the *English*, Son of *Edmund*, was King of a part of *England*, and after of the whole Isle, by the Death of his Brother *Edwin*, in 959. After he had subdued the *Scots*, imposed an annual Tribute of a Number of Wolves Heads on the Province of *Wales*, to clear the Country of those Creatures, and reduced a part of *Ireland*, he set himself to polish his Subjects, and reform the Manners of the Church, at the Persuasion, and by the Assistance of Pope *John* XII and of St *Dunstan*. He died, after a Reign of Sixteen Years, over all *England*, on the first of *July*, in 975. *See* Osbert's Vie de St. Dunstan, *and* Du Chesne's Histoire d'Angleterre.

JAMES

JAMES I. was anointed, with *Anne* his Queen, Daughter of the King of *Denmark*, *July* the 24th, 1607, at *Westminster*, near *London*. He had been already crown'd King of *Scotland*, at two Years old; and as King of *England*, he was anointed on the Head, the Forehead, between the Shoulders, on the Arms, the Hands, the Feet, and the Queen only upon the Head and Neck (*f*)

The Coronation of Q. *Anne*, Consort of Prince *George* of *Denmark*, was more magnificent than any in *England* till that time.

This Princess was anointed and crown'd Queen of *Great Britain* and *Ireland*, on St. *George*'s Day, the Patron of *England*, in *Westminster-Abbey*, by the Archbishop of *Canterbury*, in the Year 1702.

On the Coronation-Day, the Queen left the Palace at *St. James's* early in the Morning, and went thro the Park to the Abbey, with Kettle-Drums beating, and Trumpets and other Instruments playing.

The Baronesses of *England* began the Procession, the Viscountesses came after, follow'd by the Countesses, Marchionesses, and Dutchesses, all in Train, one after another; habited after the *Roman* Manner, in Robes and long Mantles, fasten'd on the Shoulders with Diamond Buckles.

All these Ladies were dress'd with a great Number of Jewels, and each bore in her Hand a Coronet, set with Pearls and Diamonds, larger or smaller, according to their Rank and Quality (*g*).

(*f*) See *Tho Smith*, Of the Government of *England*; translated from *English* into *Latin* by *J. Bulnæus*.

(*g*) The Court was then at *St. James's*, *Whitehall* having been burnt many Years before.

After this numerous and shining Court, walking two and two; came the Barons, Viscounts, Earls, Marquisses, and Dukes; dress'd likewise in the antient Manner, each bearing in his Hand a Coronet: two Lords, one representing the Duke of *Normandy*, the other the Duke of *Aquitain* (*h*), clos'd the Train (*i*). Pr. *George* of *Denmark*, her Majesty's Spouse, went single, just before her.

The Queen was in her Royal Robes, and three young Ladies of the first Rank in the Kingdom bore her Train, in this Majestick Figure she enter'd the Church, and placed herself in the Choir, beneath a Pavilion, erected for that purpose. The Sermon was preach'd by the Archbishop of *York*, from these Words, *Kings shall be thy Nursing Fathers, and Queens thy Nursing Mothers*. Then she receiv'd the Communion, and took the accustom'd Oath (*k*), after which, she was anointed by the Archbishop of *Canterbury*, and crown'd Queen of *Great Britain*, *France*, and *Ireland* (*l*).

(*h*) It is only in *France* and *England*, among Christian Princes, that the Presence of Peers at a Coronation is spoken of, *England* has adopted these Dignities, on the Score of her Pretensions to *France*.

(*i*) They had Caps cover'd with Golden Tissue, in imitation of Straw, because they, whom they represented, had the same.

(*k*) This Oath is to defend the Church, according to the Form establish'd by *Edward* VI to render Justice, and maintain the Laws of the Kingdom. *See* Davity's Description Generale de l'Europe

(*l*) N. B *Here the Author, who is a* Roman-Catholick, *has this Note.*

The Mass is not mention'd in this Coronation, because *England*, which had preserv'd the *Roman* Religion for many Ages, had separated from it, and given Entrance to Heresy under *Henry* VIII. in 1514. In 1557, the *Roman*

Then the Church resounded with the Acclamations of the People, who express'd their Joy by loud Huzza's. The Queen departed with the Imperial Crown upon her Head, with the Globe in one Hand, and the Scepter in the other. The Ladies, that went before, wore their Coronets. The Queen was seated in the Chair of St. *Edward* (*m*), after which she was conducted into *Westminster-Hall*, where the Coronation-Feast was to be celebrated (*n*).

During the Feast, the Champion appeared on horseback, according to Custom, armed Cap-a-pee, and throwing one of his Gauntlets upon the Ground, he made this Challenge *If any one pretends that* Anne Stuart *is not lawful Queen of* Britain, *let him take up this Gauntlet, and he shall find me ready to answer him.*

No Person accepting the Challenge, the Champion makes several Rounds and Flourishes with his Horse (*o*), and the Queen drinks his Health in a Golden Cup (*p*), which she presents to him afterwards, and drinking

man Service was let fall in *England*; and *Elizabeth*, succeeding her Sister *Mary* in the Throne, entirely abolish'd the Mass in 1558.

(*m*) Call'd, *The Aged*, King of *England*, who ascended the Throne in 900, and died, after a glorious Reign, in the Year 924.

(*n*) They who relate this Ceremony, tell us, that it was Seven in the Evening when the Queen sat down to Table. *See* Les Memoires du Temps, *printed in* Holland, *in* 1721.

(*o*) If he does it without falling, the *English* take it for a very good Omen, for if the Champion be dismounted, or Horse makes a Trip, they reckon it an ill Presage to that Reign.

(*p*) Half full of Wine.

it

it off, takes it as his Perquisite. After Dinner the Queen went to take her Seat in Parliament, and then returned to *St. James's* in the same Order she went thither.

Queen *Anne*, after a Reign of 12 Years, died on the 12th of *August*, 1714. without leaving any Issue, the Nobles and People of *England*, with one common Consent, agreed to invite over and to proclaim the Prince *George*, Elector of *Brunswick-Lunenbourg*. This was done five hours after the Death of the Queen, and Prince *George Lewis* I. Elector (*q*) of *Hannover*, at present on the Throne, was anointed and crowned King of *Great Britain*, *France*, and *Ireland*, at *Westminster-Abbey*, by the Archbishop of *Canterbury*, *Oct.* 31. 1714. with great Pomp, and the same Ceremonies that were observed at the last Coronation, except that the Train consisted only of Lords, and the Ladies were only Spectators. The Sermon was preach'd by the Bishop of *Oxford*; his Text was, *Psalm* 118. 24. *This is the Day which the Lord hath made, we will rejoice and be glad in it.*

(*q*) The Right of King GEORGE to the Crown of *Great Britain*, is not only from Blood, as Son of the Princess *Sophia*, Grand-daughter of *James* I. who succeeded Queen *Elizabeth*, but a solemn Act, by which, during the Life of King *William*, he was declared sole and only Heir of the Crowns of *Great Britain*, and lawful Successor of Queen *Anne*, if she died without leaving Issue, as it happen'd.

The *Historical Journals* say, that this Prince, before he was crown'd, caused his Son and his eldest Daughter to be declared Prince and Princess of *Wales*, *Octob.* 3 1714. and that the Crown which he wore at his Coronation, made for that purpose, cost a Million, and the Coronet of the Prince of *Wales*, his Son, was almost of the same Value.

SEC-

SECT. V.

Of the Anointing and Coronation of the Kings of Portugal.

AFTER *Henry* of *Burgundy* had conquer'd (*a*) *Portugal* from the *Moors*, and driven the Infidels out of that Kingdom, and by his Marriage with *Teresa*, Daughter of *Alphonso* VI. King of *Castile*, came to the peaceful Possession of this Realm, and *Alphonso* I. call'd *Henriquez*, his Son, was Crown'd King of *Portugal*, after a Defeat of Five Petty Kings, or Generals, of the *Moors*, at *Ourique*, on the *Tayo*, *July* the 17th, 1139.

(*a*) A Kingdom of *Europe*, It is Hereditary, and tho' it is no more than about 110 *French* Leagues in Length, and about 50 in Breadth, yet it is one of the most Considerable, for its Fertility and Opulence: It is wash'd by the *Tayo*, and three other Great Rivers, that discharge themselves into the Sea. It is surrounded with *Spain*, Its Commerce to the *East-Indies* is very great and advantagious to the People. It is so populous, that they compute in it above 600 Towns, and 4000 Parishes The Eldest Son of the King, bears the Title of Prince of *Brazil*

See Antonio de Souza, de l'Excellence de Portugal Gaspard d'Estaro, des Antiquitez de Portugal. Abrege de l'Histoire de Portugal, by the Sieur Mangin, Printed in 1707

Only the Catholick Religion is receiv'd in the Kingdom of *Portugal*; Her Kings are Anointed and Crown'd in the same Manner as the Kings of *Spain*; and they take at their Coronation, the Orders of Knighthood of *Christ*, of *Avis*, and of St. *James*, of which they are Grand-Masters born.

SECT. VI.

Of the Anointing and Coronation of the Kings of Denmark.

THE (a) Kingdom of *Denmark* was Elective, 'till the Year 1660, but from that Time, the Nobility have lost their

(a) *Denmark* is a Kingdom of *Europe*, bounded by the Ocean on the West and North, the *Baltic* on the East, and *Germany* on the South. It is the Country of the Antient *Cimbri* The *Danes* were formerly very powerful, and made several Descents in *England* and *Scotland* At present, it is 80 or 90 Leagues from South to North; and 45 or 50 from East to West. The King is likewise Sovereign of *Norway*, *Groenland*, the Isles of *Island* and *Fero*, of *New Denmark* in *America*, and of some Places in *Guinea*. He also takes the Titles of Count of *Oldemburg*, of *Delmenhore*, &c. *See the* Tractatus Varij de Regno Daniæ & Norwegiæ, Lug. Batav 1629. & Les Memoires de M. Molesworth, Envoy from *England* to *Denmark*, on the State of it, 1692. Done from the *English* in 1694.

their Antient Privileges, and the Kingdom is Hereditary.

Since the Year 930, when *Harold*, or *Herold* I. of the Name, was converted to Christianity, the Kings of *Denmark* have been Anointed at their Coronation, like the other Christian Kings of *Europe*, with Ceremonies very much resembling those of their Neighbours; that is, the *Swedes* and *Germans*.

SECT. VII.

Of the Anointing and Coronation of the Kings of Sweden.

THE Kingdom of *Sweden* was formerly Elective, tho' the Preference given by the Senators to the Issue of their Kings, seems to have made it at last Hereditary. In important Affairs, the King assembled the States, which are compos'd of the Nobility, the Clergy, the Men of Trade, and the Peasants; but since the King was invested with an Absolute Authority in 1680, he is not oblig'd to convene the States, unless he pleases: so that this Kingdom is Monarchical, and so far Hereditary, that the Children of the King, Male or Female, succeed to the Crown, even during their Minority. In which Case, the Five first

(a) Officers of the Kingdom, call'd *The Five Great Lords*, are Tutors and Guardians to the King or Queen while a Minor, and govern the Kingdom in that Time.

Charlemagne, in the Eighth Century, sent *Herbert* to preach the Christian Faith in *Sweden*, who founded there the Church of *Lincopinc*. And under the Empire of *Louis the Debonnair*, St. *Aucbertus*, a *Frenchman* by Birth, a Religious, and afterwards Bishop of *Corby*, preach'd the Gospel in that Kingdom, and founded there the Church of *Birke* in 829 So that from this Time, the Commerce of the *Swedes* with the other Christian Countries, has introduc'd the same Ceremonies of Anointing at a Coronation, that are practis'd in those Places.

The first *Swedish* King that we find was Anointed at his Coronation, was *Eric* VIII. who ascended the Throne, in 980. From that Time, immediately after the Decease of the last King, he who has the Right to succeed, appoints a Day for the Coronation, assembles the Nobility, and

---

(a) *Sweden* is a Northern Kingdom of *Europe*, bounded to the West by *Denmark* and *Norway*, to the North by *Lapland*, to the East by *Finland* and *Muscovy*, and to the South by the *Baltick* The Five Great Officers of the Crown, are, The Grand Justiciary, the President of the Council of War, of the Admiralty, of the Chancery, of the Exchequer, and of the Council of Commerce.

the Principal Officers, and goes in Pomp to the Church of *Upsal*, Seven Leagues distant from *Stockholm*, the Capital of *Sweden*, to be there Anointed and Crown'd by the Archbishop of that Church, who claims that Right from all Antiquity, as being the Successor of one of the first Apostles of this Nation.

The King then takes the Oath, To preserve the Peace of the Kingdom, to render Justice to his Subjects, and maintain their Privileges, General and Particular. Then he falls upon his Knees, and demands the Benediction of the Prelates, who assist at that Ceremony, and prays to God, for Grace to improve in Virtue, and to vanquish and surmount the Enemies of the Faith. This done, he is array'd in the Royal Robes, and Anointed by the Archbishop of *Upsal*, who girds him with the Sword, puts the Crown upon his Head, and the Scepter into his Hand, then, accompany'd by the chief Lords of the Kingdom, he conducts him to a lofty Throne, to be view'd by the People, and says to him, *Stand, and keep the Place appointed for thee by God.* The whole Ceremony is carry'd on with Prayers, not much unlike those of our Coronation.

By (*a*) the Treaty of Peace between *Frederick* I. of *Hesse-Cassel*, King of *Sweden*, and *Peter* I. Emperor of all *Russia*, otherwise call'd Czar of *Muscovy*, sign'd at *Neustad* in *Finland*, *August* the 10th and *September* the 30th, 1721. it is agreed, That the King of *Sweden*, and his Successors, shall not for the future, take any other Title, but that of King of *Sweden*, the *Goths* and *Vandals*.

SECT. VIII.

Of the Anointing and Coronation of the Kings of Poland.

POLAND, whose Government is at present Monarchical, because it owns a King; and Aristocratical, (*b*) because the King cannot by his own Authority,

(*a*) *See* Le Discours de l'Etat & Couronne de Suede, *&c.* containing an Abridgment of the History of the Kings of *Sweden*, Printed at *Paris* in 1633; and the present State of *Sweden*, with an Abridgment of the History of it, done from the *English*, and Printed in *Holland*, in 1695, & le Jour Hist de Verd. for *May* 1722

(*b*) *Poland*, is an Elective Kingdom of *Europe*; it comprehends the Antient *Sarmatia Germanica*, and the Eastern Part of *Germany*, towards the *Vistula*.

with-

without the Consent of the Senators, direct the Affairs of the State; has been long govern'd by Dukes and Palatines, of whom *Miscelaus*, or *Mesko*, is the first who embrac'd the Christian Religion: He was baptiz'd by the Archbishop, and in the City of *Gnezna*, in the Year 964. His Son *Boleslaus*, succeeded him in 999, and the Emperor (*b*) *Otho* gave him the Title of King about the Year 1001, conducted him to the Church, conven'd the Bishops, and caus'd him to be Consecrated and Anointed King of *Poland*, by the Archbishop of *Gnezna*, who has kept the Privilege of Crowning the Kings of *Poland*. After his Unction, the Emperor himself install'd him in the Royal Seat, put the Crown upon his Head, and set him free from his Obedience, and Subjection to himself and all his Successors in the Empire. But *Boleslaus* II. surnamed *The Cruel*, Son of *Casimir* I. having put to death St. *Stanislaus*, Bishop of *Cracow*, *Poland*, by way of Punishment for his Crime, forfeited the Title of a Kingdom, and was reduc'd to a Principality, which was given to *Uladislaus*, in the Year 1082.

(*b*) To make him an Acknowledgment for his Magnificent Reception of him, when he went to the Church of *Gnezna*, to visit the Tomb of St. *Aldebert*, who was kill'd by the *Prussians*.

It did not recover the Name of a Kingdom, 'till *Primislaus* II. who was chosen by the Nobility, and was anointed and crown'd in the Church of *Gnezna*, towards the Year 1295. He was succeeded by *Ladislaus* II. call'd *The Small*; who, to maintain this Dignity of a King, sent Ambassadors to the Pope, who ordain'd, That he should be solemnly anointed in the Church of *Cracow*, in the Year 1320.

It is on the Score of this Recovery of the Kingdom, that the Church of *Cracow* has had the Privilege to be the Place where the Kings of *Poland* are anointed and crown'd. But the Archbishop of *Gnezna* still performs the Ceremony, because he baptiz'd the first Christian King.

(c) From this Time, on the Death of the

(c) Tho' the Children of the King of *Poland* have no Right to the Crown, yet commonly one of them is Elected. They pay the same Regard to the Daughters, as it happen'd after the Death of *Louis* King of *Poland* and of *Hungary*, in 1382; who left two Daughters, one marry'd to *Sigismund* Marquis of *Brandenburg*, the other call'd *Hedwig*, who was chosen Queen, and marry'd to *Jagello* Duke of *Lithuania*, who became a Christian to espouse Her, and be King of *Poland*. The Widows of the Kings are also favour'd. Thus *John Casimir* was elected, on a Condition of marrying the Queen *Maria Louisa*, Relict of *Vladislaus* IV. But these Rules have not been without Exception. For, after the Death of *John Sobieski*, the Princes his Sons have been excluded from the Crown.

King,

King, that Archbishop, who is Primate born and Great Chancellor of the Kingdom, which he governs in an *Interregnum*, has the Right to assemble the Nobility for the Election or Nomination of a New King.

This Diet or Assembly, is held in a large Plain, half a League from *Warsaw*, under a Great cover'd Hall, surrounded with a Ditch, and open at three Gates, which are built at the Expence of the Republic.

At the Opening of the Diet, they celebrate the Mass of the Holy Ghost, in the Church of St. *John* at *Warsaw*, after which the Senate and Nobility go to *Szopa*, where the Nobility immediately chuse the Marshal of the Agents, or Deputies of the Lesser Diets; Then Audience is given to the Ambassadors of all the Princes pretending to the Crown, or recommending a Candidate. It is on this Account that the Pope sends his Nuntio to the Diet, to represent to the Republic, the Interest which the Church has in their Electing a Catholic King. Then the Diet retires, in good Order, to the Place assign'd for the Assembly, and there proceed to the Choice of a King.

Assoon as he is chosen, before he is proclaim'd, they make him take an Oath, call'd by the *Poles*, the *Pacta Conventa*, to keep the Capitulation, so call'd, inviolably, which is then made with the New elected

King,

King, the Senate, and the Nobles. The Principal Articles of it, are,

I. That the King ſhall not appoint any Perſon to be his Succeſſor.

II. That he ſhall leave to the Republic the Right of Coining Money.

III. That he ſhall not declare War againſt any Prince, without the Conſent of the Republic.

IV. That he ſhall have no Foreigners in his Council, of whatſoever Rank they may be; nor ſhall give them any Offices, Dignities, or Governments of Places.

V. That he ſhall not marry without the Conſent of the Senate.

VI. That he ſhall have no Royal Furniture or Proviſion for his Table, than what the Republick has regulated, for the Kings his Predeceſſors.

VII. That he with his Council, ſhall ſettle the Forces, Horſe and Foot, ſo that the Republic ſhall have no Occaſion for Foreign Troops; and that all Naval Force ſhall be rais'd with the Conſent of the Nobility and the Senate.

VIII. That he ſhall by no means diminiſh the Treaſury at *Cracow*, but augment it, as much as poſſible.

IX. That he ſhall borrow no Money, but by the Conſent of the Republic.

To

To these ordinary Conventions, others are sometimes added, according to the Necessity of the Time and the Quality of the King Elected

After this Election, the King makes his Entry into the Capital City of *Poland*, which is *Warsaw*; where he is receiv'd under a Canopy, born up by Senators, with great Magnificence, to the Sound of Trumpets, and other Musical Instruments; and with a Discharge of all the Artillery. Ordinarily two Days after this Entry, he is Anointed and Consecrated King in the Church of *Cracow*, by the Archbishop of *Gnezna*; who Anoints him on the Head, and between the Shoulders, sets the Crown upon his Head, and gives him the Sword, the Globe, and Scepter; with Prayers and Ceremonies much like to those of our Nation (*a*).

Yet *Stanislaus* I. was Anointed and Crown'd in the Church of St. *John* at *Warsaw*, *October* 4, 1705. on Account of the Troubles then in *Poland*, and the Party

(*a*) See Mart Cromeri, Polonia, sive, De Situ, Populis, Moribus, &c. & la Relat Hist de le Pol Pouvoir de ses Rois, leur Elect Couron. &c By the Sieur *Hauteville*, Printed at *Paris* in 1686. Histoire de la Sciffion ou Division arrivee in Pol. in 1697 By Mons de la *Rizardiere*, Printed in 1699; & Les Mem de Pol de Suede, & de Saxe; Printed at *Paris*, in 1705, and 1706.

of

of King *Augustus*, Elector of *Saxony*, who was dispossess'd of his Throne in 1704.

SECT. IX.

Of the Anointing and Coronation of the Kings or Emperors of Muscovy.

THE *Muscovites* boast of having receiv'd the Christian Religion by the Ministry of the Apostle St. *Andrew*; yet we do not find, that they renounc'd Paganism till the End of the Ninth Century; (*a*) and *Wolodimir* is the first Great Duke, Prince, or King of this Country, who was

(*a*) *Muscovy* is a large Country of *Europe*, call'd also *Russia*, on the North, it reaches to the Frozen or Northern Ocean, on the East it is divided from *Great Tartary* by the Rivers *Oby*, *Tanais*, &c. On the South it has the *Lesser Tanais*, and the Lesser *Tartary*; and on the West, the *Narva*, *Poland*, *Sweden*, and *Norway*. Its Length from North to South, is above 6 or 700 Leagues, and its Breadth from West to East, is almost the same. So that it is one of the most spacious Dominions in *Europe*. The Czar of *Muscovy*, call'd *Pe*-[illegible] I. Emperor of all *Russia*, at present Reigning, has, since the Year 1696, when he came to the Throne, very much taken off the Wildness of his People, he applies himself to increase the Commerce and Navigation of *Muscovy*, he has made the Tour of *France*, and of all *Europe*, to instruct himself in what may render his Kingdom Powerful and Formidable

converted

converted to the Catholick Faith. He took the Name of *Basil* at his Baptism, in the Year 988, *Wolodomir* is the first Soveieign of *Muscovy*, who took the Title of *Czar*, which signifies King or Emperor; which *Peter* I. *Czar* of *Muscovy*, at present reigning, has inlarg'd with the Title of Emperor of all *Russia*, according to his Treaty with the King of *Sweden* at *Neustad* in *Finland*, in *August* and *September*, 1721. Thus, since *Basilius*, the *Czars* have been Anointed and Crown'd like the other Christian Kings.

The Ceremony is perform'd in the Church of our Lady at *Moscow*, which is the Capital of the Country, by the Primate or Metropolitan, who takes the Quality of Patriarch, and is acknowledg'd Head of the *Muscovite* Church, as the Pope is of the *Roman*, and is not less Absolute in the Spiritual, than the *Czar* is in the Temporal Authority.

(*a*) On the Day of the Coronation, the Streets and Ways thro' which the *Czar* is to

---

(*a*) The Primate of *Muscovy* holds himself to be Independent of the Church of *Rome*, and will have no Correspondence with it; having the same Aversion for the *Latins* that they have for the *Jews* The *Muscovites*, in Religion, follow the *Greek* Ceremonies, communicate in both Kinds, and give the Holy Sacrament to Infants, at the Age of Seven Years. They have Confession

to paſs from his Palace to the Church, are cover'd with Scarlet, Cloth of Gold, and other Rich Tapeſtries, on which he walks, attended by his whole Court, to the Place of his Coronation, which is the Church of our Lady at *Moſcow*, where he is waited for by the Patriarch, and all his Clergy. Then Maſs is ſung; during which, the Primate Anoints the *Czar*; who afterwards takes the Crown, the Scepter, and the Imperial Globe, (or Apple) which are deliver'd to him by the Patriarch, with Prayers and Ceremonies almoſt like ours, or thoſe of *Sweden*. Then the Patriarch communicates the Emperor in both Kinds. After which, his *Czariſh* Majeſty, in his Robes of State, departs from this Church to go to *Archangel*, (another Church, where the *Ruſſian* Monarchs are bury'd) to pray for the Kings deceas'd, his Predeceſſors (*b*).

Along

Confeſſion, Faſts, and Times of Abſtinence very rigorous Of all Feaſts of the Year, they only obſerve that of the Annunciation, and that of St. *Nicholas*, their Patron, their Prieſts do not ſay Maſs out of Churches conſecrated by their Biſhops, and all the *Muſcovites* ſay daily the Horologe, that is, the Canonical Hours. *See* the Treatiſe of *F Poſſevin* de Rebus Moſcoviticis

(*b*) The firſt Kings of *France*, and many of the Third Race, went to the Church of St *Denys*, after their Coronation, to pray at the Tombs of the Martyrs,

Along the way he makes a Largeſs to the People of ſmall Pieces of Gold, ſtruck for that purpoſe. Then, amidſt the Acclamations of his People, he returns to his Palace, where he has a Royal Feaſt, and an Open Table, for all that aſſiſted or were preſent at the Ceremony.

CHAP. XV.

Of the Coronation of the Dukes and Sovereign Princes of Europe.

AS the ſole Title of Sovereign Prince makes thoſe who carry it equal in Authority and Power (with regard to their Subjects) to Kings in their Dominions; ſo, the Ceremony of their Coronations has often come near to that of our Kings, excepting the Sacred Unction, which is only given to Emperors and Monarchs. Thus the Dukes of *Savoy*, of *Lorrain*, of *Brabant*, and others, receive, in the Principal Churches of the Capital

---

tyrs, and beg the Divine Protection to their Reign, by their Interceſſions *See* La Relation Nouvelle de Muſcovie, by Monſ de la *Neuville*, Printed at Paris in 1698; and le Journ. de Verd. for *May* 1722.

Towns

Towns of their Dominions, by the Hands of Bishops and Prelates appointed for it, the Crowns, the Orders of Knighthood, the Swords, and Marks of their Sovereignty, take the accustom'd Oaths, and receive that of their Subjects; with Ceremonies almost like those of the Princes of *Italy*, except the Dukes of *Savoy*, who, since *Amadeus* VIII. (in Favour of whom the County of *Savoy* has been erected into a Dutchy, by the Emperor *Sigismund*, in 1416) do not receive, as formerly, from the Archbishop of *Turin*, or any other Prelate, the Ring of St. *Maurice*, which is the Mark and Symbol of the Investiture of that Dutchy; but take it themselves from the Altar, and put it on their Finger, after having receiv'd the Ducal Crown, and other Ornaments of their Sovereignty (*a*).

(*a*) *See* Guichenon, sur l'Hist de Savoy, La Chron. de Sav by *Pradin* Du Chêne, Hist de Bourgogne. Abreg de l'Hist de Sav by *Thom le Blanc*. Hist de Bar, de Du Chêne Godefr & Sainte Marthe, de l'Orig. de la Mais de Lor

CHAP.

CHAP. XVI.

Of the Anointing and Coronation of the Queens of France.

THE Salique Law excludes Women from the Succession to the Crown, and absolute Government; so that tho' the Widows of Kings have been already Queens, yet they cannot ascend the Throne to govern solely and in their own Name. But they may have the Regency of the Kingdom during the Minority of the Kings their Sons; it being granted to them, in this case, as a Guardianship.

Tho' the Queens of *France*, according to the Fundamental Law of the Kingdom, are not rais'd to the Throne, by way of Government, but only as lawful Consorts of our Kings, yet as they do, in some measure, shew the Excellency and Greatness of Majesty which belong to them in Point of Honour as the Wives and Mothers of Kings, it is just to distinguish them above all other Princesses, not only by outward Appearances, but by the Invisible and Mysterious Gifts of the Holy Unction; which setting a publick Character upon them as Queens, puts them more particularly under the Protection of God, and makes them more awful to their Subjects, and more worthy of Society with the Sacred Person of the Kings their Spouses.

Hence, from all Antiquity, the Queens of *France* are publickly Anointed and Crown'd, with proper Solemnities and Ceremonies; not indeed with the Oyl of the Holy Vial, which is reserv'd for our Kings, but with the sacred Chrism (*a*).

Yet we do not find, that the Queens of the first Race of our Kings were Anointed; however, it is plain, that almost all of the Second and Third receiv'd the Unction with the Crown; to begin with *Bertha*, the Consort of *Pepin*, Founder of the Second Race. As we prove by the following Table.

(*a*) *Non in unctione*, &c. Not with the Unction sent from Heaven, but the plain sanctify'd Oyl; as we are told by the MS. Ritual of *Rheims*. See Aim l 5 Flod. in Chron. Mezeray. Favin. Marlot. Theat d'Hon.

CHAP.

CHAP. XVII.

A Chronological and Historical TABLE *of the Anointing and Coronation of the Queens of* France, *of the Second and Third Race.*

(*a*) *BERTHA*, Wife of King *Pepin*, was Anointed and (*b*) Crown'd in the Church of St. *Dennis* (*c*) by Pope *Stephen* III. with the King her Husband, and her

---

(*a*) She was the Daughter of *Charibert*, Count of *Laon*.

(*b*) This Ceremony was done in Time of Mass, which has ever since been observ'd. *See* the Annals of St *Bertin* of *Metz*.

(*c*) St *Dennis*, or *Denys*, a small Town, known thro all *Europe*, situate about two Leagues from *Paris*, in the Isle of *France* It is renown'd for its Great Church and Royal Abbey, whose Name it bears, which was founded upon the Sepulchre of St *Denys*, the Apostle of this Kingdom, and of his Companions, *Rusticus*, and *Eleutherus*, the first Martyrs of *France*. They say, That the first Chapel built here by *Catula*, a Pious Lady, being ruin'd, *Dagobert* I at the Instance of St. *Genevieve*, erected a Church in that Place in 630, to the Honour of St *Denys*, and his Companions, which he adorn'd with the finest Work of that Time, covering with Silver Plates the Part that was over the Holy Bodies He founded there a Rich Abbey, where he ordinarily resided, and held his

 Audiences,

her Two Sons *Charles* and *Carloman*, in *August* 754. *Hermengarde*, Daughter of *H[illegible]*, of the House of *Saxony*, first Wife of *Louis* I. call'd *The Debonnair*, was Anointed and Consecrated at *Rheims*, with the King her Husband, by Pope *Stephen* V. in the Year 816. It is observ'd, That this Pope being come to *France*, purely to Crown *Louis* I. as Emperor of the West, (*a*) brought with him Two Crowns of Gold, one set with Jewels for the King, and the other plain for the Queen.

Judith, Daughter of *Welf*, Count of *Ravensberg*, Second Wife of *Louis* I. was Anointed and Crown'd on her Wedding-Day at *Frankfort*, in 819.

Audiences, and after gave his Apartments to the Religious, when he retir'd to his Palace of *Clichy*. But this Church being spoil'd by the Infidels, *Pepin* undertook to rebuild it more Magnificently, and it was not finish'd, till *Charlemagne*. Since *Dagobert*, our Kings have paid a particular Devotion to the Saints aforesaid, by adding to the Riches and Beauty of it. Many have been Crown'd there; and most of them are wont to go just after their Coronation, to pray for the Intercession of these Saints, in order to the Publick Welfare. They have also chosen it for their Burial-Place. The Queens of *France* have long been Crown'd there, and we may fairly say, That no Place contains more Things of Value, than what the Bounty of our Kings has put into the Treasury of this Church. *See* le Moines Vie de Dagob. & Mezeray Hist. de Fr. Tom. 1. l. 8.

(*a*) *Louis* had already been Crown'd as King of *Aquitain*, in 800.

Hermentrude,

Hermentrude, Wife of *Charles the Bald*, and Daughter of Prince *Vodon*, was Anointed at *Soissons* by *Hincmar* Archbishop of *Rheims*, in the Year 866 (*a*).

Frederune, the first Wife of *Charles the Simple*, was Anointed in the Church of St. *Remy*, by *Hervé* Archbishop of *Rheims* (*b*), *April* the 18th, 907.

Emmine, Wife of *Raoul*, was crown'd at *Rheims* by the Archbishop *Seulphe*, in 923.

Gerberge, Daughter of the Emperor *Otho*, Wife of *Louis d'Outremer* was anointed and crown'd at *Rheims* by the Archbishop *Artald*, on her Wedding-Day, in 942.

Constance, Daughter of *William* Count of *Arles*, and of *Blanche* of *Anjou*, Wife of King *Robert*, was anointed at *Orleans* by *Sevinius*, Archbishop of *Sens*, in the Year 990 (*c*).

After *Constance*, we do not find that *Mathilda*, and *Anne* of *Sclavonia*, the first and second Wives of *Henry* I. were anointed, no more than *Bertha* Daughter of *Florent* I. Count of *Holland*, Wife of *Philip* I *Alice* of *Savoy* Daughter of *Humbert* II.

(*a*) *See* Flodoard Hist Eccles Rem l. 1, 2, 3, & 4 Guill. Marlot Metrop Rem. Hist

(*b*) Melange Curieux du P Labbe

(*c*) Doublet Hist. de France.

Count of *Maurienne*, and Prince of *Piedmont*, Wife of *Louis le Gross*, It appears, that this Ceremony was interrupted under these Three Reigns, and did not revive till *Louis* VII. call'd *The Younger*, who had Three Wives, The first was call'd

Eleonor, Daughter of *William* Duke of *Guienn*, she was anointed and crown'd at *Bourdeaux*, with King *Louis* VII. her Husband, in *August* 1137. The second was call'd

Constance of *Arragon*, Daughter of *Alphonso* King of *Castille*, she was anointed and crown'd at *Orleans*, with King *Louis* VII. her Husband, by *Hugo* Archbishop of *Sens*, in 1152. And the third call'd

Adelle, or *Alice*, Daughter of *Theobald the Great*, Count of *Champagne*, was anointed and crown'd Queen of *France* by *William Theobald*, Archbishop of *Rheims*, her Brother, in 1158, in the Church of *Rheims*, with her Husband King *Louis* VII.

Elizabeth, or *Isabella*, Daughter of *Baldwin*, Count of *Hainault*, first Wife of *Philip the August*, was anointed and crown'd Queen at St. *Denys*, *May* the 29th 1180, by *Guy* Archbishop of *Sens*, with *Philip the August* her Husband, who had been already crown'd at *Rheims* in 1179

Blanche, Daughter of *Alphonso* VIII. King of *Castille*, Wife of *Louis* VIII. was anointed and crown'd, with the King her Husband,

band, in the Church of *Rheims*, *August* the 6th, 1223, by *William de Janville*, then Archbishop; the King of *Jerusalem* assisted at this Ceremony.

Margaret de Provence, eldest Daughter of *Raymond Beranger*, Wife of St. *Louis*, was anointed and crown'd Queen of *France*, in the Church of *Notre Dame* at *Paris*, by *Galserus* Archbishop of *Sens*, in the Year 1224.

Mary, Daughter of *John* Duke of *Brabant*, Wife of *Philip the Hardy*, whom he marry'd at the Castle of *Vincennes*, in *August* 1274, was anointed in the Year following, in the Holy Chapel at *Paris*, by *Pierre de Barbes*, Archbishop of *Rheims*, notwithstanding the Remonstrances and Opposition of the Archbishop of *Sens*, the Metropolitan; to which the King answer'd, *That the Holy Chapel was exempt from his Jurisdiction.*

Jane of *Navarre*, Wife of *Philip the Fair*, was anointed and crown'd at *Rheims* by the same Archbishop in *August* 1285.

Clemence, second Wife of *Louis le Hutin*, and Daughter of *Charles Martel*, King of *Hungary*, was anointed at *Rheims* by *Robert de Courtenay*, *August* the 13th, 1315.

Jane, Daughter of *Hue* Count of *Burgundy*, Wife of *Philip the Long*, after her Marriage at *Corbeil*, was anointed and crown'd at *Rheims*, by the Archbishop

Robert de Courtenay, in the Year 1316, with the King her Husband.

Jane of *Burgundy*, Daughter of *Robert* II. Spouſe of *Philip de Valois*, was anointed and crown'd, with the King her Husband, at *Rheims*, by *William de Trye*, her Uncle, Archbiſhop and Cardinal, *May* the 27th, 1328.

Jane of *Boulogne*, ſecond Wiſe of *John* I. and Daughter of *William* Count of *Boulogne*, and of *Margaret d'Evreux*, was anointed and crown'd at *Rheims*, with the King her Husband, by *Hue* Archbiſhop, *September* 26, 1350.

Jane of *Bourbon*, Daughter of the Duke of *Bourbon*, and Wife of *Charles* V. was anointed and crown'd at *Rheims* with her Husband, by Archbiſhop *Craon*, *May* the 19th, 1364.

Iſabelle of *Bavaria*, Wife of *Charles* VI. was married, anointed and crown'd at *Amiens*, by *Richard de Picque*, Archbiſhop of *Rheims*, *Auguſt* 12, 1389. From this Queen it is obſerv'd, that almoſt all the reſt have been anointed and crown'd at St. *Denys*, preferably to any other Church.

Anne of *Bretagne*, Daughter of *Francis*, Count *d'Etampes*, and laſt Duke of *Bretagne*, Wife of *Charles* VIII. was married, anointed and crown'd at St. *Dennis*, in the Year 1504 She gave her Golden Crown, inriched with Pearls, and adorned with

Nine

Nine Flowers-de-Lys, to this Church. They who have written upon this Coronation, say, That the Queen was dress'd in a Robe of White Sattin, that the officiating Prelate, who is not nam'd, put the Holy Chrism on her Breast, and between the Shoulders; that the Duke of *Orleans* supported her Crown on her Head, it being too large and weighty, that near the Queen was Madam *de Bourbon*, and other Ladies of the Court, and Princesses; who wore their Coronets, according to their Quality; that the Queen receiv'd the Body of our Lord at Mass, at which assisted above Twenty Archbishops and Bishops.

Claude of *France*, first Wife of *Francis* I. and Daughter of King *Louis* XII. was crown'd at St. *Denys* by Cardinal *du Mens*, otherwise call'd of *Luxembourg*, who anointed her on the Breast and Forehead, then gave her the Scepter, the Hand of Justice and the Ring.

Eleonor of *Austria*, Daughter of the Emperor *Charles* V. Second Wife of *Francis* I. was anointed and crown'd at St. *Denys*, *March* the 5th, in the Year 1531, by the Cardinal *de Bourbon*. The Pope's Legate, who was present at this August Assembly, gave the solemn Benediction, and full Absolution to those who assisted at this Coronation.

Catharine

Catharine de Medicis, Wife of *Henry* II. was anointed and crown'd at St. *Denys* on *Whitsunday*, by *Louis* Cardinal *de Bourbon*, in 1549 (*a*).

Mary Stuart, Queen of *Scotland*, Daughter of *James Stuart* V. King of *Scotland*, and of *Mary de Lorrain*, was married to *Francis* II. in the Church of *Notre-Dame* at *Paris*, where ſhe was likewiſe anointed and crown'd *April* the 24th, 1558.

Elizabeth of *Auſtria*, Wife of *Charles* IX. was married at *Mezieres*, and was anointed and crown'd at St. *Denys*, by *Charles* Cardinal of *Lorrain*, Archbiſhop of *Rheims*, in 1571.

Mary de Medicis, Daughter of *Francis de Medicis*, Great Duke of *Florence*, ſecond Wife of *Henry* IV. after having been married by his Proxy, the Duke *de Bellegard*, his Maſter of the Horſe, *October* 5, 1600, was again married to him in Perſon at *Lyons* (where the King met her *November* the 3d enſuing) by Cardinal *Aldobrandini*, who perform'd the Ceremony before at *Florence*; and this Princeſs Nine Years after was anointed and crown'd at St. *Denys* by the Cardinal *de Joyeuſe*, *May* the 11th, 1610, with the utmoſt Magnificence,

(*a*) Pope *Paul* III. gave Indulgences to thoſe who aſſiſted at this Coronation. *See* Doublet. Hiſt. Page 1344.

in

in Presence of the King (*a*), all the Princes, Princesses, Ladies, and Lords of the Court.

This Princess is the last Queen, that has been anointed to this Time (*b*).

CHAP. XVIII.

By (c) *whom, and where, the Queens of* France *are to be Anointed.*

AFTER the Observations made in the Table above, it is easy to prove, that tho' many Authors would insinuate, that the Right of Anointing and Crowning the Queens of *France*, as well as of Blessing

(*a*) Who assisted at this Ceremony in a Gallery made for him on the side of the High Altar.

(*b*) Queen *Anne* of *Austria*, eldest Daughter of *Philip* III. King of *Spain*, Wife of *Louis* XIII. and Queen *Maria-Teresa*, of *Austria*, the Infanta, Daughter of *Philip* IV King of *Spain*, Wife of *Louis* XIV. of Glorious Memory, not being anointed, as the others were; whether to avoid the Expence, or for other particular Reasons, Historians have not inform'd us

(*c*) *See* Ivo Carnot Epist. Aimoin. Favin Theat d'Hon. Flodoard, Marlot. Hist. de l'Egl. de Reims.

the Nuptial Bed, belongs from all Antiquity to the Archbiſhop of *Rheims*, like the Archbiſhop of *Mentz* in *Germany* and other Kingdoms, where the Prelate who anoints the Kings, does alſo crown and anoint the Queens, yet it is certain, that this Privilege does not of Right belong to him, nor to any other Biſhop, and that at preſent our Kings pitch upon any Prelate they pleaſe, for it, and it is done now in one Church, and then in another, ſometimes by the Popes, ſometimes by the Archbiſhop of *Rheims*, and ſometimes by Cardinals, or other Prelates, there having been neither Place nor Prelate particularly appointed for it, till the Coronation of *Iſabel*, Wife of *Charles* VI. Since whom, the Queens of *France*, have been Anointed and Crown'd at St. *Denys*, not only on account of the Nearneſs of it to the Capital City, and Reſidence of our Kings, but chiefly, for the Devotion which our Princes have for the Holy Martyrs the Protectors of *France*, whoſe Bodies are Interr'd in that Church; where it is probable, that our Kings would likewiſe be Anointed and Crown'd, if the Holy Vial, ſent from Heaven for their Coronation, had not been preſerv'd at *Rheims*.

CHAP.

CHAP. XIX.

Of the Ceremonies of the Anointing and Coronation of the Queens of France.

THESE have a great Reſemblance with thoſe of our Kings, and are almoſt as Antient.

Nothing is omitted to make the Entry and Reception of the Queen in the Town of St. *Denys*, ſtately and magnificent: The Preparation of the Church of the Abbey of that Name where the Ceremony is uſually done, is much the ſame with that at *Rheims*, for the King. The Church is lin'd with the richeſt Tapeſtries of the Crown; and the Choir is cover'd with Crimſon Velvet, powder'd with Flowers-de-Lys, in Golden Embroidery.

Over-againſt the High Altar, is rais'd a Theatre eight or nine Foot high, twenty eight long, and twenty two in breadth, with eight or ten Steps aſcending to it; and in the Middle of this Theatre is plac'd another leſſer, about a Foot high, for the Throne and Praying-deſk of the Queen, covered with purple Velvet, powder'd with

with Flowers de-Lys, in Golden Embroidery; over which is a Canopy of the ſame.

The Great Maſter of the Ceremonies orders likewiſe Theatres, Ranges of Seats, Galleries and Scaffolds, on the Right and Left, for the Princes, Prelates, Embaſſadors, Great Officers, Miniſters, Gentlemen, and others that are preſent.

He cauſes to be erected on the Right-ſide, near the Altar, a Gallery or Pew glaz'd, for the King; cover'd with Tapeſtry and purple Velvet, Embroider'd with Golden Flowers-de Lys.

On the Left ſide of the Altar, over-againſt the King's Gallery, is a long Bench, cover'd with Cloth of Gold, for the Cardinals; and another behind, for the Archbiſhops, and Biſhops, aſſiſting at the Coronation. Next to the Altar, on the ſame ſide, is a Table for the Great and Leſſer *(a)* Crown, the Scepter, the Hand of Juſtice, and the Ring, appointed for the Coronation of our Queens.

On the Right, at the Goſpel-ſide, is another Table, for the Offerings, to be deliver'd

(*a*) The Great Crown, is that of *Jane d'Evreux*, Wife of *Charles* IV It is of Gold, ſet with Rubies, Saphires, and large Oriental Pearls. The Leſſer is of Gold, or Vermillion, made for the Coronation of each Queen, lighter than the other, preſented afterwards by the Queens to the Treaſury of St *Denys*

liver'd to the Ladies, who are to present them; and before this Table is a Chair of Crimson Velvet, Embroider'd with Gold, and two Cushions of the same, for the Seat of the Prelate officiating.

The Queen is dress'd in a Silver Damask, or a white Sattin; over which is a long Royal Robe of blue Velvet, lin'd with Ermines, all over powder'd with Golden Flowers-de-Lys.

The Princesses of the Blood who attend Her, have on this Day no more than three or *(a)* four Flowers-de-Lys on their Robes; and the Dutchesses and Countesses have likewise Coronets on their Heads, such as belong to each of them.

Things being thus dispos'd, the Queen, who should be at St. *Denys*, on the Eve of her Coronation, is conducted in the Morning to the Church, by two Cardinals *(b)* or Archbishops, with all the Pomp and Retinue suitable to this great Ceremony. The hundred *Swiss*, the two hundred Gentlemen of the King's Houshold, Drums,

---

(a) Mary de Medicis, Wife of *Henry* IV was in a Bodice of Green Velvet, cover'd with Flowers-de-Lys of Gold-Wire; the Gown over it was of Ermines, set with precious Stones, and her Royal Robe of Velvet, powder'd with Flowers de-Lys of Gold, and furr'd with Ermines.

(b) At the Coronation of *Mary de Medicis*, they were the Cardinals *de Gondy*, and *de Sourdis*.

Trumpets, and Heralds, form the Procession; The Knights of the Order of the Holy Ghost come after, and two Ushers of the Chamber, with their Maces. The Princes, the Great Master, the Great Chamberlain bearing the Cushion on which the Queen is to kneel at the Coronation.

The Dauphin, if there be one, with the first Prince of the Blood following him, bear up the Lappets of the Queen's Robe, Three other Princes, each following according to their Rank of Proximity of Blood, carry the Crown, Scepter, and Hand of Justice.

Three Princesses of the Blood bear the Train of the Royal Robe.

The Queen thus conducted, advances to her Oratory, set up before the Altar, and after the accustom'd Prayers, she prostrates herself before the Altar, and is Anointed by a Cardinal or Prelate officiating, on the Head and (*a*) Breast, and in no other Place (*b*), saying the Prayers proper to the Crowning of Queens: It was

(*a*) Two Princesses of the Blood, prepare the Queen for it; At the last Coronation, Madam undress'd her Head, and Queen *Margaret* open'd the Cloths that cover'd her Breast.

(*b*) To shew, that Queens have no Authority by themselves; and should enterprize nothing without the Assistance of the King

the

the Cardinal *de Joyeuse*, assisted by Cardinal *Peron*, and many Bishops, who officiated at the Coronation of *Mary de Medicis*.

The Great Almoner of *France* presents the Crown to the officiating Prelate, who puts it upon the Queen's Head, without quitting it, reciting the Prayer, *Accipe Coronam*, &c. Take the Crown of Glory, Honour and Delight, that thou mayest shine with Lustre, and be Crown'd with eternal Exaltation, thro' our Lord, &c.

Ordinarily, as it is the Crown of *Jane D'Evreux* which is us'd at the Coronations of our Queens, and is very Weighty, two of the first Princes support it on their Heads; as the Dukes of *Anjou* and *D'Alenzon*, did to *Elizabeth* of *Austria*, Wife of *Charles* IX. *Monseigneur* and *Monsieur* to *Mary de Medicis*, for the Peers do not act as such in the Coronation of a Queen, tho' they do in that of a King.

After the Coronation-Prayer, the same Lords set on the Queen's Head a lesser Crown, set with Pearls and Diamonds.

This done, the Prelates officiating present to the Queen the Ring, Scepter, and Hand of Justice, without any Prayer. We must observe the Queen's Scepter is less than the King's.

Then she goes back from the Altar to a Throne, in the same Order as she went to it, holding the Scepter and Hand of Justice.

The same Prince or Lord who carry'd the Great Crown, re-conveys it to the Throne of the Queen, where he places it before her on a high Cushion cover'd with Cloth of Gold: The other Lords, who bore the Scepter and Hand of Justice, attend likewise the Queen to the Throne. Then one of her principal Ladies rises up, and after some Reverences, presents the Horary and Prayer-book to the Princesses, who are to deliver them to the Queen; this they do with three Reverences, to the Altar, the Queen, and the Ladies.

After this, Mass is begun by the Prelate or Cardinal officiating, and the Gospel is carry'd to the Queen, for her to kiss it, with Ceremonies like those of a King's Coronation.

After the *Credo*, the Masters of the Ceremonies give the Offerings to three Ladies, appointed to carry them to the Lady of Honour, on the great Scaffold, which they ascend, making two Reverences, one to the Altar, the other to the Queen.

After this, the Queen descends from her Throne to make her Offering, in the same Order as she was conducted to be Crown'd: The Offerings are carry'd by Three Princesses or Great Ladies, on rich Cushions, cover'd with Mantles of White Damask, fring'd with Gold.

At

At the Coronation of *Mary de Medicis*, they were the Dutcheſſes of *Vendôme*, Madam *de Guiſe*, and Madamoiſelle *de Vendôme*.

Theſe Offerings are, Wine in two ſmall Casks of Silver Gilt, the Loaf of Silver, the Loaf of Gold, and a Wax-Taper, garniſh'd with 13 Pieces of Gold.

The Queen receiving theſe Offerings from the Hands of the Princeſſes, gives them herſelf immediately to the Prelate officiating.

While the Queen is at the Offering, the Princes or great Lords carry the Scepter, the Hand of Juſtice, and the Crown; and after the Offerings, ſhe returns to the Throne in the former Order.

At the Elevation, the Queen falls on her Knees, and in the mean time the firſt Prince holds the Crown.

About the End of Maſs, the Queen deſcends from her Throne, and is conducted the third time before the Altar in the former Order.

She kneels, and lays the Crown ſhe has on her Head upon a Cuſhion prepar'd for her, and after ſhe has been Abſolv'd, ſhe receives the Holy Communion from the Prelate officiating.

At the *Agnus Dei*, the ſecond Prelate aſcends the Scaffold to the Throne, and gives the *Kiſs of Peace* to her Majeſty (*a*).

The Ceremony is uſually clos'd with Largeſſes made by the Heralds to the People, of a great Number of Pieces of Gold and Silver, purpoſely ſtruck for the Coronation; and the Queen is re conducted to her Appartment in the Palace in the ſame Order as ſhe left it. The Bearers of the Royal Ornaments go immediately before her, with Muſick playing, and the Acclamations of the People.

(*a*) The Cardinal *de Goudy* had the Honour to give the Kiſs of Peace to *Mary de Medicis* at her Coronation.

A

RELATION

Of what Passed

At the Ceremony *of the* Coronation *of* LOUIS XV. *and of what went before and follow'd it.*

THE King having fix'd a Day for His Anointing and Coronation, on *Sunday* the 25th of *October*, 1722, and commanded to follow in this Great Pomp, the Form of Ceremonies, that had been obſerv'd at the Anointing and Coronation of *Louis* XIV. of Glorious Memory, his Great Grandfather; his Majeſty left the Caſtle of *Verſailles* on the 16th of that Month, and lay at his Palace of the *Thuilleries* at *Paris*; from whence he ſet out on the 17th for *Rheims*, where he arriv'd on the 22d, about Three in the Afternoon; having paſs'd thro' *Dammartin*, *Villers Cotterêts*, *Soiſſons* and *Fimes*. All along the Road, he was attended in his Coach by the Princes of the Blood, and the Duke *de Charoſt* his Governor, and eſcorted by the *Night-Guards du Corps*, the *Quarter Guards* of the *Gens-d' Arms*; The *Light Horſe Guards* of *Gray Musketeers*, the *Black Musketeers*, and the *Guards* of the *Chamber*, with the Officers belonging to each, at the Head of them.

The *Night-Life Guards* follow'd his Majeſty's Coach; the *Gens-d'Arms* clos'd the March, and after them was a numerous and magnificent Retinue of Coaches and Equipages belonging to the King, the Miniſters, and Lords that attended him.

Monſieur the Duke of *Orleans* was at great Expence in his Caſtle of *Villers-Cotterêts*, for the Reception of his Majeſty. The Count *d'Evreux* Governor of the *Iſle of France*, at the Head of the Officers of the City of *Soiſſons*, preſented the Keys of it to him; who afterwards was complimented by the Officers of the Town, the Preſidial, the Treaſurers of *France*, and the Court of Election, with the Ordinary Ceremonies; as alſo by the Univerſity.

There were Feaſts, Illuminations, and Public Rejoycings, where-ever the King made

made a Stay, or Lodg'd; and all the Ways thro' which he pass'd, from *Paris* to *Rheims*, were lin'd by vast Numbers of People, and Persons of all Ranks, who by their Zeal, and continual Acclamations of *Vive le Roy*, assur'd him of their Submission, and the Sincerity of their Wishes.

The Arrival *of the* KING *at* Rheims.

AT some Distance from *Rheims*, the Troops of the Houshold, and the Regiments of *French* and *Swiss* Guards, were drawn up in Battalia, under the Command of the Duke of *Villeroy*, Captain of the Life-Guards. The Prince *de Rohan*, Governor of *Champagne*, with the Marquiss *de Grand Pré*, Lieutenant-General of the Province, went before the King, at the Head of the Town-Officers, and presented him with the Keys of the City of *Rheims*, into which he made his Entry in the following Order.

The Detachments of the Two Companies of Musketeers, who always attended the King during his Journey, march'd at the Head, then a Coach of the Duke of *Chartres*, two of the Duke of *Orleans*, one of of the King's, the Guards of the Chamber, another Coach of the King's, in which were Prince *Charles* of *Lorrain*, Great Master of the Horse of *France*, the Prince *de Turenne*, Great Chamberlain, the Duke *de Gêvres*, first Gentleman of the Chamber, and the principal Officers of the King's Houshold.

The Pages of the Great and Small Equerry, the King in his Coach of State, with the Dukes of *Orleans*, of *Chartres*, and *Bourbon*, the Count of *Clermont*, the Prince of *Conty*, and the Duke *de Charost*. The Prince of *Rohan*, and the Marquiss *de Grand Pré* were on Horse-back, before the Coach; and at the Boot, on the King's side, on Horse-back, was the Duke *D'Harcourt*, Captain of the Quarter-Guards; all round the King's Coach were Twenty-four Valets on Foot, the Night Life-Guards, the Horse Grenadiers, the Four Companies of Li e Guards, the Two Companies of Musketeers, the Light-Horse following the King's Coach, and the *Gens-d'Arms* of the Guard clos'd the March.

The Grand Master, and the Master of the Ceremonies, had also their Places in the Procession.

The Town-Officers of *Rheims* had rais'd Triumphal Arches at the Field-Gate, and the Gate of *Vesle*, and near the Great Square of the Metropolitan Church, adorn'd with proper Emblems and Inscriptions; and they were guarded by the Burghers under Arms.

The

The Arrival *of the* KING *at the Church.*

THE King croſs'd the great Street of the Suburb of *Veſle*, between the Regiments of *French* and *Swiſs* Guards, who were plac'd in a Line under Arms from the Gate of *Veſle*, to the great Gate of the Church. The King alighting from his Coach, was receiv'd at the Church-Door by the Archbiſhop Duke of *Rheims*, at the Head of his Chapter, the Canons being in Copes of Cloth of Gold, aſſiſted by *John-Joſeph-Languet*, Biſhop of *Soiſſons*; *Nicholas Charles de Saulx de Tavanne*, Biſhop and Count of *Châlons*; *Charles de St. Albin*, Biſhop of *Laon*, Peer of *France*; *Francis Trudaine*, Biſhop of *Senlis*, *Francis-Honoré-Antoine de St. Aignan*, Biſhop and Count of *Beauvais*; *Pierre Sabaſtier*, Biſhop of *Amiens*; and by *Francis de Chaſteauneuf de Rochebaune*, Biſhop and Count *de Noyon*, his Suffragans, all in their Pontifical Habits.

The King fell upon his Knees at the Church-Door, on a Rich Cuſhion ſet ready for him, and after a ſhort Prayer, and kiſſing the Book of the Goſpels, he roſe up, and receiv'd Standing the Compliment of the

the Archbiſhop of *Rheims*. Then the Chanter of the Church ſung the *Reſponſe, Ecce ego mitto*, and while it was continu'd by the Muſick, the Clergy enter'd the Choir in Proceſſion, and the King, walking the laſt after the Prelates, was conducted to a Pew, under a Canopy, in the middle of the Choir, before the High Altar, where he aſſiſted at the *Te Deum*, perform'd by the Muſick and Organ, with a continu'd Diſcharge of the Cannon and Fire-Arms.

During the *Te Deum* a coſtly Sun of Silver Gilt was brought from the Sacriſty, weighing about 125 Marks, which the King preſented to the Church of *Rheims*; the Duke of *Orleans* receiving it from the Duke *de Villequier*, firſt Gentleman of the Chamber, preſented it to the King, who laid it upon the Altar, with the ordinary Ceremonies.

The *Te Deum* ended, the Archbiſhop, after ſome Prayers, gave the Benediction; after which the King retir'd into the Archiepiſcopal Palace, that was adorn'd with the fineſt Furniture of the Crown. Here he was complimented by the Chapter of *Rheims*, the Abbot *Batchelier* Dean and Deputy of the Chapter, making the Harangue to him.

The Body of the City made their uſual Preſents; the Univerſity paid their Devoirs to him by the Sieur *Gerard* their Rector;

Rector, as did also the Courts of Presidial and of Election, of *Rheims*.

On the 23d and 24th in the Morning, the King visited several Churches, and on the 24th in the Afternoon, attended by the Duke of *Orleans*, the Princes of the Blood, the Duke *de Charost*, follow'd by the whole Court, went to the Metropolitan Church, where he plac'd himself in the middle of the Choir, in a Pew erected beneath a Canopy of Purple Velvet, powder'd with Flowers-de-Lys of Gold, with the Princes of the Blood on his Right, his Governor on his Left, and the Principal Officers about him. The Cardinal *de Rohan*, Great Almoner of *France*, was on the Right of it, and the Cardinals *de Bissy*, *du Bois*, and *de Polignac*, on the Left.

The Archbishop and Bishops invited by the King to the Ceremony, were placed near the Altar on the Right, and the Places on the other side were fill'd by the Lords of the Court. His Majesty assisted at the first Vespers of the Coronation, sung by the Archbishop of *Rheims*, who was in the first Seat of the Choir, on the Right, and they were continued by the King's Musick, and that of the Church.

After Vespers, the Bishop of *Angers* preach'd a very Eloquent Sermon on the Ceremony of the Coronation, from this Text, Samuel *took a Viol of Oyl, and anointed him,*

him, &c. *and from that Day the Spirit of the Lord was upon* David, 1 *Sam.* Chap. x. and xvi.

The Sermon ended, the King left the Church in the former Order, and return'd to the Archbiſhop's Palace, where he Confeſs'd to *F. de Ligneres*, Jeſuit, His Confeſſor in Ordinary.

Sunday, *the Coronation Day*, October 25, 1722.

THE Metropolitan Church of *Nôtre-Dame* at *Rheims*, had been prepar'd with great Magnificence; the High Altar was ſet out with Cloth of Silver, lac'd with Gold, and charg'd with the Arms of *France* and *Navarre* in Embroidery, which, with the Copes, had been preſented by the King the Evening before.

The Throne where the King was to ſit after his Coronation, was in the Middle of the Lobby, that divides the Nave from the Choir, under a Rich Canopy of Purple Velvet, powder'd with Flowers-de Lys of Gold: The Oratory before the Throne was cover'd in the ſame Manner with that of the Choir, and all the Seats or Benches on which were plac'd the Peers, the Great Offi-

Officers, and all that had any Function, or were invited, were likewise so cover'd.

And, as the Ceremony began early in the Morning, they took the Precaution to illuminate the Church by a great Quantity of Sconces, and Branches of Tapers.

While the first Canonical Hour was sung, the Archbishop of *Rheims*, who had in the Sacristy dress'd himself in his Pontifical Robes, seated himself in a Chair that was set ready for him, over-against the King's Oratory, with his Face turn'd towards the Choir. The Bishops of *Soissons* and *Amiens*, who discharg'd the Offices of Deacon and Sub Deacon, plac'd themselves on each side of him; and the Bishops of *Senlis*, *Nantes*, *Verdun*, and St. *Papoul*, who were to sing the Litanies, took their Places on the Right side of the Altar.

The Cardinal *de Rohan*, Great Almoner of *France*, the Cardinals *de Bissy*, *de Gêvres*, *Du Bois*, (Prime Minister) and *de Polignac*, all in their Rochets and Cardinals Caps, were on a Form something above, but less advanc'd forward then the Bench of the Ecclesiastical Peers.

The Archbishops of *Tholouse*, *Bourdeaux*, *Sens*, *Alby*, the Bishop of *Toul*, nominated to the Archbishoprick of *Tours*, the Bishops of *Metz*, *Angers*, *Chartres*, *Rennes*, *Blois*, *Troyes*, *Cisteron*, *Avranches*, *Puy*, and *Leitoure*, who were invited by the King, were in in their Rochets and Purple Camails, on Forms behind the Ecclesiastical Peers: The Abbots *de Brancas*, and *de Premeaux*, Agents of the Clergy, were behind the Bishops; as were the Abbots *Milon*, *de le Vieuxville*, *d'Argentré*, *de Froulay*, *Caulet*, and *de Pezé*, Almoners of the King, in their Rochets, and Black Robes over them.

The Sieurs *Amelot*, *Bignon de Blanzy*, *Le Pelletier des Forts*.

The Abbot *de Pomponne*, the Count *de Luc*, and the Sieurs *d'Angervilliers*, *d'Argenson*, *d'Harlay*, and *d'Odun*, Counsellors of State, the Sieurs *d'Herbigny*, *Bernard*, *de le Grandville*, *Orry*, *de Vatan*, *de Fontanieu*, *de Talhoüet*, *d'Ombreval*, *de Vanolles*, and *le Pelletier*, Masters of Requests, all in their Robes of Ceremony, were also invited, and sat below the Archbishops and Bishops; and the Sieur *Noblet* representing the Sieur *Ranchin*, Dean of the King's Secretaries.

Perin, as first Procurator Syndic.

Poisson, in Quality of Syndic.

Le Noire de Cindré, as Third Syndic.

Archembault, and *Carpot*, as Ancient Secretaries of the King, Deputies of the Company, according to the King's Letter *de Cachet*, were behind the Masters of Requests.

The Ecclesiastical Peers, in their Pontifical Robes, were by the Altar, on the Epistle-side.

The

The Mareschals *d'Estreés*, *de Tessé*, and *d'Huxelles* who were to bear the Royal Ornaments at this Ceremony, were on a Bench behind that of the Lay-Peers.

The Marquis *de la Vrilliere*, the Count *de Maurepas*, and the Sieur *le Blanc*, Secretaries of State, were on a separate Bench beneath, and more retir'd than that of those Three Marshals of *France*.

The Marshals *de Matignon*, and *de Bezons*, and other Lords of the Court, and principal Officers of his Majesty, were all upon Benches and Forms, set for them by the Great Masters, and Masters of the Ceremonies, according to Custom.

The Pope's Nuntio, and the Ambassadors of *Spain*, *Sardinia* and *Malta*, were invited, and conducted in the usual manner to their Gallery, on the Left side of the Altar; and with them were the Chevalier *de Sainctot*, and the Sieur *de Rémond*, Introductors of Ambassadors.

On the other side of the Altar, to the Right, in a Gallery, was *Madame*, accompany'd with Madame the Dutchess of *Lorrain*, the Infante Don *Emanuel*, Brother of the King of *Portugal*, and the Princes and Princesses of *Lorrain*, who came *Incognito* to *Rheims*, to view the Coronation

Then came the Lay-Peers, who, after the ordinary Ceremonies and Reverences, were

were conducted by the Maſter of the Ceremonies to their Bench near the Altar on the Goſpel-ſide, dreſs'd as they are deſcrib'd above, with their Coronets over a Cap of Purple Sattin.

The D. of	*Orleans*	Repreſenting the	Duke of	*Burgundy*
	Chartres			*Normandy*
	Bourbon			*Aquitaine*
The C. of	*Charolois*		Count of	*Toulouſe*
	Clermont			*Flanders*
The Pr. of	*Conti*			*Champagne*

The 3 former wore the Ducal Coronet, the 3 latter that of a Count; the Dukes of *Orleans* and *Bourbon*, and the Prince of *Conti*, had upon their Robes the Collar of the Order of the Holy Ghoſt.

Beſides the Places we have ſpoken of, there were erected between the Pillars on both Sides of the Choir, above the Seats of the Canons, Galleries in the Form of an Amphitheatre for Perſons of Diſtinction; and there was a particular Amphitheatre for the King's Muſick, behind the High Altar.

Things being thus diſpos'd, the Six Lay-Peers, and the Five Eccleſiaſtical Peers, approaching the Archbiſhop Duke of *Rheims*, deputed by Conſent the Biſhops

of

of *Laon* and *Beauvais*, to go and ſeek the King, which they did in order of Proceſſion, with the Ceremonies above deſcrib'd; only the Hundred Gentlemen Penſioners were not preſent, the King having diſpens'd with them by an Arret in *Auguſt* 1722, on Account of the great Age and Infirmities of the Duke *de Lauſun*, their Captain, without drawing it into Conſequence.

The King being arriv'd at the Church through a large Open Gallery, built from the Hall of the Archbiſhop's Palace to the Church-Door, dreſs'd only in a Coat of Crimſon-Sattin, as above is deſcrib'd, was conducted by the two Biſhops aforeſaid, firſt to the Foot of the Altar, then to a Seat prepar'd for him beneath a Canopy, in the middle of the Choir, as we likewiſe intimated above.

The Dukes of *Villeroy* and *Harcourt*, Captains of the Guards in their ordinary Habits, but very Magnificent, took their Places on the Right and Left of the King's Seat, the Marquis *de Courtenvaux*, Captain of the Hundred *Swiſs*, in his Habit of Ceremony, took his Place on the Right Side of his Majeſty's Seat, and the Six Guards of the *Sleeve*, dreſs'd as aforeſaid, with their Partizans in their Hands, were plac'd lower, on each Side the Choir, the Marſhal *de Villars*, repreſenting the Conſtable, habited like the Lay-Peers, was ſeated near the King, having on each side the Sieurs *Millet*, and *de Varennes*, Ushers of the Chamber, in White Sattin, with their Maces. The Sieur *d'Armenonville*, Keeper of the Seals, discharging the Place of Chancellor of *France*, in his Habit of Ceremony, was on another side something more distant.

The Prince *de Rohan*, performing the Office of Great-Master of the King's-Houshold, with his Staff of Command in his Hand, was on a Bench behind the Chancellor, having on his Right the Prince of *Turenne*, Great Chamberlain of *France*, and the Duke *de Villequier*, first Gentleman of the Chamber on his Left; all three Habited like the Lay-Peers, with the Coronet of a Count upon their Heads.

Prince *Charles* of *Lorrain*, Master of the Horse of *France*, who is to take the Cap of his Majesty when he puts it off in the Ceremony, and was appointed to bear the Train of the Royal Robe, was near the King on his Right Hand. The Duke *de Charost*, Governor of the King, was on a Seat before the Bench of the Secretaries of State, the Marshal Duke of *Tallard*, the Count *de Matignon*, the Count *de Medavy*, and the Marquiss *de Goesbriant*, Knights of the Order of *The Holy Ghost*, appointed to carry the Offerings in the Habit, and large Robe of Ceremony of the Order, were in the four first High Seats of the Choir, belong-

belonging to the Canons, on the Epistle-side. The Marquis *de Dreux*, Great Master of the Ceremonies, and the Sieur *des Granges*, Master of the Ceremonies, took their proper Places, dress'd as above.

When the Places were thus taken, the Archbishop Duke of *Rheims*, presented the Holy Water to the King, and the rest that were Invited, or had any Office at the Ceremony; then the *Veni Creator* was sung; after which the Canon for the Week begun the Third Hour, and in the mean Time the Holy Vial came to the Church-Gate, where it was receiv'd by the Archbishop of *Rheims*, in the Order, and with the Ceremonies above-mention'd. It was brought by Father *Gaudart*, Grand Prior of the Abbey of St. *Remy*, under a Canopy born up by the Sieurs *de Romaine*, *Godet*, and St. *Catharine*, Knights of the Holy Vial, dress'd in White Sattin and a Robe of Black Silk, and by the Sieur *Clignet*, Bailiff of the Abbey of St *Remy*, and was conducted by the Marquiss *de Prie*, the Count *d'Estaing*, the Marquiss *d'Alegre*, and the Marquis *de Beauvau*, whose Ranks were drawn by Lot, and they went with their Squires before them, in the Order recited before, preceded by the Friers Minims, the Canons of the Collegiate Church of St. *Timothy*, and the Religious of the Abbey of St. *Remy*.

When the Archbishop plac'd the Vial upon the Altar, the Four Barons or Lords who attended it, seated themselves in the Four first Chairs of the Canons, on the Gospel side, and their Gentlemen in the lower Chairs, holding their Escutcheons before them; the Grand Prior, and Treasurer of the Abbey of St. *Remy*, were at the side of the Altar, during the Ceremony, as well as the Grand Prior, Treasurer, and one of the Ancient Religious of the Abbey of St *Dennis*, who brought the Royal Ornaments from the Treasury, and staid to keep them ready for the Coronation.

In the mean Time, the Archbishop went behind the Altar to put on the Necessary Habits for Mass, and at his Return, he receiv'd the King's Promises of Protection to all the Churches subject to the Crown, and after the Antient Formalities, the King pronounc'd, holding his Hands upon the Holy Gospels, the Oath of the Kingdom, those of the Orders of the Holy Ghost, and of St. *Louis*, and that of observing the Edict upon Duelling.

Then the Duke *de Villequier*, first Gentleman of the Chamber to the King, took off his Long Robe, and put it into the Hands of the first *Valet de Chambre*; and Prince *Charles* of *Lorrain* receiving the Cap of his Majesty, gave it to the first

Valet

Valet of the Wardrobe. After which the King took ſome of the Royal Ornaments.

The *Litanies* were ſung by the Biſhops of *Senlis*, of *Verdun*, of *Nantes*, and of St *Papoul*, and the Unctions were made by the Archbiſhop, and the Biſhops of *Laon* and *Beauvais*, they opening the King's Habit, after which the King receiv'd the Holy Unctions from the Hands of the Archbiſhop (that is of *Rheims*, which is always meant in this Relation) and the Two other Biſhops aſſiſted him in cloſing his Habit with the Ties of Gold-Lace, then, when the King has taken the Gloves, after the Benediction of them, the Ring, the Scepter, and the Hand of Juſtice, the Sieur *d'Armenonville*, Keeper of the Seals of *France*, repreſenting the Chancellor, goes up to the Altar and calls the Peers in Order, as above, then the King was Crown'd with the Ordinary Ceremonies.

So likewiſe he was Enthron'd with the General Acclamations of *Vive le Roy*, the Salvo's of the Artillery, the Drums beating, Trumpets and other Inſtruments playing, and Gold and Silver Medals were diſtributed, repreſenting on one Side the King's Buſt, with this Inſcription.

LUD. XV. REX CHRISTIANISSIMUS.

Louis XV. *Most Christian King.*

And on the Reverse, the Time of his Coronation, with this Inscription or Legend.

REX CÆLESTI OLEO UNCTUS.

The King, Anointed with Heavenly Oyl.

And in the *Exergue*,

REMIS, 25 OCT. 1722.

At Rheims, Oct. 25, 1722.

These Medals were distributed in the Choir, and in the Body of the Church by the Heralds at Arms, and after the *Te Deum* begun by the Archbishop of *Rheims*, and sung in full by the King's Musick, Mass is solemnly celebrated by the Archbishop, at the High-Altar, and Low Mass is begun at the Altar in the Lobby, according to Custom; it was said thrice by M. the Abbot *Guynot*, Chaplain in waiting, and it was serv'd by the Sieurs *Paulmier*, and *Evrard*, Clerks of the Chapel, in their Surplices. On the side of the Altar, were on their Knees, Monsr the Abbot *Milon*, the King's

King's Almoner, in his long Habit, and in his Rochet, the Abbot *Bayle*, Chaplain in Ordinary, likewiſe in his long Habit, and the Abbot *Pernot*, Clerk of the Chapel. In the mean time the Biſhop of *Soiſſons* ſung the Goſpel of the ſolemn Maſs, the Book of which was after brought to the King on his Throne to be Kiſs'd by him, with the Accuſtom'd Ceremonies and Reverences.

The Offerings were made as uſual; the Marſhal Duke of *Tallard* carry'd the Veſſel of Silver Gilt, in which was the Wine preſented by the King at Arms, the Count *de Matignon* carry'd the Loaf of Silver, the Count *de Medavi* the Loaf of Gold, and the Marquiſs *de Goesbriant* the Thirteen Pieces of Gold in the Purſe, having received them all from the Heralds at Arms. When the King was at the Altar to offer them, he gave the Scepter to the Marſhal *de Teſſé*, and the Hand of Juſtice to the Marſhal *d'Huxelles*; afterwards, he reſum'd them, and re aſcended the Throne in the Order as he deſcended from it.

When the Archbiſhop had given the ſolemn Benediction, the Great Almoner of *France* went to receive the Kiſs of Peace from Him, and going up to the Throne, he approach'd the King, and gave it to his Majeſty, as did after the Peers, Eccleſiaſtical and Laical, as uſual.

Before the Offertory, the Abbot *Milon*, the King's Almoner, having try'd and tasted the Bread that was to be Consecrated for Communicating the King, brought it from the Lobby to the High Altar.

The Mass ended, the King goes down from his Throne to Communicate, as he went to Offer; and being before the Altar, Monsieur the Duke of *Orleans*, representing the first Peer, took off his Crown, which he deliver'd to the Marshal *d'Estreés*; and the King gave his Scepter and Hand of Justice to the Marshals *de Tessé* and *d'Huxelles*.

Then he is *Reconcil'd* under a Pavilion near the High Altar on the Epistle side, by *F. Ligniers* his Confessor, and falls on his Knees at the Foot of the Altar, and receives the Absolution of the Archbishop, and the Communion in both Kinds.

While he Communicates, the Communion-Cloth is spread on the Side of the Altar, by the Cardinal *de Rohan*, Great Almoner of *France*, and by *Henry Charles du Cambort de Coislin*, Bishop of *Metz*, first Almoner; and on the King's side, by the Dukes of *Orleans* and *Chartres*, as first Princes of the Blood.

When the King has Communicated, the Archbishop returns the Great Crown of *Charlemagne* to the King, which he holds for some Time upon his Knees, while he performs his Thanksgiving Devotions, and after

after the Archbiſhop has purify'd the Chalice, he takes that Crown from the King, gives it to the Marſhal *d'Eſtreés* for him to carry it, and another that is lighter to his Majeſty, made for the Purpoſe, and enrich'd with the fineſt Jewels of the Crown; then the King reſumes his Scepter and Hand of Juſtice, and after a profound Reverence to the Altar, he returns to the Archbiſhop's Palace, thro' the ſame Open Gallery we ſpoke of before, in the following Order.

In the mean Time, the Holy Vial is remitted to St. *Rhemy*, in the ſame Manner as it was brought in the Morning.

The KING's *Return to the Archbiſhop's Palace.*

THE Count *de Montſoreau*, Grand Provoſt of the Houſhold, at the Head of his Company began the Proceſſion.

The Marquiſs *de Courtenvaux*, Captain of the Hundred *Swiſs* Guards, at the Head of them, marching two and two.

The King's Hautbois, Drums, Trumpets.

The Heralds at Arms.

The Grand Masters, and Masters of the Ceremonies.

The four Knights of the Order of the Holy Ghost, who carry'd the Offerings.

The Marshals *de Tessé* and *d'Huxelles*, who bore the Scepter and Hand of Justice; with the Marshal *d'Estreés* in the midst of them, bearing the Great Crown of *Charlemagne*, on a Cushion of Purple Velvet.

The Marshal *de Villars* representing the Constable, bearing the Royal Sword; having the two Ushers of the Chamber on each side of him, with their Maces.

The King in his Royal Robes wearing his Crown, and holding the Scepter and Hand of Justice, amidst the Six Peers in their Ducal Mantles and Coronets, and the Six Ecclesiastical in their Copes and Mitres, walking on either Hand in Parallel Lines.

The Archbishop Duke of *Rheims*, on the Right next the King, and supporting his Arm; preceded by his Cross and Pastoral Staff, and assisted by Two Canons in their Copes.

Prince *Charles* of *Lorrain*, bearing the Train of the Royal Robe, the Dukes of *Villercy* and *d'Harcourt*, Captains of the Guards, and the Six Guards of the Sleeve, on each side of the King; and the Duke *de Charost* his Governor.

The

The Sieur *Fleuriau D'Armenonville* representing the Chancellor, by himſelf, immediately after the King.

After him the Prince of *Rohan*, performing the Charge of Grand Maſter, with the Prince *de Turenne* on his right, and the Duke *de Villequier* on his left.

The Officers of the Life Guards clos'd the Proceſſion, which held from the Church, to the Door of the King's Apartment.

When he enter'd it, he put off his Gloves and Linnen that had touch'd the Holy Unction, and gave them to the Biſhop of *Metz*, his firſt Almoner, to be burnt according to Cuſtom.

In the mean Time, Five Tables were prepar'd in the Archbiſhop's Hall, for the Feaſt of the Coronation. That of the King was ſet as uſual before the Chimney over-againſt the Door of his Majeſty's Apartment, on a Floor, rais'd four Steps, about two Foot high, under a large Canopy of Purple Velvet, powder'd with Flowers-de-Lys in Golden Embroidery.

The Tables of the Eccleſiaſtical and Lay-Peers, were on the Right and Left ſide of the Hall, at ſome diſtance from the Platform of the King's, and about two Foot lower.

At the End of the Eccleſiaſtical Peers, which was on the Right by the Windows, was another, plac'd on the ſame Line for the Embaſſadors who were invited; where the

the Pope's Nuncio held the first Rank. At the End of the Table of the Lay-Peers, a fourth was plac'd on the same Line, call'd the Table of Honours, for the Great Chamberlain and the other Lords, who had a Right to sit there.

The Tables thus set ready, the Duke *de Brissac*, Grand Pannetier of *France*, or Master of the Pantry, commanded the King's Table to be spread, and brought the Large Royal Cup, and Padlock of his Office to his Majesty, accompany'd by the Marquiss *de Lanmery* Great Cupbearer, carrying the King's Salver, Glasses, and Decanters, and by the Marquiss *de le Chesnay*, Great Squire Carver, bearing the Royal Spoon, the Fork, and Carving Knife. These three Great Officers were in Habits and Robes of black Velvet, turn'd up with Cloth of Silver.

The Grand Master of the Ceremonies, having given Notice to the Great Master of the Houshold, that the Service for the King's Table was ready, and the Prince of *Rohan* (who supply'd this Place, Monsieur the Duke of *Bourbon*, representing one of the Ancient Peers,) having his Majesty's Order to command it to be brought up; he went as Great Master of the Household, where the Dishes were prepar'd and order'd up, the first Course in this Method.

First,

First, were the Hautbois and Flutes of the King's Chamber, playing such Marches and Flourishes as were proper.

The six Heralds at Arms.

The Grand Master, and Master of the Ceremonies.

The Twelve Masters of the Houshold, two and two with their Staves.

The Marquiss *de Livry*, first Master of the Houshold.

The Prince *de Rohan*, with his Staff of Command, going immediately before the Service; the Duke *de Brissac*, carrying the first Dish, follow'd by the Gentlemen Waiters, who brought up the other Dishes.

The Marquiss *de la Chesnay*, plac'd in order the Dishes on the Table, uncover'd them, tasted them, cover'd them again; while the Prince *de Rohan*, preceded by the same Retinue, went to signify it to the King, who came to his Table in this Manner.

The Hautbois, Trumpets and Flutes.

The Six Heralds at Arms.

The four Knights of the Order of the Holy Ghost.

The Marshal *d'Estreés*, with the Great Crown of *Charlemagne*, on a Cushion of purple Velvet, between the Marshals *de Tessé* and *d'Huxelles*.

The Prince of *Rohan*, between the Prince *de Turenne*, and the Duke *de Villequier*.

The

The Marſhal Duke of *Villars* with the Sword, and the two Uſhers of the Chamber with their Maces, on each ſide of him.

The King with his magnificent Crown of Diamonds upon his Head; and the Scepter, and Hand of Juſtice, the Eccleſiaſtical Peers in their Copes and Mitres, on his Right, and the Lay-Peers habited as above, on his Left.

The Two Captains of the Guards, and the King's Governor following him; and the ſix Guards of the Sleeve, or the *Scotch* Guards, marching in two Lines after the Peers.

The Archbiſhop of *Rheims*, leading the King by the Right Arm, Prince *Charles* bearing the Train of the Royal Robe, and the Keeper of the Seals behind the King, clos'd the Train.

When the King came to his Table, the Archbiſhop gave the ordinary Bleſſing to it; and while the Great Crown, Scepter, and Hand of Juſtice, were diſpos'd on Cuſhions of Purple Velvet, at the right and left Corners of the King's Table, the Twelve Peers went to take their Places at their Tables, each according to his Rank, and the Order of the Call, and all on the ſame Side. The Archbiſhop of *Rheims* had behind him Two Canons aſſiſting in their Copes, and oppoſite to him, Two Eccleſiaſticks in their Surplices, holding his Croſs

Crofs and Crofier; The Bifhops of *Soiffons*, *Amiens* and *Senlis*, his Suffragans, were at the fame Table, over-againft the three laft Ecclefiaftical Peers, only in their Rochets and purple Camails.

At the Ambaffadors Table, the Pope's Nuncio took the firft Place; oppofite to him was the *Spanifh* Embaffadors, the *Sardinian* on the Nuncio's fide; oppofite to him the *Dutch* Embaffador, and the *Maltefe* next to him. The Keeper of the Seals was over againft the Embaffador of *Malta*, below whom was the *Chevalier de Sainctot*, and the *Sieur de Rémond*, Introductors of Embaffadors.

At the Table of Honours, on the fame Side and Line, were the Great Chamberlain, the firft Gentleman of the Chamber, and the four Knights of the Order of the Holy Ghoft, who bore the Offerings, all drefs'd as they were in the Morning of the Coronation.

When the Entertainment came in, the Prince *de Rohan* prefented the Napkin to the King, as alfo after Dinner; he was ftanding all the Time near the Table, on the Right of his Majefty.

The Marfhal *de Villars*, with the two Ufhers on each fide of him, bearing their Maces, was before the Table over-againft the King, and held the naked Sword all the Time.

Prince

Prince *Charles* of *Lorrain* was behind the King's Chair; on each side of him were the two Captains of the Life Guards. The Master of the Pantry, the Great Cup-bearer, and the Great Squire Carver were before the Table, to discharge their Duties, The Master of the Pantry chang'd the Plates, the Napkins, and the Covers; The Great Cup-bearer serv'd the King at his drinking, and when-ever he call'd for Wine or Water, went for the Glasses and Decanters, and had them all tasted before the King. The Great Squire Carver took off and replac'd the Dishes, and put those near his Majesty which he pleas'd to eat of.

The Three Marshals abovesaid, who bore the Great Crown, Scepter, and Hand of Justice, were plac'd near to each that was respectively carry'd by them.

The Abbot *Milon*, the King's Almoner in waiting, was at the farthest Corner of the Right side of the Table, where the Box of Table Linnen was, to open it whenever the King was inclin'd to change the Napkins.

All the Services of the King's Table were brought by his Officers, with the same Order and Train as the first, and always with a Flourish of the Musick.

There were only three Courses, taking in that of Fruit, and the last was serv'd up

by

by the Duke *de Brissac*, Great Master of the Pantry.

The two Tables of Peers, those of the Ambassadors, and of Honours, were serv'd by the Officers of the City of *Rheims*, and by the most considerable Burgesses, all at the Expence of the City; which also defray'd the Charge of that of the King, according to Custom.

The Dutchess of *Lorrain*, and many Foreign Princes, who were with her *Incognito*, saw the Coronation Feast, from a Gallery rais'd for them in the Hall, on the Left of his Majesty's Table.

Assoon as the King had din'd, the Archbishop of *Rheims* advanc'd towards the Table, and said Grace: Then the King resum'd the Scepter and Hand of Justice, and retir'd into his Apartment, whither he was re-conducted in the same Order and Ceremony as he parted from it, to come to his Table. He then dismiss'd all the Peers, Great Officers, and Lords who attended him, and withdrew into his Closet, about Three in the Afternoon.

The Archbishop and the Spiritual Peers return'd to the Church, to put off their Pontifical Habits.

Then the Marshal of *Villars*, the Prince *de Rohan*, the Marshals *d'Estreés*, *d'Uxelles*, and *de Tessé*, the Dukes *de Villeroy*, and *d'Harcourt*, Captains of the Life Guards, the Marquiſs *de Courtenvaux*, the Grand-Maſter, and Maſter of the Ceremonies, the Maſter of the Pantry, the Grand Cup-bearer, the Great Squire Carver, and the firſt Maſter of the King's Houſhold, went to the Town-Hall of *Rheims*, to a Table that was ſet ready for them. So likewiſe the Count *d'Eſtaing*, the Count *de Beauveau*, and the Marquiſs *de Prie*, who attended the Holy Vial, with many other Lords of the Court, had likewiſe a diſtinct Table. Both were ſerv'd by the Town-Officers and moſt Eminent Burgeſſes, and at the City Charge; with all the Affluence and State ſuitable to ſo great a Day.

On the Morrow of the Coronation, *October* 26th, the King, according to Ancient Cuſtom, went in Cavalcade to hear Maſs, at the Abbey of St. *Remy*. The Regiments of *French* and *Swiſs* Guards lin'd the Way from the Archbiſhop's Palace to the Abbey; It was in this Order.

The Horſe Grenadiers, the two Companies of Musketeers, the Light Horſe-Guards, with their Officers at the Head of them. The Foot-Guards of the Provoſtſhip of the Houſhold, two and two, the Grand Provoſt of the Houſhold on Horſeback, at the Head of them; and a conſiderable Number of Lords and Courtiers, nobly dreſs'd and mounted.

Three

Three of the King's led Horses, richly Equip'd and Caparison'd with blue Velvet, rais'd with Embroidery of Gold and Silver, led by the King's Equerries on Foot.

Twelve Pages on Horseback, of whom six were of the Chamber, three of the Great, and three of the Small Stables of His Majesty.

The Trumpets of the Chamber.

The Hundred *Swiss* in their Habits of Ceremony, on Foot, with the Marquiss *de Courtenvaux* their Captain, on Horseback, at the Head of them. Many Marshals of *France*, and Knights of the Orders of the King, all on Horseback, without observing any Rank amongst them.

Prince *Charles* of *Lorrain* was on Horseback, immediately before the King. His Majesty was not dress'd in the Antique Manner, but in a Modern Habit of Blue Velvet, Embroider'd with Silver, mounted on a Horse very Magnificently furnish'd; the Reins were held by Two Equerries: Four more were about him on Foot: The two Captains of the Guards were on Horseback on each side of him, and the Six *Scotch* Guards were on Foot on the Wing of them.

Immediately after the King, were on Horseback the King's Governor, the Prince *de Rohan*, the Duke *de Chaulnes* the Great Chamberlain, the first Gentleman of the

Chamber, and the Marquiſs *de Beringhen*, Firſt Maſter of the Horſe.

The Dukes of *Orleans*, *Chartres*, and *Bourbon*, the Counts of *Charolois*, and *Clermont*, and the Prince of *Conti*, were on Horſeback about his Majeſty, the Duke of *Orleans* was attended by his firſt Gentleman of the Horſe, and the Captain of his Guards, and the other Princes of the Blood, by one of their principal Officers.

Then came the Officers of the Life-Guards in Attendance, the Night Guards *du Corps*, the four Companies of the Life-Guards, and the *Gens-d'Arms* of the Guard clos'd the March, which was made with Extraordinary Pomp, and Repeated Acclamations of the People.

The King at the Abbey Gate of St. *Remy* was receiv'd and commended by the Sub-Prior, at the Head of all the Religious in their Copes.

He enter'd the Choir, where he heard Low Maſs, during which, the King's Muſick perform'd a Compoſition ſet for the Occaſion.

After Maſs, he went behind the High-Altar, to pay his Devotions at the Tomb of St. *Remy*, he view'd the Shrine of that Saint, and the Holy Vial: Then, in the former Method, return'd to the Archiepiſcopal Palace.

On

On the ſame Day about Three in the Afternoon, the Commanders and Officers of the Order of the Holy Ghoſt, held a Chapter at the Apartments of the Duke of *Orleans*, where they regulated the Proceedings of the Day following, in the Ceremony of the Knighting, when the King was to be made Grand Maſter and Sovereign of that Order.

The 27th the King heard Low Maſs, and a Compoſition ſung by the Muſicians of the Chapel, in the Church of the Jeſuits; at the Gate of which he was receiv'd and complimented by Father *Robinet*, their Provincial.

In the mean time the Metropolitan Church, where the Ceremony of Knighting was to be perform'd, was prepar'd for it by Order of the Sieur *de Breteuil*, Provoſt and Maſter of the Ceremonies of the Order.

The High Altar was ſet off with the Ornaments of the Order, which are of Green Velvet, rais'd with Flames of Gold Embroider'd. Two Thrones were ſet for the King, under two Canopies cover'd with the ſame, one at the firſt place entring the Choir, where the King was to be at Veſpers, the other near the Altar on the Goſpel ſide, under which the King was to ſign the Oath he made at his Coronation, and receive the Mantle and Collar of the

 Order.

Order. Over the Stalls were the King's Arms and those of the Knights, according to the Rank of their Reception into the Order; The greatest part of the Benches and other Places were left almost in the same manner as they had been dispos'd at the Coronation.

An Hour before the King came to Church, the Duke of *Orleans* conferr'd the Order of St. *Michael* on the Duke of *Chartres* and the Count of *Charolois*, who were to receive that of the *Holy Ghost*, Soon after the Cardinals *de Bissy*, *de Gêvres*, *du Bois*, and *de Polignac*, as well as the Archbishops and Bishops who were invited to this Ceremony, being come in a Body to the Gate of the Choir, were receiv'd and conducted, with the Ordinary Ceremonies, into the Chancel, to certain Forms near the Altar on the Epistle-side. The King's Almoners were behind the Bishops, the Keeper of the Seals was below the Forms or Benches of the Clergy, on an Arm-Seat, without a Back to it, With him were the Counsellors of State, the Masters of Requests, the King's Secretaries, who took the same Seats they had at the Coronation.

Opposite to the Clergy and the Council, on the Gospel-side, were the Principal Officers and Lords of the Court.

Two Galleries were reserv'd for the Dutchess of *Lorrain*, and other Foreign Princes,

Princes, who, as before, came *Incognito*. But the Dutchefs could not be there on the Knighting.

About Three in the Afternoon all the Commanders, Knights and Officers of the Order of the *Holy Ghoft*, being affembled in the King's Apartment, in the Grand Habit of the Order, the Sieur *de Breteuil*, in his Robe of Ceremony, went to inform his Majefty, that all was in Readinefs for it, then the King proceeded, as at the Coronation, through the fame open Gallery.

The Grand Provoft and Guards of the Provoft-fhip of the Houfhold, began the Proceffion. Then came the Hundred *Swifs* of the Guard, in their Habits of Ceremony, led by their Captain, Drums beating, Colours difplay'd; the Drums, Fifes, and Trumpets of the King's Stables, the Six Heralds at Arms, the Sieurs *Chevrard* and *Halle*, one Ufher, the other Herald of the Orders of the King, the firft bearing the Mace, and both in the Habits of the Order of the *Holy Ghoft*, going before the Sieur *de Breteuil*, who went between the Sieurs *Crozat*, Great Treafurer of the Order on his Right, and *de Montargus*, Secretary of it on his Left, in the Habits of Ceremony of the Order.

The Abbot *de Pomponne*, Chancellor of the Orders of the King, went alone in his

Habit of Ceremony, follow'd by the Count of *Charolois*, and the Duke of *Chartres*, each going single in the Habit of Probationers for the Order, then, by two and two, the Marquis *de Goesbriant*, and the Count *de Medavi*, the Count *de Matignon*, and the Marshal *d'Uxelles*, the Marshals of *Tallard* and *Villars*, *Jessé* and *Estreés*. The Prince of *Conti* alone, the Duke of *Bourbon* alone, the Duke of *Orleans* alone: All Knights, in the Robes and Collar of the Order. After them the King in his Habit of Probationer for the Order, with the Cardinal *de Rohan* on his Right, and the Bishop of *Metz* on his Left, both Commanders of the Order; the Marquiss *de Nesle* bore up the Train, and about his Majesty were the Duke of *Charost*, the two Captains of the Guards, the Great Chamberlain, the first Gentleman of the Chamber, the two Ushers of the Chamber with their Maces, dress'd in their Habits of White Sattin, the Six *Scotch* Guards Habited as at the Coronation, and many others Great Officers and Lords of the Court.

All walk'd with their Heads cover'd, from the King's Apartment, to the Entrance of the Choir, where the Chancellor, Provost, and Master of the Ceremonies, the Great Treasurer, and Secretary of the Order, preceded by an Usher and an Herald,

Herald, advanc'd to the midſt of it, made the uſual Reverences, and then took their Places one againſt another. That of the Abbot *de Pomponne* was a Stool with a looſe covering of Green Velvet, Embroider'd with Flames of Gold, over againſt the Throne the Sieurs *de Breteuil*, *Crozat* and *Montargis* ſate upon a like Stool farther advanc'd in the Choir, *de Breteuil* being in the midſt between the others; the Herald was alone before them, and the Uſher was likewiſe alone on the ſame kind of Stool, almoſt at the middle of the Choir.

The Duke of *Chartres* having enter'd, and the Count of *Charolois* after him; they made the uſual Reverences, and took their Places as Probationers oppoſite to one another, at the loweſt part of the Choir as you enter on the Left Hand; then all the Knights enter'd two and two, according to their Rank, and after their Reverences, they ſtood at the Foot of their Places till the King came in. As ſoon as he enter'd the Choir, he made his Reſpect to the Altar, and aſcended the firſt Throne that was ſet for him.

The Duke of *Orleans* took the firſt Place on the Right of the King; on each ſide of his Majeſty were the Dukes of *Villeroy* and *Harcourt*, the Duke of *Charoſt*, the Great Chamberlain, the firſt Gentleman of the Chamber, and the Marquiſs *de Neſle*, appointed

pointed to bear his Train. Then all the Knights went up to the High Stalls that are their ordinary Places.

The Cardinal *de Rohan* plac'd himſelf in one of the Lower Stalls beneath the King.

The Biſhop of *Nantes*, firſt Almoner of the Duke of *Orleans*, ſate below his Royal Highneſs, next to the Cardinal *de Rohan*.

The Biſhop of *Metz*, firſt Almoner of the King, as Commander-born of the Order, was in the Chancel on a Bench ſet for the Eccleſiaſtical Commanders, which was after the Arm Chair of the Archbiſhop of *Rheims*, officiating in his Cope and Mitre, and the Seats of his Aſſiſtants, who were Three Chaplains of the Chapel of the King's Muſick, ſitting on either ſide of him. Three Clerks of the ſame Chapel ſtood before the Archbiſhop.

When all theſe Seats were taken, the Abbot *de Pomponne* Chancellor of the Order, the Sieurs *de Breteuil*, *Crozat*, and *Montargus*, preceded by the Herald and Uſher of the Order, left their Places to go and make the accuſtom'd Reverences; after which they ſate down, cover'd, as did likewiſe the King and all the Knights; then *de Breteuil*, with the Uſher and Herald before him, began again to make a Reverence to the Altar, and one to the King, to know whether they were to begin the Office, of which he gave Notice to the Archbiſhop.

The

The ſame Reverences were repeated before the Hymn, to give the King a Signal to be uncover'd and kneel down; and at the *Magnificat* for him to ſtand up.

Veſpers were ſung by the Muſicians of the Chapel of the King's Muſick; When they were ended, the four Great Officers of the Order, preceded by the Herald and Uſher, began again their Reverences at the Foot of the Altar; after which, they ſeated themſelves on the Floor of the ſecond Throne, that was rais'd near the Altar, on the Goſpel-ſide, each taking the Right or Left of the Throne, according to their Dignity. So that the Chancellor, the Provoſt, and Maſter of the Ceremonies, were neareſt to his Majeſty; the Herald and Uſher of the Order, were at the Foot of the Platform, to the Right and Left.

The Knights likewiſe quitted their Stalls, and after their Reverences at the Foot of the Altar, they went up and plac'd themſelves at the Paſſages, that led to the Throne, according to their Rank and Dignity.

Then the King deſcended from the Throne, where he had heard Veſpers; and, preceded by the two Uſhers of his Chamber, with their Maces, and the ſix *Scotch* Guards, and follow'd by his Great Almoner, the two Captains of his Guards, his

his Governor, his Great Chamberlain, the Marquiſs *de Neſle*, and many other great Officers and Lords, he went to the Foot of the Altar, made his Reverences, and then aſcended his Throne near the Altar.

When the King was plac'd there, the Archbiſhop of *Rheims* ſeated himſelf in an Arm-Chair, that was ſet for him on the Platform of the Throne, and demanded, Whether his Majeſty would ſign the Oath of the Order of the Holy Ghoſt, which he took at his Coronation? To which the King having agreed, the Secretary of the Order, preſented him the Regiſter where the Writing was, that his Majeſty ſign'd, as well as the Profeſſion of Faith, which all the Kings of *France* and Knights have ſign'd ever ſince the Eſtabliſhment of the Order of the Holy Ghoſt.

Then the King roſe up, put off his Cap, and gave it to the Great Almoner: The Great Chamberlain took off his Cloak of Probation, and his Majeſty kneeling on a Cuſhion, the Archbiſhop put about his Neck the Croſs of the Order faſten'd with a blue String, then the Provoſt and Maſter of the Ceremonies, put the Mantle of the Order over his Majeſty's Shoulders, The Great Treaſurer preſented the Great Collar of the Order to the Archbiſhop, who put it about the King's Neck, and having receiv'd from the Sieur *de Clerambault*, Gene-

Genealogist of the Orders of the King, the Office of the Order, with a String of Beads of ten Courses, he presented them to his Majesty.

This done, the King cover'd himself and took his Seat; the Archbishop return'd to his Place near the Altar, and all the Knights went to the Throne, the highest in Dignity going first, to kiss the King's Hand, as Great Master and Sovereign of the Order; then they return'd to their Stalls. The Officers of the Order had likewise the Honour to kiss the King's Hand, and they stay'd on the Platform of the Throne.

After this, the Archbishop sung the *Veni Creator*, which was carry'd on by the King's Music, and in the mean Time, the Provost and Master of the Ceremonies, preceded by an Herald and an Usher, after a Reverence to the King, went down from the Throne, and went to admonish the Dukes of *Orleans* and *Bourbon*, who were to be Sponsors to the Duke of *Chartres* and the Count of *Charolois*, to conduct them to the Throne; after which, he went for those two Princes, at the lower End of the Choir, where they were plac'd as Candidates; and they, after the usual Reverences, conducted by their Sponsors, preceded by the Provost, the Herald, and Usher of the Order, went up to the Eminence where the Throne

Throne was erected, where falling on their Knees, on Cushions, before the King, the Secretary of the Order presented to them the Oath, which they read and sign'd on their Knees, as well as the Profession of their Faith, written in the same Register, which was sign'd by the King, while the Chancellor of the Order held the Book of the Gospels open, on the Knees of the King.

The Herald took off from these two Princes, their Cloak of Probation; The Great Treasurer presented the Blue String to his Majesty, with the Cross of the Order, which the King put about their Necks, over the Habit of Probation, beginning with the Duke of *Chartres*.

The Provost put the great Robe of the Order upon them; over which the King put the great Collar of the Order; which the Great Treasurer had presented to him for that purpose, Then the two New-created Knights rose up, made a Reverence to the King, went down from the Throne, and seated themselves on their Bench near the Altar.

In the mean Time, the Master of the Ceremonies having made a Reverence to the King, all the Officers of the Order, who were on the Platform of the Throne, descended from it, and began to make their Reverences again, over-against the Altar,

Altar, preceded by the Herald and Usher; then they return'd to their first Places, that is, the Stools where they had sate during the Vespers.

The King then descended from his Throne; and, follow'd by all his Attendants, he began his former Reverences at the Foot of the Altar; after which he return'd to his Throne, at the bottom of the Choir, where he heard the *Compline*, sung by the Musicians of the Chapel of Musick.

This ended, the four Great Officers of the Order, preceded by the Herald and Usher, quitted their Places, made their Reverences to the Middle of the Choir, and near the Altar; and then put themselves in Motion to re-conduct the King: The Knights did the same, and follow'd them in Rank, as they came to the Church. The King descended from his Throne, in the Collar and Large Robe of the Order; the Marquis *de Nesle* bore the Train; His Majesty made one Reverence to the Altar, and returned to the Archbishop's Palace, in the same Manner, through the open Gallery, as he came from it.

When the Commanders, Knights, and Officers of the Order, were come to the King's Chamber, they put themselves in a Line to the Right and Left, the King passed through the midst of them, and when he had entered his Closet, they retired.

On

On the 28th Day, about Ten in the Morning, the Prelates who made up the Clergy, that were invited to the Coronation, were conducted to an Audience of the King, with the ordinary Ceremonies, and the Archbishop of *Toulouse*, appointed to speak for them, complimented his Majesty, in the Name of the Clergy, and thanked him for the New Assurances of Protection which he had given them on the Day of his Coronation.

The same Day, in the Afternoon, the King, attended by the Duke of *Orleans*, the Princes of the Blood, and the Duke *de Charost*, went in his Coach to a Camp formed near the City of *Rheims*; there the King mounted on Horseback, and made a Review of the Troops of His Houshold, and the Regiment of *French* and *Swiss* Guards, having at his Side the Duke *De Villeroy*, who commanded these Troops during the Encampment.

The Touching of the SICK.

THE King not being able to go to *Crobenit*, or *Corbigny*, to pay his Nine Days Devotion before the Shrine of St. *Marcoul*, according to antient Usage; partly

partly on account of the Difficulty of the Roads, which were become almoſt impracticable, and partly from the advanced Seaſon of the Year; He thought it proper, to order that Shrine to be brought in Proceſſion from St. *Marcoul*, into the Church of the Abbey of St. *Remy* at *Rheims*; where the King appeared in Ceremony, on the 29th about 9 or 10 in the Morning, to begin there the Nine Days Devotion; which was continued by the Abbot *d'Argentré*, one of his Almoners, as *Louis* XIV. his Great Grandfather, had done before.

The King was in a Robe of Cloth of Gold, with the Collar of the Order of the Holy Ghoſt over it; attended in his Coach by the Dukes of *Orleans*, *Chartres*, and *Bourbon*, the Count *de Clermont*, the Prince *de Conty*, and the Duke *de Charoſt*.

He was received by the Prior and Religious, in their Copes, at the Church Door, with the ordinary Ceremonies; and being conducted to the Middle of the Quire, to a Seat prepared for him, the Cardinal *de Rohan* ſaid Low Maſs; during which the King communicated, The Dukes of *Orleans* and *Chartres* held the Napkin on the Side of the King, and the Abbots *Milon*, and *de le Vieuxville*, Almoners in Waiting, held the Two other Ends of it, on the Altar-ſide: After Maſs, the King went to ſay his Prayers before the Shrine of St. *Marcoul*, ſet near the Altar, on the Goſpel Side; then he went into the Abbey and broke his Faſt; after which, he returned into the Church to hear a Second Maſs; which was ſaid by a Chaplain, belonging to the Chapel of the King's Muſic.

Maſs ended, The King went into the Park of the Abbey, to the Walks, where there were above 2000 that had the King's Evil, and were touched by him in the following Order, beginning with the *Spaniards*, and ending with the *French*. The King was preceded by the Guards of the Provoſtſhip of the Houſhold, the Hundred *Swiſs* Guards, the Life Guards, *&c.* Great Numbers of Lords; after them were the Two Uſhers of the Chamber, bearing their Maces, the Sieur *Dodard*, firſt Phyſician, and many of the King's Phyſicians and Surgeons. The Dukes *de Villeroy*, and *d'Harcourt*, on each Side of the King, and about him the Six *Scotch* Guards: The Cardinal *de Rohan* immediately after him. The King was uncovered, and while he touched the Diſeaſed, extended his Right Hand from the Forehead to the Chin, and from one Cheek to the other, making the Sign of the Croſs, and ſaying theſe Words,

Dieu te gueriſſe, le Roy te touche.
God cure thee, the King toucheth thee.

The

The first Physician supported his Hand on the Head of each of them, the Duke *d'Harcourt* held their Hands closed, and as soon as they were touched, the Great Almoner distributed the King's Alms amongst them.

On the Day of this Ceremony, the Cardinal *de Rohan*, in his Camail and Rochet, assisted by the Sieurs the Abbots *Milon*, and *de la Vieuxville*, went to the Prisons of *Rheims*, where he pronounced to more then 600 Criminals, the Liberty indulged to them by the King, on the Account of his Coronation; and his Orders to dispatch Gratis all their Pardons, and give Succours to the Needy, in order to their Return Home: Then, after a very Pathetic Exhortation to merit the King's Favour, he returned to the Archbishop's Palace, to give an Account of it to the King, and of the Exactness with which the Sieurs *d'Herbigny*, *d'Ombreval*, *de Vanolles*, and *le Pelletier*, Masters of Requests (whom he presented to his Majesty) had discharged their Commission, to examine, by Information, into those that were to be admitted to Pardon, or excluded from it. The Prisoners who were inlarged, followed the Cardinal *de Rohan*, 'till they came about the King's Apartment; and gave Expressions of their Joy and Acknowledgment, by Acclamations of *Vive le Roy*, making the Palace resound with them, which put an End to the Ceremony of the Coronation.

During the King's stay at *Rheims*, as well before as after his Coronation, he visited many Churches and Convents, and went to see Madame, lodging at the Abbey of St. *Peter*, with the Nuns, and the Dutchess of *Lorrain* who, tho' she came to *Rheims* Incognito, visited likewise the King in the Archbishop's Palace.

On the the 30th of *October*, the King set out from *Rheims*, to return to *Versailles*, and was saluted by several Volleys of the Artillery on the Ramparts. The Prince *de Rohan*, at the Head of the Body of the City, reconducted him to some Distance from it. In the King's Coach, were the Duke of *Orleans*, the Princes of the Blood, and the Duke *de Charost*. He was preceded and followed by the Brigades in Attendance; the *Gens d'Arms*, and the Light-Horse of the Guard, Detachments of the Two Companies of Musketeers, and of the Night Life-Guards, with their Officers at the Head of them. The King lay that Night at *Fimes*, and made a Stay at *Soissons* on the 1st of *November*, being *All-Saints* Day. The Bishop of the Place officiated Pontifically, and Preached before him; The King parted thence at Two, and about Four, came to *Villers-Cotterêts*, to the House of the Duke of *Orleans*, and at Eight, to *Chantilly*, another House of the Duke's,

Duke's, where he was diverted and entertained with the greateſt Regularity and Magnificence that has been known. On the 8th of *November*, he came to St. *Dennis* about Three in the Afternoon, the Bailiffs, Officers, and Sheriffs of the Town, received him at the Gates of it, and preſented him with the Keys: He went to the Abbey-Church, where he was received under a Canopy, ſupported by the Religious The Prior, at the Head of all the Religious in their Copes, preſented the Holy Water to him, and complimented him, then the King went to kneel at an Oratory that was ſet for him in the Choir, and while he ſaid his Prayers there, the Anthems of S. *Dennis* and S. *Louis* were ſung; after which, going up to the Altar, he paid his Devotions before the Shrines of the Holy Martyrs, and that of St. *Louis*, and ſaid One *De Profundis* before the Image of the deceaſed King *Louis* XIV. his great Grandfather, after which, having viewed the Tombs of the Kings his Predeceſſors, he ſpent a long Time in conſidering the Rarities in the Treaſury of the Abbey; and about half an Hour after Four, he took Coach again, and ſet out for his Palace of the *Thuilleries*, where he arrived about Six in the Evening, having been received in the Suburb of St. *Dennis*, by the Duke *de Trême*, Governor of *Paris*, and complimented by the Sieur *de*

Chateauneuf, *Prevôt des Marchands*, at the Head of the Sheriffs, the Body of the City, and the Guards, commanded by the Sieur *Buret*, their Colonel.

On the 9th about Ten in the Morning, the King was Complimented on his Happy Return, by the Supreme Courts, and the Body of the City, The Sieur *de Mesmes*, first President, at the Head of the Parliament, spoke in the Name of them; The Sieur *de Nicolaï*, first President of the Chamber of Accounts, the Sieur *Richard*, President of the Court of Aids, and the Sieur *de Chateauneuf*, *Prevot des Marchands*, had the Honour to do the same, each at the Head of their Companies or Societies.

In the Afternoon, the Grand Council, and the Court of the *Mint* (or of the Public Monies) complimented the King on the same Subject. The Sieurs *de Vertamont*, and *Hosdier*, first Presidents of those Bodies, being at the Head of them: The University and the *French* Academy had the Honour to do the same, the Heads of them speaking in their Name. All these Societies were presented to the King by the Count *de Maurepas* Secretary of State, and conducted by the Sieurs the Marquisses *de Dreux*, and *des Granges*, Grand-Master, and Master of the Ceremonies, according to Custom.

On

On the Day following, being the 10th, the King set out from *Paris*, and returned to the Castle of *Versailles*, about Evening.

We ought not to omit it in this Recital, that the Cardinal *de Noailles*, Archbishop of *Paris*, always animated with the Spirit of Religion, and a Holy Zeal for the Prosperity of the King, and the Welfare of the People, had, by an Express Injunction of *October* the 16th last past, appointed Public Prayers, throughout all his Diocess, on occasion of the King's Coronation; which was imitated by the greatest Part of the Archbishops and Bishops in their Churches: Much less ought we to conceal it from Posterity, that the first Care of the King, after his Anointing and Coronation, was to give Thanks for it to God, and beseech Him to support his Reign, for the Glory and Advantage of the Nation, and the Good of his People; and to engage his first Pastor, and all the other Bishops, his Subjects, to joyn their Prayers with his; as he declared himself by his Letter, dated at *Rheims*, the Day after his Coronation, *October* the 26th, written to Cardinal *de Noailles*, to enjoyn a *Te Deum* to be sung, by way of Thanksgiving, and to obtain a Happy and most Christian Reign.

In pursuance of this Letter, *Te Deum* was sung in the Church of *Nôtre-Dame*, at *Paris*, *November* the 12th, 1722. The supreme

Courts, and Body of the City, assisted at it, being conven'd with the ordinary Ceremonies, which was followed with Bonfires, Illuminations and Public Rejoycings.

We must farther observe, that this Journey of the King to *Rheims*, has been the most Magnificent that has yet appeared, and that all was regulated in it, with the greatest Judgment and good Order.

The Ministers and Great Lords, kept their Tables there with the utmost Expence and Delicacy: Among which, after the Princes, we must distinguish those of the Cardinal *du Bois*, Prime Minister, and the Duke *de Villeroy*, Captain of the Life-Guards, and Commander in Chief of all the Troops that Encamped near *Rheims*, on occasion of his Majesty's Coronation; the Memory of which will be Immortal.

A LIST *of the Princes of the Blood, Cardinals, Archbishops, Bishops, Abbots, Priors, Religious, and other Ecclesiasticks; Great Officers of the Crown, Captains of the Guards, Marshals of* France, *and other Lords, Ministers, Counsellors and Secretaries of State, Masters of Requests, Secretaries of the King, and other Officers of his Majesty, who perform'd any Function at, or were invited to the Coronation of* LOUIS XV. *King of* France *and* Navarre; *perform'd in the Metropolitan Church of* Rheims, October *the 25th,* 1722.

The NAMES *of the Princes, who represented the Antient* LAY-PEERS.

M. PHILIPPE, *Duke* D'ORLEANS, Grandson of *France*, Regent of the Kingdom, Uncle of the King, represented *the Duke of* BURGUNDY.

M. LOUIS, D'ORLEANS, *Duke de* CHARTRES, First Prince of the Blood, Uncle of the King, represented *the Duke of* NORMANDY.

M. LOUIS

M. LOUIS HENRY, *Duke de* BOURBON, Prince of the Blood, Coufin of the King, reprefented *the Duke of* GUYENNE.

M. CHARLES *de* BOURBON, *Count de* CHAROLOIS, Prince of the Blood, Coufin of the King, reprefented *the Count de* TOULOUSE.

M. LOUIS *de* BOURBON, *Count de* CLERMONT, Prince of the Blood, Coufin of the King, reprefented *the Count of* FLANDERS.

M. LOUIS-ARMAND *de* BOURBON, *Prince de* CONTI, Prince of the Blood, Coufin of the King, reprefented the *Count de* CHAMPAGNE.

The NAMES *of the* ECCLESIASTICAL PEERS.

ARMAND JULES *de* ROHAN, Archbifhop Duke of RHEIMS, and Peer of *France*, perform'd his Function.

CHARLES *de* ST. ALBIN, Bifhop Duke of LAON, Peer of *France*, perform'd his Function.

FRANCIS *Honoré Antoine de Beauvilliers de* St. AIGNAN, Bifhop, and Count *de Beauvais*, Peer of *France*, reprefented the Archbifhop Duke of LANGRES.

NICOLAS CHARLES *de* SAULX *de* TAVANNES, Bifhop and Count of *Châlons*, Peer of *France*,

France, perform'd the Function of the Bishop Count de BEAUVAIS.

FRANCIS *de Chateauneuf, de Rochebonne*, Bishop and Count of *Noyon*, Peer of *France*, perform'd the Function of the Bishop of CHASLONS.

ANTOINE *Hercule de Fleury*, the Ancient Bishop of *Frejus*, Preceptor of the King, perform'd the Function of the Bishop and Count of NOYON, Peer of *France*.

The Names of the Prelates *and other* Ecclesiasticks, *who had any Functions.*

The Great Almoner of France,

ARmand *Gaston de Rohan*, Bishop and Prince of *Strasburg*, Commander-born of the Orders of the King, did his Office.

The First Almoner,

Henry Charles du Cambout de Coislin, Bishop of *Metz*, Commander of the Order of the Holy Ghost, Duke and Peer of *France*, did his Office.

The King's Confessor,

The Reverend Father *de Lignieres*, Jesuit.

The

The Deacon and Sub-deacon,

John Joseph Languot, Bishop of *Soissons*.
Pierre Sabatier, Bishop of *Amiens*.

The Preacher,

Michael Pomet de la Riviere, Bishop of *Angers*, preach'd on the Eve of the Coronation-Day.

The four Bishops, who sung the Litanies,

Louis de la Vergne de Tressan . . .	Bp. of *Nantes*.
Francis Trudaine . .	Bp. of *Senlis*.
N. Dromesuil . . .	Bp. of *Verdun*.
Gabriel Florent de Choiseul	Bp. of St. *Papoul*.

The King's Almoners,

The Abbots *Milon*, *de la Vieuville*; *d'Argentré*, *de Froulay*, *Caulet*, and *Pezé*.

The King's Chaplain in Ordinary,

The Abbot *Bayle*.

The Chaplains in Waiting,

The Abbots *Guinot* and *Josiot*.

Clerk

Clerk of the Chapel in Ordinary,

The Abbot *Pernot.*

Clerks of the Chapel in Waiting,

The Abbots *Pomier* and *Evrard.*

The Grand Priors and Religious of the Abbeys of St. Remy *and St.* Dennis,

Pierre Gaudard, Grand Prior of St. *Remy,* brought the Holy Vial, aſſiſted by the Treaſurer and the Religious.

The Grand Prior, Treaſurer, and one Religious of St. *Dennis,* brought and prepar'd the Royal Ornaments.

The Names of the Great Officers of the Crown.

The Great Almoner of France,

ARmand Gaſton de Rohan, Biſhop and Prince of *Strasburg,* Great Almoner of *France,* perform'd his Charge.

The Conſtable,

Louis Hector, Duke of *Villars,* Peer and Marſhal of *France,* Knight of the Three Or-

Orders of the King, and of the Golden Fleece, represented the Constable.

The Chancellor,

Gaston Jean-Baptist Fleuriau d'Armenonville, Keeper of the Seals of *France*, did the Office of Chancellor.

Grand-Master of the King's Houshold,

Hercule de Rohan, Prince *de Soubize*, Duke *de Rohan*, Peer of *France*, did the Office of Great-Master; Monsieur the Duke of *Bourbon*, who is invested with it, representing the Third Lay-Peer.

Grand-Chamberlain,

Frederic Maurice Casimir de la Tour d'Auvergne, Prince *de Turenne*, Great-Chamberlain in Reversion, did his Office.

First Gentleman of the Chamber,

Louis Marie, Duke *d'Aumont*, call'd of *Villequier*.

The Three Marshals of France, *who bore the Royal Ornaments,*

Victor Marie, Count *d'Estreés*, Grandee of *Spain*, bore the Crown.

Nicolas

Nicolas Chelons du Blé, Marquiss *d'Huxelles*, the Scepter.

René de Froulay, Count *de Tessé*, Grandee of *Spain*, the Hand of Justice.

All three Knights of the Order of the Holy Ghost.

The Four Knights of the same Order, who bore the Offerings,

Camille d'Hostung, Count *de Tallard*, Duke *d'Hostung*, Peer and Marshal of *France*, carry'd the Vessel fill'd with Wine.

Jacques de Matignon, Count *de Thorigny*, and Lieutenant General, the Golden Loaf.

Jacques Leonore Rouxel de Medavy, Count *de Grandcay*, Lieutenant-General, the Silver Loaf.

Vincent Louis, Marquis *de Goesbriant*, Lieutenant-General, the Purse with Thirteen Pieces of Gold in it.

The Great-Master of the Horse of *France*, Prince *Charles* of *Lorrain*, bore the Train of the Royal Robe, and receiv'd the Cap of his Majesty, when he put it off during the Ceremony.

The Four Lords Lieutenants General of the King's Armies, who attended and reconducted the Holy Vial,

Yves, Marquiss *d'Alegré*.

Francis,

Francis, Count *d'Estaing*.

Pierre Magdelaine, Count *de Beauvau*.

Louis, Marquiss *de Prié*, Sponsor to his Majesty.

The Four Knights of the Holy Vial, who supported the Canopy,

The Sieurs *de Romaine*, *Godet*, *de Sainte Catherine*, and *Clignet*, Bailiff of the Abbey of St. *Remy*.

The Guard-du-Corps,

Francis de Neufville Duke of *Villeroy*, Captain of the Life-Guards, did the Office of first Captain of the *Scotch* Guards, and Commanded the Camp near *Rheims*.

Francis, Duke *d'Harcourt* Captain of the Life-Guards, being in Attendance, did his Office.

Antoine, Duke of *Grammont*, Peer of *France*, Colonel of the Regiment of *French* Guards, did his Office.

Louis Cæsar le Tellier, Marquiss *de Courtenvaux*, Captain of the Hundred *Swiss* of the Guard, did his Office.

The Masters of the Ceremonies,

Thomas Dreux, Marquiss *de Brezé*, Grand-Master.

Michel

Michel Ancel des Granges the Son, Master of the Ceremonies, perform'd their Duties.

Two Ushers of the King's Chamber, with their Maces,

The Sieurs *Millet* and *de Varenne.*

The Names of the Great Officers who perform'd their Functions out of the Church, on the Day of the Coronation.

The Great-Master of the Pantry,

Timoleon Louis de Cossé, Duke *de Brissac*, did his Office at the Coronation Feast.

The Great Cup-bearer,

Marc Antoine Front de Beaupoil de St. Aulaire, Marquiss *de Lanmary*, and *de Chabanne*, and *Coutures*, Baron *de Milly*, Seigneur *d'Angerville*, and *de Rovres*, did his Office.

The Great Squire Carver,

John Baptiste de la Chenaye, Governor of *Meulau*, did his Office.

The first Master of the Houshold,

Louis Sanguin, Marquiss *de Livry*.

The Twelve Masters of the King's Houshold.

The Gentlemen-Waiters of the King.

The Great Provost of the Houshold,

Louis de Bouchet, Knight, Lord, Count *de Montsoreau*, Marquiss *de Sourches* and *du Bellay*, Lord of *Abendant*, Lieutenant General of the Armies of the King, Provost of the Houshold, did his Office.

The Names of the Cardinals, Archbishops, and Bishops, who were invited to the Coronation, and assisted at it.

THE Cardinals *de Rohan*, *de Bissy*, *de Gêvres*, *du Bois*, and *de Polignac*.

The Sieurs

De Nesmond . .	Abp. of *Toulouse*.
D'Argenson. . .	Abp. of *Bourdeaux*.
De Chavigni . .	Abp. of *Sens*.
De Castries . .	Abp. of *Alby*.
De Camilly, .	Bp. of *Toul*, nam'd to the Arch-bishoprick of *Tours*.

Trudenne

Trudenne . . .	Bp. of *Senlis*.
Poncet	Bp. of *Angers*.
De Coislin . . .	Bp. of *Metz*.
Merinville . . .	Bp of *Chartres*.
De Dromenil . .	Bp. of *Verdun*.
Turpin Croiset de Sanzay . .	Bp. of *Rennes*.
De Caumartin .	Bp. of *Blois*.
De Choiseul . .	Bp. of St. *Papoul*.
Bossuet	Bp. of *Troyes*.
Lafitau	Bp. of *Cisteron*.
Le Blanc	Bp. of *Avranche*.
De Conflan . .	Bp. of *Puy*.
De Beaufort . .	Bp. of *Leictoure*.

All in their Rochets and Purple Camails.

The Names of the Great Officers, and other Officers of the Order of the Holy Ghost, who perform'd their Functions on the Day of the Ceremony of Knighting.

A*Rmand Jules de Rohan*, Archbishop Duke of *Rheims*, officiated and said Mass.

The Abbot *de Pomponne*, Chancellor of the Order.

The Sieurs *de Breteuil*, Provost and Master of the Ceremonies; *Crozat*, Great Treasurer, *Le Bas de Montargis* Secretary; *Hallé*,

Hallé, Herald of the Order, *de Clerambault*, Genealogist; and *Chevrard*, Usher.

The Marquiss *de Nesle* bore the Train of the Royal Robe on the Day of the Knighting.

The Names of the Prelates and Officers who serv'd in Touching of the Sick.

ARmand *Gaston de Rohan*, distributed the Alms.

The Abbot *d'Argentré*, continued the Nine Days Devotion, begun by the King.

The Duke *d'Harcourt*, held the Hands of the Diseas'd clos'd.

The Sieur *Dodard* first Physician, held their Heads.

Many other Physicians and Surgeons to the King.

The Sieurs *Millet* and *de Varenne*, Ushers of the King's Chamber, carry'd their Maces before his Majesty.

The Names of the Counsellors and Secretaries of State, the Masters of Requests, and the Secretaries of the King, who assisted at the Coronation in their Robes and Habits of Ceremony; being Invited to it.

Counsellors of State.

The Sieurs

Amelot.

Bignon de Blanzy.

Le Pelletier des Forts.

L'Abbé de Pomponne.

The Count *du Luc.*

D'Argenvilliers.

D'Argenson.

D'Harlay.

Dodun.

Secretaries of State.

The Marquiss *de la Vrilliere.*

The Count *de Maurepas.*

The Sieur *le Blanc.*

The

The Masters of Requests.

The Sieurs

D'Herbigny.	*De Fontanieu.*
Bernard.	*De Talhonet.*
De la Grandville.	*D'Ombreval.*
C[illegible]ry.	*De Vanolles.*
[illegible]an.	*Le Pelletier.*

The Sieurs

Noblet, *Pernin,* *Poisson,* *Le Noire,* *Archambault,* and *Carpot.*	Secretaries to the King, deputed by the Company, pursuant to the *Letter de Cachet.*

The

The Names of the Marshals of France, *Ambassadors and Lords, who were likewise invited to the Coronation, and were present.*

THE Marshals *de Matignon*, and *de Bezons*, and the Duke *de Charost*, Governor to the King, having always attended the Duke *de Chaulnes.*

The Pope's Nuncio.

The Ambassadors of *Spain*, *Sardinia*, and *Malta*, and with them in their Gallery, the Sieurs *de Sainctot*, and *de Remond*, Introductors of Ambassadors, and other Lords not invited.

The Princes and Princesses, un invited, who were present.

Madame, and with her in her Gallery Madame the Dutchess of *Lorrain*, with the Princes and Princesses of *Lorrain*, her Children, and the Infante *Don Emanuel* Brother to the King of *Portugal*; who came

Incognito to *Rheims*, to ſee this Auguſt Ceremony; and other Lords and Ladies of their Court.

The Names of Perſons appointed by the King, to enlarge the Priſoners and Criminals, whom his Majeſty thought fit to Pardon, on the Account of his Coronation.

THE Cardinal *de Rohan*, Great Almoner, to whom it belong'd by virtue of his Office.

The Sieurs *d'Herbigny*, *d'Ombreval*, *de Vanolles*, and *le Pelletier*, appointed by the King to examine the Informations and Proceedings extraordinary on the Crimes for which the Accuſed implor'd the King's Pardon.

The Sieur *de Vatan*, Procurator General of the Commiſſion, and, as the others, Maſters of Requeſts.

The APPROBATION *of the* RELATION.

I Signify'd *September* the 4th in my Approbation, That M. *Menin*, Counsellor to the Parliament of *Metz*, promis'd an *Exact Relation of the Ceremony of the Anointing and Coronation of* Louis XV. He has done it: I have perus'd it. It comes up to the Magnificence of this Great Feast, in the View of giving the greater Enhancement to his Work. Hence this Magistrate ends by That his *History of the Coronation*. It is extremely just to convey it down to Posterity with his Book, which will never be look'd upon as a *fleeting Work*, but a *standing Design*; since it will ever have an *Air of Novelty*, which will carry a Man to inquire into the Ceremonies of the Coronations of the Kings of *France*, and of all the Sovereign Princes of *Europe*.

At *Paris*, *November* 14. 1722.

The Abbot RICHARD,
Censor-Royal.

The

The Privilege *of the* KING.

LOUIS, by the Grace of GOD, King of *France* and *Navarre*, To our Beloved and Faithful Counſellors, The Perſons holding our Courts of Parliament, The Maſters of the Ordinary Requeſts of our Houſhold, The Great Council, the Provoſt of *Paris*, the Bailiffs, Stewards, or their Lieutenants-Civil, and other our Juſtices to whom it ſhall appertain, *Greeting*.

Our Beloved and Faithful Counſellor in

do permit him, by these Presents, to Print the same in such Volumes, Form, Margin, Character, jointly and separately, as often as he shall please, and to sell or cause it to be sold throughout all our Kingdom, for Eight Years following, from the Date of these Presents.

We prohibit all Persons to bring a Foreign Impression into our Dominions; and all Booksellers, Printers and others, to print, sell, or cause to be printed or sold, or to counterfeit the said Book, in Whole or in Part; or to make any Extracts from it, under any Pretence; to Increase, Correct, change the Title, or otherwise, without his Leave, or that of others from him, on Pain of Confiscation of the Counterfeit Copies, and 1500 Livres; of which a Third shall come to *Us*, a Third to the [illegible]

Incognito to *Rheims*, to see this August Ceremony, and other Lords and Ladies of their Court.

The Names of Persons appointed by the King, to enlarge the Prisoners and Criminals, whom his Majesty thought fit to Pardon, on the Account of his Coronation.

THE Cardinal *de Rohan*, Great Almoner, to whom it belong'd by virtue of his Office.

The Sieurs *d'Herbigny*, *d'Ombreval*, *de Vanolles*, and *le Pelletier*, appointed by the King to examine the Informations and Proceedings extraordinary on the Crimes for which the Accused implor'd the King's Pardon.

The Sieur *de Vatan*, Procurator General of the Commission, and, as the others, Masters of Requests.

The

The APPROBATION *of the* RELATION.

I Signify'd *September* the 4th in my Approbation, That M. *Menin*, Counsellor to the Parliament of *Metz*, promis'd an *Exact Relation of the Ceremony of the Anointing and Coronation of* Louis XV. He has done it: I have perus'd it. It comes up to the Magnificence of this Great Feast, in the View of giving the greater Enhancement to his Work. Hence this Magistrate ends by That his *History of the Coronation*. It is extremely just to convey it down to Posterity with his Book, which will never be look'd upon as a *fleeting Work*, but a *standing Design*; since it will ever have an *Air of Novelty*, which will carry a Man to inquire into the Ceremonies of the Coronations of the Kings of *France*, and of all the Sovereign Princes of *Europe*.

At *Paris*, *November* 14. 1722.

The Abbot RICHARD,
Censor-Royal.

The Privilege *of the* KING.

LOUIS, by the Grace of GOD, King of *France* and *Navarre*, To our Beloved and Faithful Counſellors, The Perſons holding our Courts of Parliament, The Maſters of the Ordinary Requeſts of our Houſhold, The Great Council, the Provoſt of *Paris*, the Bailiffs, Stewards, or their Lieutenants-Civil, and other our Juſtices to whom it ſhall appertain, *Greeting*.

Our Beloved and Faithful Counſellor in our Court of the Parliament of *Metz*, the Sieur *Menin*, having repreſented to us, That he deſir'd to publiſh a Work, intituled, *An Hiſtorical and Chronological Treatiſe of the Anointing and Coronation of the Kings of* France, *from* Clovis *to this Time*, *and of the other Princes of* Europe *Compos'd by the Sieur* Menin If we would grant him our Letters of Privilege neceſſary for it. For theſe Reaſons, we being inclin'd to uſe the ſaid Sieur *Menin* in a Favourable Manner, and acknowledge his Zeal, have permitted, and do do permit him, by these Presents, to Print the same in such Volumes, Form, Margin, Characters, jointly and separately, as often as he shall please, and to sell or cause it to be sold throughout all our Kingdom, for Eight Years following, from the Date of these Presents.

We prohibit all Persons to bring a Foreign Impression into our Dominions, and all Booksellers, Printers and others, to print, sell, or cause to be printed or sold, or to counterfeit the said Book, in Whole or in Part; or to make any Extracts from it, under any Pretence; to Increase, Correct, change the Title, or otherwise, without his Leave, or that of others from him, on Pain of Confiscation of the Counterfeit Copies, and 1500 Livres; of which a Third shall come to *Us*, a Third to the *Hôtel Dieu* of *Paris*, and a Third to the *Author*, and all Expences, Damages and Interests: On Condition, that this be Register'd intire in the *Register* of the *Company of Booksellers and Printers* of *Paris*, within Three Months from the Date hereof: That it shall be printed only in our Kingdom, on good Paper and Characters, according to the Regulations of that *Company*. And before it be here any way printed, it shall, as it is, be approved by our Well-beloved and Faithful Knight the Keeper of the Seals *Fleuriau d'Armenonville*, and

and Two Copies ſhall be depoſited, one into the Library of the *Louvre*, the other into that of the Keeper of the Seals, on Pain of the Nullity of theſe Preſents; By which we give the Author a full and quiet Poſſeſſion of it, without Moleſtation.

Theſe Preſents printed at the Beginning or the End of this Work, ſhall be held to be duly ſignified; and the Copies compar'd by our Counſellors and Secretaries, ſhall be deem'd as Originals.

We command our Firſt Uſher or Sergeant to make all the neceſſary Acts for the Execution of theſe Premiſſes, without other Permiſſion, and notwithſtanding the *Clameur d' Haro*, *Charte Normande*, and Letters contrary to this. *For ſuch is our Pleaſure.*

Given at Paris, November 10, 1722. *and of our Reign the Eighth.*

By the KING *in His Council.*

Sign'd,

CARPOT.

With his proper Flouriſh made to his Name.

IT is Ordain'd by the King's Edict of *August*, 1686. *That the Books whose Impression is permitted to be sold by the Privilege of His Majesty, can only be sold by a Bookseller or Printer.*

Regifter'd, *together with the Cession, in the* Fifth Regifter *of the* Company of Bookfellers and Printers *of* Paris, *Page* 242. N°. 372. *conformably to the* Regulations *and the* Arrêt *of Council* Auguft 13. 1703.

At *Paris*, *November* 16. 1722.

BALLARD, *Syndic.*

FINIS.

BOOKS Printed for W. MEARS, at the Lamb without Temple-Bar.

1 THE *Chronological Historian*, containing a regular Account of all material Transactions and Occurrences Ecclesiastical, Civil and Military, relating to the *English* Affairs, from the Invasion of the *Romans*, to the present Time With the Creations and Promotions of the Nobility and Baronets, Ministers of State, Generals, Judges, Attorneys, and Solicitors-General, as they stand in Order of Time, whereby that Confusion, which generally mis-leads the Reader in the Perusal of our Historians for want of an exact Chronology, is prevented, and other Defects and Omissions supply'd Illustrated with the Effigies of all our *English* Monarchs, curiously Engraven from Original Paintings, by Mr *Vertue*.

2 *Vertot*'s Miscellanies, consisting of, 1 A Dissertation upon the true Original of the *French*, by a Parallel of their Manners with those of the *Germans* 2 On the Rise of the *Salique* Law. 3. On the *Sainte Ampoulle* or *Holy Vial* at *Rheims*, used in the Coronation of the Kings of *France* 4 On the Antient Form of Oaths used among the *French* By M the Abbot of *Vertot* of the Royal Academy of Inscriptions and *Belles Lettres* 5 On the Antient Burial Places of the Kings of *France*, by *R. F. Mabillon* 6 On the Time of the Nativity of Christ, discover'd from Antient Medals, by M *Vaillant*, Both Members of the same Academy Done from the *French* by *John Henley*, M A

3 The History of *Sweden*, from the most early and Authentic Accounts of that Kingdom, to the erecting of it into an Absolute Monarchy, and the Establishment of the Reformation By *J Henley*, M A

5 *Monasticon Hibernicum*, or the Monastical History of *Ireland*, containing, 1 All the Abbies, Priories, Nunneries,

ries, and other Regular Communities which were in that Kingdom. 2. The Time when, and the Titles under which they were founded. 3 The Name and Quality of their Founders, 4 The Provinces, Counties, Cities, or Towns in which they were seated, &c. With a Map of *Ireland*, and Draughts of their several Habits.

5. A Commentary upon the Prophet *Ezekiel*, by *W. Lowth*, Prebendary of *Winchester*

BOOKS Printed for S. CHAPMAN, *at the* Angel *in* Pallmall.

THE Survey of *Cornwall*, and an Epistle concerning the Excellencies of the *English* Tongue Now first published from the Original Manuscript By *Richard Carew* of *Antoine*, Esq, With the Life of the Author By *H——— C – –* , Esq,

The History of the Royal Society of *London*, for the Improving of Natural Knowledge. By *Tho Sprat*, D D Late Lord Bishop of *Rochester*. The Third Edition Corrected.

A Description of the most beautiful Pieces of Painting, Sculpture and Architecture, at and near *Rome*. The Second Edition

Fables and Dialogues of the Dead. By the Archbishop of *Cambray*, Author of *Telemachus*.

The *Arabian* Nights Entertainment The 9, 10, 11, and 12 Parts. In Two Volumes. Never before in *English*.

Love in Excess, or, The fatal Enquiry A Novel In Three Parts Compleat. By Mrs *Haywood*

Just

Just Publish'd,

MEmoirs and Original Letters of King *Charles* II. Queen Mother, the Duke of *York*, the Duke of *Lorrain*, the Archbishop of *Tuam*, Lord Viscount *Taaffe*, &c. giving an exact Account of the Civil Transactions in the Kingdom of *Ireland*, from *February* 1650. to *August* 1653, and particularly of the Treaty between the *Irish* and the Duke of *Lorrain* against the Parliamentarians; whereby the Intrigues of both Parties are laid open, and the Historians who writ of those Transactions, are supplied, and corrected. The whole collected and digested by the Marquiss of *Clanricarde*, Earl of St. *Albans*, &c. Deputy Lieutenant and General Governor of *Ireland*, in the Absence of the Marquiss of *Ormond*, Lord Lieutenant of that Kingdom.

—— *He* (the Marquiss of *Clanricarde*) *left behind him so full a Relation of all material Passages, as well from the Beginning of that Rebellion, as during the Time of his own Administration, that I have been the less particular in the Accounts of what passed in the Transactions of that Kingdom, presuming that more exact Work of his, will, in due time be communicated to the World*

Lord *Clarendon*'s Hist of the Rebell *Book* 13.

N B. There is prefix'd to it (tho' not mention'd in the Proposals) a Dissertation illustrating several Passages in that Book, with a Digression concerning the Education and Studies of the *Irish* Bards, or Antient Poets, and of their Works, out of which the learned Doctor *Keating* has compiled his History of *Ireland*, with some Account of Dr *Keating*'s Life, and the Occasion of his writing that History

CPSIA information can be obtained at www.ICGtesting.com
Printed in the USA
244267LV00002B/302/P